Neo-Victorian Freakery

Also by Helen Davies

GENDER AND VENTRILOQUISM IN VICTORIAN AND NEO-VICTORIAN FICTION: Passionate Puppets

Neo-Victorian Freakery

The Cultural Afterlife of the Victorian Freak Show

Helen Davies

palgrave
macmillan

First published 2015 by
PALGRAVE MACMILLAN

Palgrave Macmillan in the UK is an imprint of Macmillan Publishers Limited, registered in England, company number 785998, of Houndmills, Basingstoke, Hampshire RG21 6XS.

Palgrave Macmillan in the US is a division of St Martin's Press LLC, 175 Fifth Avenue, New York, NY 10010.

Palgrave Macmillan is the global academic imprint of the above companies and has companies and representatives throughout the world.

Palgrave® and Macmillan® are registered trademarks in the United States, the United Kingdom, Europe and other countries.

ISBN 978–1–137–40255–4

This book is printed on paper suitable for recycling and made from fully managed and sustained forest sources. Logging, pulping and manufacturing processes are expected to conform to the environmental regulations of the country of origin.

A catalogue record for this book is available from the British Library.

A catalog record for this book is available from the Library of Congress.

Typeset by MPS Limited, Chennai, India.

Contents

Acknowledgements

I am extremely grateful to Teesside University for the research sabbatical I received in Autumn/Winter 2014 in order to complete this book, and for the support from my colleagues in the English department during this period and beyond. In particular, I would like to thank Rachel Carroll for her advice on this project in the early stages. Thank you to the reader of the project, who offered invaluable advice in shaping the book from proposal to manuscript, and to Paula Kennedy and Peter Cary at Palgrave Macmillan for their assistance during the entire process.

Teesside University also provided funding for me to carry out some research for Chapter 3 at the North Shore Archives and Anna Swan Museum at the Creamery in Tatamagouche, Nova Scotia in September 2013. During this visit, I was fortunate to receive the expert guidance of Dale Swan, one of Anna's relatives, and I am indebted to him for his knowledge, generosity, and kindness.

Thank you to James Mcgrath for his thoughtful feedback on the early chapters of this book, to Nadine Muller for inviting me to deliver a keynote address based on Chapter 2 at the 'Neo-Victorian Cultures: The Victorians Today' conference in at Liverpool John Moores University July 2013, and for Claire O'Callaghan for her comments on my initial proposal for this book project. I am privileged to have James, Nadine, and Claire as friends as well as colleagues. Especial thanks to Claire for her ongoing support as a research collaborator, and her patience in managing our other projects whilst I was preoccupied with this book. I am delighted that Adam Paxman agreed to provide the original artwork for the front cover of *Neo-Victorian Freakery*, and I am so appreciative of his creativity, talent, and time.

My thanks are inadequate to express the support I have received from Madge and Peter Davies during the writing of this book, and in every other way. I am lucky to have them as my family, and as my friends.

Introduction: Distorted Images and Re-membered Bodies: Constructing Neo-Victorian Freakery

What are the politics of representation that are involved in neo-Victorianism's 'reflections' upon the nineteenth-century freak show? Reflection – or the mirror – has been a significant metaphor in critical accounts of neo-Victorian engagements with the nineteenth century. For example, the titular concept of Simon Joyce's *The Victorians in the Rearview Mirror* (2007) invokes the motif of 'looking back' at Victorian culture to make sense of past, present and future. However, he emphasises that the representations we perceive are 'mediated image[s]': for him, there is a process of 'the inevitable distortion that accompanies any mirror image, whether we see it as resulting from the effects of political ideology, deliberate misreading, exaggeration, or the understandable simplification of a complex past' (Joyce, 2007, p. 4). Ann Heilmann and Mark Llewellyn's influential definition of neo-Victorianism considers the genre as a process of self-conscious '*(re)interpretation, (re)discovery and (re)vision concerning the Victorians*' (Heilmann and Llewellyn, 2010, p. 4; original emphasis). They elaborate upon one of these key terms – '*(re) vision*' – in a chapter focusing upon 'Spectrality and S(p)ecularity', suggesting that 'neo-Victorian literature sets up a mirror-like or reflective stance between our own period and that of the nineteenth century' (Heilmann and Llewellyn, 2010, p. 144). Yet they also highlight the ways in which such 'reflections' are not accurate forms of representation. The 'glass' of neo-Victorianism's mirroring of the nineteenth century contains 'shadows, spectres and written ghosts that never quite materialise into substantive presences but instead remain simulations of the "real"' (Heilmann and Llewellyn, 2010, p. 145). In other words, reflections are never realities, but offer only distorted images of the Victorian past, twisted and misshapen by contemporary culture's desires. Sometimes we might see our own images in the nineteenth century as a process of identification, but also sometimes we seek to distance ourselves from the 'otherness' of the Victorians.

My gloss of reflective imagery in neo-Victorian criticism deliberately invokes the vocabulary of deformity, as the concept of the mirror has also been important for understanding the combination of fear and fascination attached to making a spectacle of extraordinary bodies. Elizabeth Grosz gives the following account of why the display of people with unusual anatomies can be a source of horror and allure:

> The freak illustrates our [...] fascination with our mirror-images [...] The relation we bear to images of ourselves is drawn from this simultaneous and ambivalent reaction: the mirror-image threatens to draw us into its spell of spectral doubling, annihilating the self that wants to see itself reflected. At the same time, it gains pleasure from the access it gives to the subject's exteriority, from an illusory mastery over its image. [...] The freak confirms the viewer as bounded, belonging to a proper social category. The viewer's horror lies in the recognition that this monstrous being is at the heart of his or her own identity, for it is all that must be ejected or abjected from self-image to make the bounded, category-obeying self possible.
>
> (Grosz, 1996, p. 65)

According to Lacanian psychoanalysis, the child gazing at her or his reflection begins to develop a sense of independent self by perceiving their image as an illusory wholeness. This is, of course, a delusion: a disjuncture between the reflected representation of 'complete' self and the fragmented reality of an infant unable to fully control its body and movements. Nevertheless, there is a pleasure in this looking. Furthermore, a distinction between self and other begins to develop.[1] In Grosz's example of the 'freakish' body as a distorted mirror, there is also pleasure for the subject who looks – a power relationship of gazing which designates the audience as 'normal' and the unusual body as 'other'. But this demarcation of boundaries is also an illusion, for the 'monstrous' other also bears some resemblance to the 'normal' self in terms of representing all of that prior fragmentation and amorphousness that has been repressed, 'ejected' or 'abjected'.[2]

And perhaps it is in this sense of rejecting that which has come before that these two deployments of mirror metaphors – the neo-Victorian and the freakery studies perspective – coalesce. Marie-Luise Kohlke and Christian Gutleben have already made this connection in their introduction to *Neo-Victorian Gothic: Horror, Violence, and Degeneration in the Re-Imagined Nineteenth Century*: 'On psychological and ideological levels, the Victorians function as our threatening doubles and distorted freak show/funhouse mirror images, disclosing something akin to rejected atavistic or archetypal selves, our superseded progenitors who are nonetheless still with us, if only as an evolutionary vestige' (Kohlke and Gutleben, 2012, pp. 4–5). In this telling formulation, Kohlke and Gutleben imply that all neo-Victorian representations of nineteenth-century subjects have the potential to be understood as 'freakish'. The Victorians might be constructed as the monstrous other, irrevocably different but still disturbingly familiar. But, to use a suitably degeneration-inflected analogy, what of the missing link that has been skipped in this chain of association? More specifically, what of neo-Victorian constructions of nineteenth-century freak shows?

An important criticism of a psychoanalytic explanation for understanding the complex reactions to and meanings placed upon extraordinary bodies is that it does not take into account the social and cultural contexts for constructing 'otherness' at any given historical moment. As disability activists and scholars have argued, what is deemed 'abnormal' – or, indeed, 'normal' – in terms of the body is not fixed or essential.[3] So, to return to the metaphor of the neo-Victorian mirror, what does contemporary culture wish to see when looking back at the people who performed in nineteenth-century freak shows, and the audiences who came to view them? How are nineteenth-century narratives of freak show performers revisited by neo-Victorian culture, and what are the politics of such re-presentations? To what extent does the representation of freak show performers in neo-Victorianism think beyond oppressive and exploitative understandings of bodily difference in the Victorian era and our own cultural moment, extending the ethical work of neo-Victorianism in terms of redressing past inequalities of gender, sexuality, race, and class? Or does neo-Victorianism distort freak show performers beyond all recognition, compounding nineteenth-century abuses of vulnerable people?

Neo-Victorian Freakery: The Cultural Afterlife of the Victorian Freak Show is a study of how the lives of nineteenth-century freak show performers have been revisited and reinterpreted by contemporary literature and culture. A chapter will be devoted to each performer: Sarah Baartman, exhibited as 'The Hottentot Venus' in early nineteenth-century Europe; Chang and Eng Bunker, the original 'Siamese Twins'; Anna Swan, a Canadian woman of height who was exhibited as a 'giantess' in P. T. Barnum's American Museum; Charles Sherwood Stratton (billed as 'General Tom Thumb') and Lavinia Warren, his wife who was also of shorter stature; and Joseph Carey Merrick (the 'Elephant Man'). Through exploring both nineteenth-century and neo-Victorian representations, I debate the extent to which neo-Victorianism challenges some of the more exploitative aspects of freak show conventions, and interrogate issues about social identity, oppression and agency that are apparent in neo-Victorian reflections of these performers. As an additional strand to this discussion, the Afterword of the book will address the representation of P. T. Barnum in neo-Victorian fiction. However, before offering a more detailed outline of the book's contents, I want to introduce the key critical and historical contexts for the themes of my work: neo-Victorianism and freakery studies, and the productive intersections between these fields.

Neo-Victorianism and the politics of 're-membering'

There has been a significant amount of critical debate about the terminology that should be used to define contemporary fiction and other cultural productions which are set in the nineteenth century, but 'neo-Victorian' has now become established as the most commonly used appellation for this genre of work.[4] As my discussion of Ann Heilmann and Mark Llewellyn's key definition of neo-Victorianism has indicated, and as I have argued elsewhere,[5] one of the crucial features of neo-Victorianism is its commitment to critical engagement with the aesthetic form and ideological messages of nineteenth-century literature.[6] It is the latter impulse which is most important for my understanding of neo-Victorianism in this book. As numerous commentators have suggested, neo-Victorianism demonstrates a commitment to reimagining subjects who historically have been marginalised from the literature and culture of the nineteenth century, often on the basis of social inequalities relating to gender, sexuality, race, class, and disability.

Before exploring the complex politics of the genre, however, it is worth acknowledging that the temporal and geographical reach of 'neo-Victorianism' is neither fixed nor self-evident. The historical individuals discussed in *Neo-Victorian Freakery* often bear complex relationships to the concept of 'Victorianism' in the first instance. For example, Sarah Baartman was a Khoikhoi woman from South Africa who was born in the late eighteenth century, exhibited in Europe during the early nineteenth century and died in Paris in 1815; several decades before the beginning of Victoria's reign. Chang and Eng Bunker were born in Siam in 1811, toured Europe and America, but ultimately resided in the United States until their death in 1874. Anna Swan was Canadian, and Charles Stratton and Lavinia Warren were American. It is only Leicester-born Joseph Merrick (1862–90) who might securely be located as a 'Victorian', yet even Merrick spent time travelling Europe. However, there are two salient contexts to recognise here: the *construction* of historical epochs, and the transatlantic – and colonial – currencies of the nineteenth-century freak show. To suggest that the widespread fascination with and discussion of 'the Hottentot Venus' in the 1810s did not inform the representations and discourses surrounding performers later in the nineteenth century would be to ignore a wealth of references to Baartman throughout the Victorian era; in many ways, the ideologies of gender, race, sexuality and bodily difference which inform contemporary representation offer a prototype for subsequent constructions of Victorian 'freakery'. Following Martin Hewitt's recognition that 'historical boundaries are permeable, and questioning the nature and positioning of chronological markers helps to avoid closing off fruitful lines of enquiry' (Hewitt, 2006, p. 395), Marie-Luise Kohlke has made comparable claims for neo-Victorianism in terms of aiming to 'interpret neo-Victorianism outside of limiting and temporal identifications' which 'the Victorian' might invoke (Kohlke, 2008, p. 2). There are colonial legacies to be noted in relation to each of the performers studied in this book that are informed by 'Victorian Britain' as a point of reference, exchange, negotiation, and contestation. All of the performers discussed were exhibited in Britain at some point in their careers, and Marlene Tromp has highlighted the ways in which there has tended to be an 'either/or' approach to thinking about the relationship between North American and British 'freakery' (Tromp, 2008, pp. 4–5). What I seek to acknowledge in the following chapters, then, are both neo-Victorianism and nineteenth-century freak shows as transnational processes, whilst not losing sight of the temporal or geographic specifics of the performers discussed.

While there has been considerable critical attention paid to matters of gender, sexuality, race, and class in neo-Victorian literature, there has been a relative dearth of interest in issues of disability and/or bodily difference.[7] Bringing a disability studies perspective to neo-Victorian criticism can actually highlight some interesting – perhaps unexpected – consequences for thinking about the genre's representation of unusual bodies. Take, for example, Kate Mitchell's conceptualisation of neo-Victorian texts as 'an act of memory'. She explains:

> They remember the period not only in the usual sense, of recollecting it, but also in the sense that they re-embody, that is re-member,

> or reconstruct it. As we shall see, the dis(re)membered pieces of the past are reconstituted in and by the text, and also in the reader's imagination. The reader thus literally embodies (re-members) the reimagined past.
>
> (Mitchell, 2010, p. 7)

'Re-membering' is a suggestive metaphor for neo-Victorian engagements with the past and, as Chapter 1 explores in more detail, it has important implications for reimagining traumatic historical events marked by racial exploitation. Furthermore, as Ann Heilmann and Mark Llewellyn have identified, a key aspect of the most 'complex, metafictional, and ironic' neo-Victorian novels is the exploration of the desire to 'repossess the Victorian by performing a slippage between [...] a physical body and a textual corpus' (Heilmann and Llewellyn, 2010, p. 108). They highlight the sexual/textual politics at work in this process, and I argue that 're-membering' bodies which were marked as abnormal, freakish, or 'other' in the nineteenth century raises crucial ethical questions about the author who reanimates such bodies, and the position of the reader who is encouraged to share in the process of textual/corporeal reconstruction. Thinking about fragments of texts as 'dismembered' pieces of bodies – and the image of authors/readers putting them together in various configurations – might be understood as a process of constructing monstrosity. It evokes the image of Dr Frankenstein assembling his 'creature' from numerous body parts. But a hybrid – or monstrous – body/text is not necessarily dis-abling. Margrit Shildrick has persuasively argued that 'monsters' are generative, transformative, forcing us to rethink our definitions of bodily 'normality' (Shildrick, 2002). Indeed, perhaps this might help us to rethink Kohlke and Gutleben's image of neo-Victorian representations of the nineteenth century as 'freakish'. As I will explore in further detail below, 'freakery' is not necessarily always an oppressive concept.

More specifically, however, when applying Mitchell's 're-membering' to neo-Victorian representations of people with unusual anatomies, if the reader 'literally embodies [...] the reimagined past', do we thus have the opportunity to identify with the 'freakish' bodies re-membered for our entertainment? The ideological implications of this sense of identification are complicated. On one hand, this might work towards breaking down boundaries between the 'abnormal' other and 'normal' self, generating a sense of empathy, understanding, and acceptance towards people with a range of different bodies. In this context, perhaps 're-membering' neo-Victorian freak show performers can be perceived as a facet of the political potential of a 'universalizing' view of physical difference. As Rosemarie Garland-Thomson explains, from a feminist disability studies perspective:

> understanding how disability operates as an identity category and cultural concept will enhance how we understand what it is to be human, our relationships with one another, and the experience of embodiment. The constituency for a feminist disability theory is all of us, not only women with disabilities: disability is the most human of experiences, touching every family and – if we live long enough – touching us all.
>
> (Garland-Thomson, 2011, p. 17)

Although 'disability' and 'freakery' are certainly not precisely equivalent terms,[8] both notions speak of the prejudice towards and marginalisation of bodies figured as 'different'. Challenging this 'difference' via neo-Victorian re-memberings therefore positions this trope as part of the genre's broader sense of 'social justice' (Kohlke, 2008, p. 10). On the other hand, we should not forget that part of the dynamic of fear/fascination towards 'freaks' that was outlined by Elizabeth Grosz is a sense of recognition and identification which leads to 'horror' (Grosz, 1996, p. 65). Such a perspective certainly does not take into account the material, lived experience of the person with an unusual body, or point towards social justice.

Furthermore, in her analysis of the ways in which the freak show can offer opportunities for 'intense identification' as well as repudiation of the 'other', Rachel Adams remarks: 'each recognition is in fact a misrecognition, in which the sympathetic onlooker reads himself into the body on display, obliterating its personhood as completely as the most exploitative exhibit' (Adams, 2001, p. 31). Put another way, to appropriate the subject with an extraordinary body as a site of identification, personal or universal, runs the risk of negating the personhood of the subject on display. Adams's explanation of this potentially well-meaning, 'sympathetic onlook[ing]' at work in the politics of audience identification with freak show performers accords with Kohlke and Gutleben's definition of neo-Victorian 'after-witness': 'the fictional re-creation of trauma that both testifies to and stands in for inadequate, missing, or even impossible acts of primary witness-bearing to historical trauma' (Kohlke and Gutleben, 2010, p. 7). They elaborate further:

> Even when motivated by the best of intentions, the after-witness cannot help but appropriate trauma to some extent [...] the 'vicarious identification involved in the re-enactment or re-living of the

> other's suffering from the inside out [...] assuming *the discursively empty or unfilled place* of the sufferer.
>
> (Kohlke and Gutleben, 2010, p. 7, original emphasis)

Considering that so much of neo-Victorianism does engage with potentially traumatic experiences – whether individual or pertaining to whole groups of historical subjects – then this potential for appropriation (or even exploitation) of the Victorians is a compelling concern. To what extent can freak show performers be re-membered by neo-Victorian authors/readers in an ethical manner? This is a question that is repeatedly addressed throughout my book, and it is answered – sometimes intentionally, sometimes inadvertently – by neo-Victorian representations of freak show performers in a variety of ways. As Kohlke and Gutleben themselves acknowledge, neo-Victorian representations – traumatic or otherwise – are not always motivated by the 'best of intentions': fictional reimaginings of the nineteenth century can also be sensationalist, cynical, trivialising, coarse (Kohlke and Gutleben, 2010, p. 23); in short, prurient, exploitative, and 'othering'. Some neo-Victorian versions of the freak show, as we shall see, struggle to move beyond these characteristics.

There is another potential interpretation of 're-membering' which is relevant in different ways to all of the performers discussed in this book. The Oxford English Dictionary indicates that the noun 'member' can also refer to 'the male genitalia', or, in more obscure usages, 'the vagina, the vulva, the female genitals'. This might seem like a strangely archaic term to refer to genitalia, yet Mitchell's concept of 're-membering' becomes significant when we consider the recurring emphasis on gender and sexuality in neo-Victorian literature. The interest in scrutinising the seamier side of Victorian culture has become something of a master narrative of neo-Victorianism; whether this is in relation to prostitution and patriarchal hypocrisy, as in Michel Faber's *The Crimson Petal and the White* (2002), same-sex desire in Sarah Waters's *Tipping the Velvet* (1998), *Affinity* (1999), and *Fingersmith* (2002), or pornography – again in *Fingersmith*, and also in Belinda Starling's *The Journal of Dora Damage* (2007). The list could go on. Viewed from this perspective, 're-membering' the Victorians also suggests reimagining them as gendered and sexualised subjects, drawing attention to the genitalia, and to uses to which it might be put. As various commentators have suggested, neo-Victorian fiction regularly features both the recovery and reimagining of marginalised nineteenth-century sexualities, which is frequently couched in terms of posing a challenge to patriarchal, heteronormative versions of history.[9] However, there are attendant ethical issues in such preoccupations with Victorian sexuality. Marie-Lusie Kohlke argues:

> Neo-Victorianism [...] has become the new Orientalism, a significant mode for re-imagining sexuality in our own hedonistic, sex-surfeited age. As the spread of interdependent, globalised economies, mass tourism, and new technologies continuously diminish the unexplored geographical 'dark areas' available for reconfiguration into mirrors of our desires, a displacement occurs from the spatial to the temporal axis – even more so since 'Oriental' religion and communities are now firmly embedded into heterogeneous, 'multi-cultural' Western societies.
>
> (Kohlke, 2008b, p. 352)

Kohlke's insights here are invaluable for contextualising the ideologically problematic aspects of 're-membering' the Victorians with regards to sexuality. It is significant that the metaphor of the 'mirror' is again invoked; the nineteenth-century past becomes a site of fears and fantasies about sexual otherness, but these are projections of our own desires and preoccupations – the ambiguous combination of identification and repudiation. Of course, Kohlke's formulation of neo-Victorian representations of sexuality as being the 'new Orientalism' is particularly appropriate when thinking about when racial identity intersects with sexual prurience – themes which will become pertinent in Chapter 1's discussion of Sarah Baartman and Chapter 2's exploration of Chang and Eng. Such impulses become additionally fraught when, as critics such as Leslie Fielder and David Gerber have argued, the freak show always already has elements of sexual fascination and exploitation (Fielder, 1978, p. 335; Gerber, 1990, pp. 15–21). Elizabeth Grosz makes such dynamics explicit in her analysis of the mix of curiosity and horror that motivates the desire to gaze upon extraordinary bodies:

> [...] the initial reaction to the freakish and the monstrous is a perverse kind of sexual curiosity. People think to themselves: 'How do they do *it*?' What kind of sex lives are available to Siamese twins, hermaphrodites, bearded ladies, and midgets? There is a certain morbid speculation about what it would be like to be with such persons, or worse, to be them.
>
> (Grosz, 1996, p. 64)

I suggest that the combination of reactions which Grosz outlines – the encounter with the sexualised extraordinary body as both radical otherness and incongruous identification – offers a further dimension to Kohlke's understanding of neo-Victorianism's reimagining of nineteenth-century sexualities as the exotic other. Does neo-Victorian fiction run the risk of delineating nineteenth-century sexuality as 'freakish'? How are such risks further negotiated when the sexualised bodies under scrutiny were marked as abnormal, freakish or other in their own historical moment? One of the unifying themes of *Neo-Victorian Freakery* is the sexualised connotations of 're-membering', and both the nineteenth-century and neo-Victorian constructions of each of the performers discussed in this book demonstrate a palpable need to account for the 'sexual curiosity' involved in the contemplation of extraordinary bodies.

Reclaiming the Freak Show? Ambivalent performances

In the midst of this discussion about exploitation, prurience, and appropriation, trauma and ethics, I want to introduce a contentious question: was the nineteenth-century freak show necessarily always an oppressive phenomenon for the performers involved? According to a certain version of neo-Victorian reimagining, it is difficult to think otherwise. Consider, for instance, the images of 'John' Merrick in David Lynch's film *The Elephant Man* (1980), coerced by his 'handler' to appear in sordid conditions to the abuse and revulsion of paying audiences.[10] The very term 'freak' seems to resonate with the most heinous connotations for labelling physical difference: aberration, monstrosity, otherness. As Matthew Sweet opines: 'The professional world of the freak has come to exemplify the worst excesses and ignorances of our Victorian ancestors. It offers a thumbnail sketch of their brutality, their credulity, their willingness to exploit the unfortunate' (Sweet, 2001, p. 140). As the following chapters will indicate, there is definitely a strand of representing the Victorian freak show that taps in to this popular view. My own discussion of 're-membering' above slipped very easily from thinking about freakery to the notion of trauma. And the following chapters will demonstrate, each of the historical performers in this book were subject to oppressive – often traumatic – modes of representation in a variety of ways. I am making no claims for a wholesale rehabilitation of the reputation of nineteenth-century freak shows. Yet it is crucial to my argument to outline something more of the complex debates surrounding the connections and tensions between freakery and disability studies, and to suggest how these themes might be particularly pertinent to exploring the representation of people with unusual bodies in neo-Victorianism.

The interest in displaying and making meaning from people with unusual bodies has a history which stretches back much further than the nineteenth century,[11] but the Victorian era saw an intensification in exhibitions of and discourses about extraordinary bodies. Critics have offered various explanations for this in both British and North American contexts. Rosemarie Garland-Thomson argues that the rise in popularity of American freak shows in the nineteenth century was linked intrinsically to modernity: the rise of industrialisation, and the need to unite spectators under the banner of the 'self-governed, iterable subject of democracy – the American cultural self' (Garland-Thomson, 1996, p. 10). The extraordinary bodies on display served as a reference point against which to construct and validate the 'uniform abstract citizenry democracy institutes' (Garland-Thomson, 1996, p. 10). The 'freaks' on display thus shored up the relative 'normalcy' and physical functionality of the audiences who came to see them. In North America and Britain, the more clearly defined working week which included leisure time, coupled with new technologies of transportation which allowed for the mobility of both audiences and performers, ensured that the fairs and levees in urban environments at which 'freaks' were exhibited were accessible. Freak shows became an important component of a new working-class culture of 'commercialized leisure' in the nineteenth century (Durbach, 2010, p. 4). Yet, as Nadja Durbach has demonstrated, freak shows were not just the preserve of the working classes: in Victorian England, the repeated emphasis of the 'respectability' and educational merit of the exhibitions in the promotional materials for such events spoke to a new middle-class sensibility as well (Durbach, 2010, p. 7). Indeed, freak shows also appealed to elite consumers: Queen Victoria herself procured private audiences with several of the performers discussed in this book, including Anna Swan, and Charles Stratton.

It is important to recognise that freakery studies as an area of disability cultural history is often preoccupied with reappropriating the term 'freak', a word which 'developed its contemporary association with human anomaly' in 1847 (Tromp, 2008, p. 1). Ironically, therefore, the reinterpretation of the freak show within disability studies could actually be understood as something of a neo-Victorian enterprise. Some commentators have resolutely refused that the freak show's exploitation of bodily difference can be recuperated for the agenda of a politically-progressive disability studies (Gerber, 1996, pp. 38–54; Mitchell and

Snyder, 2005) or have rejected the word 'freak' as hurtful and stigmatising (Clare, 1999, p. 70). However, other critics have emphasised the potential for thinking of 'freakery' as a performative, constructed identity which might subvert normative understanding of visually different bodies even as it invokes them. Robert Bogdan's influential contribution to this strain of freakery studies offers the insight that the presentation of 'freaks' onstage was not a matter of revealing the essential 'otherness' of people with unusual anatomies, but a process of *construction*: '"Freak" is a frame of mind, a set of practices, a way of thinking about and presenting people. It is the enactment of a tradition, the performance of a stylized presentation' (Bogdan, 1988, p. 3). It is Bogdan's emphasis on the 'enactment of a tradition' in terms of constructing the identity of 'freaks' which I find pertinent, as it suggests a sense of historical reiteration of the conventions of freakery, a mode of constructing identity which will be familiar to those versed in Judith Butler's work on the performativity of gender. Unsurprisingly, therefore, Butler's theories have already been applied in scholarly work on the freak show, exemplified by Rachel Adams's gloss below:

> [...] *freak* is not an inherent quality but an identity realised through gesture, costume, and staging. Following Judith Butler's description of gendered performances, *freak* might also be conceived as 'an identity instituted through a stylised repetition of acts'. Repetition serves both to reinforce that identity and to destabilise it through the introduction of slight, but potentially consequential, differences [...] disabled actors [...] must also be seen as performing, not embodying the essential qualities of, freakishness. To conceive of freaks in this way is to defy the sideshow's own logic, whereby the freak's stasis on the sideshow platform mirrors the enduring and irreversible quality of her condition. Freak shows are guided by the assumption that *freak* is an essence, the basis for a comforting fiction that there is a permanent, qualitative difference between deviance and normality, projected spatially in the distance between the spectator and the body onstage. To characterise *freak* as a performance restores agency to the actors in the sideshow, who participate, albeit not always voluntarily, in a dramatic fantasy that the division between freak and normal is obvious, visible, and quantifiable.
>
> (Adams, 2001, p. 6)

Acknowledging that the identity of the 'freak' is constructed does not necessarily forestall the problematic meanings placed upon unusual bodies. As Garland-Thomson highlights, 'enfreakment emerges from cultural rituals that stylise, silence, differentiate, and distance the persons whose bodies the freak-hunters or showmen colonise and commercialise' (Garland-Thomson, 1996, p. 10). In the same way as traditional constructions of gender, race, and sexuality have demonstrated, cultural meanings placed upon extraordinary bodies might still serve to oppress, persecute, and malign. In Butlerian terms, the performative construction of identity is the reiteration of conventional norms and values.[12]

However, as indicated by Adams's commentary, the repetitions of the 'acts' required to fabricate freakish identity might be performed differently, working to challenge 'comforting fictions' of the irrevocable otherness that freakery seems to present. It is this potential for reinstalling the agency of people who performed in nineteenth-century freak shows which allows us to rethink the outright condemnation of this very Victorian institution. As I shall indicate over the coming chapters, in material terms freak shows did afford some of the performers who participated in them considerable opportunities in relation of income, travel, and companionship. In addition, the notion of performers as being the passive bearers of the prurient gazing of a united audience – the monstrous 'other' reflected in the mirror of Elizabeth Grosz's imagining – is actually disingenuous. Nadja Durbach's valuable cultural analysis of Victorian freakery reveals exhibitions as sites of interaction between performers and audience members:

> Exhibitions were often called 'levees,' suggesting that freaks were receiving guests rather than merely showing their bodies to strangers. In fact, few freaks mutely and passively displayed their abnormalities on a stage removed from the spectators. Instead they conversed with the audience, often in more than one European language, moved among them, and invited the visitors to touch them, shake their hands, and even to kiss them. They usually performed songs, dances, or tricks to amuse the public, and at times they encouraged audience participation in their acts.
>
> (Durbach, 2010, p. 9)

While this account might easily raise questions – and eyebrows – as to the dignity of such performances (the notion of 'touching' or 'kissing' performers seems particularly dubious), it does offer the potential for thinking of freak shows as arenas for mutual engagement and communication in a variety of ways, of negotiation, of prospective dialogue. I want to make clear here that my definition of the 'freak show' in this book encompasses a broad variety of practices and forums of exhibition. Robert Bogdan identifies that people performing as 'freaks' in the nineteenth century might appear in a range of locations and contexts: museums which, in this era, featured live attractions; lecture halls and theatres; circuses; buildings rented for the purpose of exhibition; carnivals (Bogdan, 1988, pp. 25–62). As the following chapters will demonstrate, the performers discussed in *Neo-Victorian Freakery* appeared in a variety of locations, with differing levels of potential for audience interaction. Even the very act of looking – the purported 'gaze' which lends itself to an analysis of unequal power relationships and objectification[13] – can be reappropriated. Rosemarie Garland-Thomson's work on 'staring' as a process of exchange between agents is vital in this respect, as she argues that this visual encounter can generate an 'interpersonal relationship':

> [...] a circuit of communication and meaning-making. Staring bespeaks involvement, and being stared at demands a response. A staring encounter is a dynamic struggle – starers inquire, stares lock eyes or flee, and starers advance or retreat; one moves forward and the other moves back. A staring interchange can tickle or alienate, persist or evolve.
>
> (Garland-Thomson, 2009, pp. 3–4)

Such exchanges are surely precarious and unpredictable, indicated by the different consequences of staring which Garland-Thomson notes. But it offers us a way of thinking beyond the displays of Victorian freak show performers as being irrevocably exploitative, and instead as having generative and transformative potential for all involved.

But the construction of nineteenth-century freakery was not limited just to the temporal events of the performances. Garland-Thomson has identified four 'narrative forms' which produced freakish identity: the 'oral spiel' or 'lecture' which would introduce the performer, often delivered by their manager; textual promotional materials – the pamphlets of 'true life stories' furnishing a (largely fictional) history for the performer, but also newspaper advertisements and features; the 'staging' of the performance (costume, choreography); and visual merchandise – illustrations or photographs (Garland-Thomson, 1996, pp. 6–7). Victorian freaks are always already narrative constructions, formed and reformed via various media, before and after the confines of the actual performance. This central role of story-telling in forming freakery is a vital aspect of this book's engagement with nineteenth-century and neo-Victorian representations of performers. Each chapter will consider the narrative depictions of performers in their own historical moment, in the form of 'true life story' pamphlets (Anna Swan, Charles Stratton, Lavinia Warren), overtly fictional portrayals in the shape of plays and short stories (Sarah Baartman, Chang and Eng Bunker), popular and professional medical accounts (Joseph Merrick). These documents, I argue, construct freakery. Furthermore, the neo-Victorian novels, plays, and films I examine continue with this process of (re)construction as well. If, as Robert Bogdan and Rachel Adams argue, the identity of freak show performers is performative, and so can be negotiated and performed differently, what are the neo-Victorian story-telling strategies and politics deployed to enact this re-membering? My previous work on neo-Victorianism has highlighted that it is a genre preoccupied with transformation via repetition, particularly in relation to nineteenth-century gender roles.[14] *Neo-Victorian Freakery* extends and develops this concept with regards to the discursive construction of freakery in both Victorian and neo-Victorian contexts. I argue that due to the narrative component of representing unusual bodies, the strand of neo-Victorianism which I focus upon is, indeed, a freak show. Yet, like the nineteenth-century freak show, this is an ambiguous forum of negotiating difference. There are some oppressive reiterations of the boundaries between self and other, 'normalcy' and the 'abnormal', but there are also possibilities for understanding and empathy, learning about different ways of being and living which can lead us to question our presumptions about 'freakish' Victorians as well as about bodily diversity in our cultural moment as well.

Neo-Victorian biofiction, freakery, and medicine

There is, however, an obvious challenge in this (re)construction of freakery, which feeds into a broader quandary about neo-Victorian representations of the past: how might we enter into a productive and ethical negotiation with subjects whose perspectives have been lost to history? One of the reasons why the re-evaluation of freakery from a disability studies perspective has remained so contentious is because there is very little existing evidence of what nineteenth-century freak show performers actually thought of their careers. Both Leslie Fielder and Matthew Sweet have bemoaned this crucial absence from the historical record: Fielder suggesting that 'true life' stories and 'autobiographies' were often written by the performer's manager (Fielder, 1981, p. 274); Sweet acknowledging that such accounts were often overtly fictionalised and that 'to some extent, what will survive of [performers] is lies. We'll never know whether Tom Thumb and Lavinia Warren, sitting in their miniature mansion in Bridgeport, were truly happy with their lives' (Sweet, 2001, p. 153). Frustrating as this might be for scholars of the history and politics of the freak show, it does offer enormous potential for imaginative rewritings of the era. In this sense, neo-Victorianism can provide a significant creative intervention in rethinking the personalities and culture of the freak show, considering its commitment to uncovering covert, marginalised or otherwise lost histories of the nineteenth century.

Nevertheless, with this license to invent comes great responsibility as well, especially when dealing with characters who are based on actual historical figures. Fictionalised accounts of Victorian personalities – particularly authors such as Henry James, Oscar Wilde, and Charles Dickens – form an important subgenre of neo-Victorianism: bio-fiction.[15] Deploying David Andress's definition of an 'ethical approach to history',[16] Mark Llewellyn stresses the accountability of neo-Victorian authors for the historical figures who they reimagine as fictional characters, which might 'undermine certain aspects of history as a lived experience':

> Appropriating the dead writers of the nineteenth century as if they were only figments of a shared cultural imagination opens up new possibilities but also new ethical dimensions to the neo-Victorian text. Like the biographer as grave robber, some neo-Victorian fiction is in danger of blurring the distinction between reality and imagination, lives lived and lives created.
>
> (Llewellyn, 2009, p. 38)

I want to extend Llewellyn's cautionary comments on the 'dangers' of neo-Victorian bio-fiction beyond nineteenth-century authors, for surely the ethical considerations in treating historical subjects as 'fictional' characters are compounded when these 'characters' were vulnerable to misrepresentation, silencing, 'othering' and exploitation in their own life times, as in the case of all of the performers I will be discussing in this book. The neo-Victorian depictions of freak show performers can be designated as 'biofiction of marginalised subjects', to use Marie-Luise Kohlke's phrase, and as she also identifies, 'Those seemingly being written a life risk being turned into poor ghosts once more', perpetually 'spoken for' by neo-Victorian authors: 'In part, this ethical cul-de-sac undermines the liberative aspirations of biofiction of marginalised subjects' (Kohlke, 2013, p. 11).

Moreover, Llewellyn's link between neo-Victorianism and 'grave-robbing' takes on especially poignant connotations when we consider the ways in which freak show performers could be exposed to further exhibition after their lives had ended. For example, Julia Pastrana, a woman billed at various points as 'the Nondescript', 'the Bear Woman', and 'the Ugliest Woman in the World' was embalmed after her death and continued to be exhibited by her husband and manager.[17] Medical professionals were often also keen to lay claim to the remains of performers for the purposes of 'research'; the preservation and display of Sarah Baartman's body is the most controversial example discussed in this book, but Chang and Eng Bunker's and Joseph Merrick's remains have also remained the property of medical museums.[18] As Chapter 1 explains with regards to Baartman, such posthumous display is extremely difficult to justify in terms of granting performers any sense of agency or dignity, for they clearly have no opportunity to control the terms of their exhibition and are irrevocably confined to the role of object rather than subject. The connections and contrasts between medical discourses and constructions of freakery is a central theme of this book. In exploring the role which medical discourse played in the construction of 'freakery' in the nineteenth century, Alice Domurat Dreger notes a shift towards the end of the century. Previously, medical professionals might contribute towards the promotional materials for freak show performers, but at the beginning of the twentieth century, there is an increasingly proprietary attitude towards medicine's right to access unusual bodies for study and research in a forum away from public audiences (Dreger, 2004, pp. 123–24).

More broadly, disability studies as a field of critical inquiry has regularly interrogated the ways in which the medical profession might seek to pathologise and/or 'correct' unusual bodies via the 'medical model' of disability.[19] In contrast, the social model of disability argues that it is any given culture's perception of physical or cognitive difference which dis-ables individuals. Tom Shakespeare offers an important definition of the distinction between these categories: 'Whereas [the social model of disability] defines disability as a social creation – a relationship between people with impairment and a disabling society – the [medical model] defines disability in terms of individual deficit' (Shakespeare, 2010, p. 268).[20] In addition, neo-Victorianism regularly features representations of medical professionals which expose abuses of power and status in the nineteenth century, particularly in relation to gender and sexuality, but also with regards to race.[21] Christy Rieger has coined a useful phrase – 'medical sensationalism' – to discuss the neo-Victorian fascination with 'scandal, illicit sexuality, the abject body, and medical misconduct' (Rieger, 2014, pp. 153–64), and the figure of the deviant, perverse, or exploitative medical professional is repeatedly represented in the coming chapters. The boundaries between freak show and medical exhibition are frequently blurred in neo-Victorianism.

Nevertheless, how far removed is medical post-mortem exhibition from the 're-memberment' enacted upon performers by neo-Victorianism? The most ethically aware of the neo-Victorian representations of performers I explore in this project self-consciously engage with the politics of textual resurrections, yet even in the case of Barbara Chase-Riboud's *The Hottentot Venus* (Chapter 1) or Stacy Carlson's *Among the Wonderful* (Chapter 3), more questions are raised than can easily be answered. Although perhaps it is in the willingness to ask these questions, to confront the reader/viewer of neo-Victorian freak shows with their own desire to consume the afterlives of performers, that neo-Victorian freakery does aspire towards something of the ambivalent dynamism of the nineteenth-century freak show. As the audience for these fictions, we might not be able to meet the stare of the historical subjects being re-membered, but we can reflect upon our own interest (prurient? pitying? curious? empathetic?) in re-visioning Victorian freakery. And so we return again to the image of the neo-Victorian mirror, with the 'distortions' we perceive of our contemporary concerns, rather than nineteenth-century 'realities'. However, as I have sought to outline, nineteenth-century freakery was already an arena of misdirection, fiction and fabrication, which, as we shall see in the coming chapters, also reflected the concerns of its time. A risk of writing about freak shows – whether creatively or critically – is to descend into hyperbole and bravado, or to place metaphorical weight upon 'freakish' bodies which relegates the actual lives and experiences of performers to symbols and icons: in effect, to participate in the discursive construction of freakery even as I seek to critique and analyse it. Commenting on the tendency of academic studies on freak shows to reproduce photographs of the performers being discussed, David T. Mitchell and Sharon Snyder remark that: 'Spectacles of prurience continue to resuscitate modes of objectification they set out to undermine' (Mitchell and Snyder, 2005, n. p.). I have made a decision not to include photographic representations of the performers that I consider in this book for this very reason, and have largely confined my study to textual constructions of Victorian and neo-Victorian freakery.[22] Of course, this in itself offers no exoneration from accusations of prurience, objectification, and exploitation, bearing in mind, as I outlined above, that textual representation was a central device in the manufacture of freakish personae.

Contemplating this very predicament, Rosemarie Garland-Thomson suggests that the critic must 'keep a steady focus on the materiality of the people who performed as freaks and the particular circumstances of their actual lives' (Garland-Thomson, 2008, p. x). Admittedly this is a difficult task when confronted with so many fictions, but my own attempt at a 'steady focus' will be to re-member these performers as human subjects with a right to dignity and respect, and to critically interrogate representations – nineteenth century and neo-Victorian – which struggle to accord this. As a reader and critic of neo-Victorianism, I am implicated in the politics of neo-Victorian freakery: I, like you, am a member of the audience. We can never have an unmediated perspective on these performers, and the boundary between representation and 'reality' is necessarily always blurred. But the complex ideological work done by cultural representation is always worthy of scrutiny, and it is in this spirit that I reflect, albeit with a stare which is partial, upon neo-Victorian freak shows.

Neo-Victorian Freakery: chapter outline

Chapter 1, 'Mixing (re)Memory and Desire: Constructing Sarah Baartman', considers the tensions between the aspiration to re-member 'The Hottentot Venus' as a woman with dignity and the danger of resubmitting Sarah to the colonial and sexualised discourses which defined her persona during her lifetime. Nineteenth-century representations of the 'Hottentot Venus' in contemporary ballads and plays hint that the signifiers of race, gender and sexuality which shape her persona are a mode of performance, which raises the question of her agency and consent in being exhibited. Considering her posthumous exhibition as a 'specimen' in a Parisian Museum, metaphors of haunting inform her neo-Victorian afterlife, but the difficulty in 're-membering' her life without prurient focus upon her body is a contentious issue in Suzan-Lori Parks's play *Venus* (1990) and Barbara Chase-Riboud's novel *Hottentot Venus* (2003). Although these texts do represent scientific exhibition as more horrific than freak show performance, they still make us aware of our own complicity as 'consumers' of Sarah's afterlife.

Chapter 2, 'Separation Anxieties: Sex, death, and Chang and Eng Bunker', highlights speculation over the sex lives of conjoined twins – and the horror of conjoined mortality – as shaping discourses upon both nineteenth-century and neo-Victorian representations of the brothers. Several of Mark Twain's texts about conjoined twins are examined, alongside William B. Pancoast's autopsy report on the Bunker twins. Morally charged judgements on the 'propriety' of the twins' lives are never far from the surface, and the impossible dream of separation emerges as a desire to impose order upon unruly desires and bodies. Darin Strauss's *Chang and Eng* (2000) and Mark Slouka's *God's Fool* (2002) offer first-person narrative perspectives from Eng and Chang respectively. Strauss's narrative, whilst critical of freak show modes of presentation, finds it difficult to represent the brothers' sexuality in anything other than a voyeuristic light, ultimately concluding that conjoined sexuality is, in itself, 'disabling'. In contrast, Slouka's novel offers metatextual insights into the potential of forming 'connections' between self and other, but is acutely aware of the way in which the desire for identification can become oppressive, especially with regards to race.

Chapter 3, 'Excessively Feminine? Anna Swan, gendering giantesses, and the genre of the "true life story" pamphlet' considers how 'big' women are depicted as troubling the conventions of gender, and how the genre of the 'true life story' pamphlet has some compelling parallels with neo-Victorian writing more broadly. Nineteenth-century representations of Anna often seek to contain her 'excess', yet Susan Swan's neo-Victorian *The Biggest Modern Woman of the World* (1983) offers Anna's size as the barometer of her feminist potential. Yet her version of Anna still struggles with patriarchal pressures that attempt to 'belittle' and mould her to the conventions of femininity. Freak show modes of presentation are an ambivalent source of agency for Anna; an outlet from Victorian domestic expectations, but also a form of commodifying her body. This link between body and text is of central importance to Ana Swift, Stacy Carlson's representation of Swan in *Among the Wonderful* (2011). Tasked with writing her own 'true life story', she seems to take control of her body and destiny. However, her writing is still subject to posthumous exhibition, a crucial metatextual reflection on the ethical implications of how neo-Victorian freakery re-members bodies for our entertainment.

Chapter 4, 'Innocence, Experience, and Childhood Dramas: Charles Stratton and Lavinia Warren' explores how Victorian constructions of childhood intersect with nineteenth-century discourses of dwarfism. Themes of precocious sexuality, and the person with dwarfism as a 'trickster' figure emerge in representations of Stratton and Warren, as do anxieties about the boundaries between the 'child' and 'adult'. However, the neo-Victorian versions of Charles and Lavinia offered in Jane Sullivan's *Little People* (2011) and Melanie Benjamin's *The Autobiography of Mrs Tom Thumb* (2011) do not consider child – or dwarf – sexuality to be a laughing matter. In both novels Charles is a traumatised, pitiable figure, and his childhood experiences of fame are tantamount to abuse. Lavinia is an intelligent and articulate woman, but her collusion with show business and tendency to invoke power inequalities of class, race, and disability offers avenues of speculation on the dangers of 'belittling' adults.

Chapter 5, 'The Strange Case of Joseph and Jack: Joseph Merrick and spectacles of deviance', analyses the disturbing points of connection between two Victorian mythical 'monsters': Joseph Merrick and Jack the Ripper. Contextualised via nineteenth-century fears and fantasies about the spectacle of disfigured prostitutes, I suggest that Frederick Treves's memoir of Merrick fashions his subject as sexualised, feminised and deviant. The theme of gendered and moral monstrosity informs neo-Victorian versions of Merrick: Bernard Pomerance's play *The Elephant Man* (1979) and David Lynch's 1980 film of the same name position Merrick as a victim of sexual prudery and sexual violence respectively, reiterating the tropes of prostitution which are implied in Treves's text. While Merrick is often associated with the role of feminised, orientalised, and victimised sex worker in the Ripper representations this chapter considers – Iain Sinclair's *White Chappell, Scarlet Tracings* (1987), Alan Moore and Eddie Campbell's *From Hell* (1999) and the Hughes Brothers film adaptation of the same name (2001) – there is a recurring implication that his physical appearance might inspire the moral monstrosity of the doctor-as-Ripper. The depiction of Merrick in the BBC series *Ripper Street* (2012–present) offers a more sympathetic re-membering of Joseph, yet themes of sexual victimisation and deviancy are never far from the surface.

The Afterword to this book – 'The Neo-Victorian Enfreakment of P. T. Barnum' – considers three neo-Victorian versions of the American showman: his 'exotic' fashioning in Carlson's *Among the Wonderful*, his 'aggrandised' construction in Benjamin's *The Autobiography of Mrs Tom Thumb*, and an imagining of his sexual failure in Angela Carter's *Nights at the Circus* (1984). What emerges is the opportunity to reflect upon negotiating the politics of exhibition, of how cultural afterlives might be re-membered in an ethical fashion, and the metatextual lessons that the 'enfreakment' of all Victorians, regardless of their bodies, can teach us as the 'audience' for the neo-Victorian freak show.

1
Mixing (re)Memory and Desire: Constructing Sarah Baartman

Sarah Baartman was exhibited as 'the Hottentot Venus' in early nineteenth-century England and France. The facts of Sarah Baartman's life – even down to her date of birth, date of death, and her name – are still contested.[1] She was a Khoikhoi woman born during the mid-1770s in South Africa.[2] Sarah spent much of her childhood living and working on colonial farms and also as a domestic servant. Whilst in the employment of Hendrik Cesars,[3] she had been persuaded to perform for male patients in a nearby naval hospital (Crais and Scully, 2009, pp. 50–51). Western ethnographic narratives had a long-established fascination with the physical appearance and cultural customs of the 'Hottentot' people, namely the purported large buttocks and elongated genitalia of the women. It should be noted here that the term 'Hottentot' is now considered to be highly derogatory; it was the name given to the Khoikhoi people by colonial settlers, meaning 'stutterers', and referred to the sound of their language. A Scottish doctor, Alexander Dunlop, heard of Sarah and met with Cesars to negotiate bringing her to England to be displayed in the fairs and exhibitions, regularly featuring anatomical 'curiosities', which were becoming increasingly popular at this historical moment. Sarah seemingly consented to this new career in Europe under the promise of fame and fortune, and was first exhibited in Piccadilly in 1810. She was presented in a tight-fitting, flesh-coloured suit to emphasise her figure, and was exhibited as part-freak, part ethnographic specimen, and received a considerable amount of press attention and publicity. During the autumn of 1810, a campaign was started for a legal investigation into Sarah's well-being, as abolitionists of the time suspected that she was an enslaved woman and objected to the degrading spectacle of her acts. The ensuing court case ruled that Sarah was performing under her own volition, and she continued to appear in public shows and private viewings. There are some absences in the surviving historical record of her life during 1811–13, but she travelled to Paris in 1814 under the management of Henry Taylor. In 1815, she was sold to a new manager, and was regularly displayed to high-society audiences. During this time, she attracted the interest of Georges Cuvier, a French naturalist, who persuaded her to submit to examination and drawings at the Muséum d'Histoire Naturelle. Cuvier was obsessed with the racist theory of separating different ethnic groups into a hierarchy of 'species', and was keen to have the body of a 'Hottentot' woman in his natural history collection. Sarah's health began to fail in 1815, and she died between 29–31 December of that year; the precise date and cause of her death is unknown.[4] Her corpse was quickly claimed by Cuvier, who made a full cast of her body and dissected and preserved her brain, genitalia, and skeleton.

Perhaps more than any of the performers discussed in this study, Baartman's life – and afterlife – has been extremely controversial and highly-publicised. Her remains were originally housed at the Muséum d'Histoire Naturelle until 1937, when they were moved to Paris's Musée de l'Homme. Her skeleton and body cast were publically exhibited until complaints from women's groups in the 1970s led to their removal into private storage; they would make a brief return to public display in 1994. It was in 1995 that the South African government began a formal campaign to have Sarah's remains returned to her homeland for burial.[5] In many ways, the 'ownership' of Sarah's remains became entwined with South Africa's political reforms towards greater equality in the 1990s, and broader debates over the legacy of colonialism. It was not until 2002 that France agreed to these requests. The repatriation and burial of Sarah Baartman in her homeland received a great deal of press attention, and offered the opportunity for both political and cultural reconsideration of the discourses of colonialism, sexism, and 'scientific' racism which led to her exhibition in the first instance.

Textual representations of Sarah played a significant role in highlighting the indignities of her posthumous possession by France; Diana Ferrus's poem, 'I've Come to Take You Home', written in 1998, was read out by French Senator Nicolas About to the French Senate on 29 January 2002, the day they finally voted to release Sarah's remains from the Musée de l'Homme for return to South Africa (Holmes, 2007, pp. 173–74). Clearly there were other complex political negotiations at work here, but the idea that a fictional reimagining of Sarah could have such an influence upon the attitudes of a nation – that such a text could offer some avenue for redressing the power relationships of empire and gender which continued into Sarah's afterlife – is compelling indeed. As an introduction to the themes that I will be discussing in this chapter, I want to offer a brief reading of Ferrus's text. The poetic voice imagines taking Sarah back to her homeland, to the 'lush green grass' of the Cape; the speaker explains: 'I have come to bring you peace' (Ferrus, 2010, p. 213). Such a formulation implies that Sarah is an unquiet spirit, who cannot find rest until her body receives a proper burial. Her posthumous exhibition in the French museum is explained in damning terms:

> I have come to wrench you away
> away from the poking eyes of the man-made monster
> who lives in the dark with his clutches of imperialism
> who dissects your body bit by bit,
> who likens your soul to that of satan
> and declares himself the ultimate God!
>
> (Ferrus, 2010, p. 213)

The medical gaze is depicted as penetrative – masculinised and sexualised. The use of the term 'monster' is loaded, considering Sarah's career as a freak show performer. As indicated by the Introduction, all 'monsters' are 'man-made' in the sense that freakery is a process of construction, defining (and sometimes thwarting) the precarious boundaries between the 'normal' and 'abnormal'. However, Ferrus's terminology suggests that 'monstrosity' lies in the medical men such as Cuvier who used Sarah's body to justify their own racist ideologies. Here, the mirror metaphor discussed in the Introduction is also relevant; the audience of a body perceived to be unusual will project their own distorted imaginings onto that form. The image of Sarah's body being taken apart – dismembered – is particularly poignant, considering the focus on her body parts in life and in death. We are reminded of neo-Victorianism's power of re-membering, of reconstructing nineteenth-century bodies that have been lost in a variety of ways. For the poetic voice to work to 'wrench' Sarah way from the anatomisation that she has suffered thus speaks of piecing together the fragments, to repair the literal and symbolic violence that she has experienced.

In this sense, we can understand Ferrus's poem as reimagining and reappropriating several facets of Sarah's oppression in her life and death. However, there are some more ambivalent images at work in the text. The speaker of the poem is consistently represented as an active presence: 'I have come to take' / 'I have come to wrench' / 'I have come to sooth' (Ferrus, 2010, p. 213). These acts of reparation offer a pointed contrast to the actions of the 'man-made monster', but he too has been an agent with 'poking eyes', dissecting powers, and the privilege of declaration. In either set of deeds, it is always Sarah who is having something done to her; she is never the active agent, but always the passive bearer of someone else's volition. Furthermore, the speaker's promised actions in relation to Sarah's body are noteworthy: 'I will cover your face with the palms of my hands, / I will run my lips over the lines in your neck, / I will feast my eyes on the beauty of you' (Ferrus, 2010, p. 213). This imagined engagement is protective, emotional, sensual, and erotic in turn. To look upon Sarah as a woman of beauty is a significant reappropriation of her image, considering her denigration as 'freakish' in some nineteenth-century accounts which will be explored below. However, the prospect of 'feasting' on Sarah's body is surely provocative, a quasi-cannibalistic image of consumption which signifies ambiguously. Even as Sarah is re-membered, the poem struggles to think of her as anything other than a passive victim, and invokes a discourse of eroticism and 'savagery' as it attempts to wrest her from the gaze of one audience to another.

The first section of this chapter begins with an analysis of the terms under which Sarah was exhibited as 'the Hottentot Venus', and examines a selection of notable textual representations dating from her lifetime. In the Introduction to this book, I highlighted Robert Bogdan's definition of the construction of freakery as 'the enactment of a tradition' (Bogdan, 1988, p. 3); as a context for exploring how neo-Victorianism revisits and re-enacts the exhibition of 'the Hottentot Venus', we need to understand something of the 'traditions' in which her original presentation were located. In Sarah's case, this involves both the freak show and ethnographic display. Much of the contemporary debate around Sarah's exhibition relied upon the distinction – or potential lack thereof – between the performance of freakery and the ethnographic show as a vehicle for colonial exploitation. In this vein, I examine a series of legal documents and letters published in newspapers dating from 1810 which debate Sarah's exhibition and the extent to which she 'chose' this, rather than being coerced as an enslaved woman. Ultimately, Sarah's exhibition was deemed lawful, but there are ambivalences in these documents which deserve further scrutiny in terms of the anxiety they reveal about her agency: an uncertainty which is also a key theme in her neo-Victorian afterlife. However, the emphasis which is placed upon the freak show as a forum for performers to exercise their own volition is also important, a theme which becomes particularly apparent in my analysis of the anonymous ballad published the year after this legal wrangle. *The Hottentot Venus: A New Song* (1811) constructs Sarah was a knowing agent in control of her own presentation. Of course, there are still racial and gendered ideologies at work in this construction, which problematize her exhibition even as it is celebrated. The final text I wish to explore in this section is the French play by Théaulon, Dartois, and Braiser, *The Hottentot Venus, or Hatred of Frenchwomen* (1814).[6] Despite the play's colonialist ideologies, it can also be interpreted as representing the boundaries between 'respectable' Western femininity and the 'otherness' of the Hottentot Venus as being permeable, performative, and unstable. The play thus might point towards the ways in which the representation of freak show performers such as Sarah offered an avenue for rethinking the borders between 'self' and 'other' in her own cultural moment, a theme which becomes central in her neo-Victorian afterlife.

Exhibition; agency; re-membering; sexuality; haunting; consumption: these are the tropes which shape Sarah Baartman's representation in neo-Victorianism. Via a brief reading of the concept of 're-memory' in Toni Morrison's *Beloved* (1987), I suggest that the metaphor of haunting becomes pertinent to conceptualising the tension between victimhood and agency in Baartman's cultural afterlife. My analysis of Suzan-Lori Parks's *Venus* (1990) highlights the play's problematizing of uncovering the 'real' Sarah via re-memberment. She is a complex, sexualised subject who is complicit in her own exploitation to an extent. However, the audience is also embroiled in her posthumous 'consumption', and we are forced to reflect upon our own participation in this feasting on her body. Barbara Chase-Riboud's *Hottentot Venus* (2003) has some significant parallels with Parks's play, for it also engages with the themes of agency, the freak show, and the politics of re-memberment. Both texts depict science – in the form of fictional versions of Cuvier – as more exploitative and objectifying than freak show presentation. As we shall see, the play and novel also are self-conscious about their own continued 'exhibition' of Sarah yet sometimes struggle to re-member her without reiterating the discourses which made her a spectacle in life and death.

Ethnographic exhibition and the enfreakment of Sarah Baartman

Sarah's billing as 'the Hottentot Venus' overtly presented her in terms of race and expectations of femininity, and the ways in which a 'Hottentot' woman would have signified to an early nineteenth-century audience demand further consideration. As we shall see throughout this book, the public exhibition of unusual bodies has always been shaped by ideologies of gender, race, and sexuality, and these are heightened in the case of Sarah. She appeared in freak shows alongside other performers with perceived physical anomalies, but her own purported differences signified as racial spectacles as well. Her exhibition was not only invested in freak show discourse, but those of ethnographic display. As Bernth Lindfors explains: 'displaying foreign peoples for commercial and/or educational purposes' has a substantial historical precedent before the nineteenth century, which is bound up with new geographical circuits of trade which emerged from 1500s onwards (Lindfors, 1996, p. 207). Of course, such overseas encounters rapidly became avenues for colonial expansion, and nineteenth-century attitudes towards 'Hottentots' were informed by accounts of the Khoikhoi people proffered by Dutch travellers and colonisers from around 1600s. Sadiah Qureshi offers the following summary of the imperialist implications of these depictions:

> Wildness and savagery characterized depictions of the Khoikhoi during the seventeenth century, quickly establishing them as the 'link' between ape and human in nature's great hierarchy. Images suggestive of cannibalism and depicting the consumption of raw flesh, alongside women with simian proportions and pendulous breasts, were characteristic.
>
> (Qureshi, 2004, p. 234)

The alleged 'savagery' of the indigenous people of European colonies acted as justification for their subjugation; spurious stories of cannibalism and bestial inclinations positioned 'Hottentots' as closer to the state of animals than humanity, and in need of controlling. Such racist ideologies continue, most troublingly, into Sarah's afterlife; the concept of 'cannibalism', as suggested by Ferrus's 'feasting', will loom large in a variety of ways. Furthermore, as Z. S. Strother has also pointed out, these stereotypes were also gendered: 'Hottentot' women were a source of especial fear and fascination in relation to their bodies, namely their supposedly overgrown buttocks and elongated labia (Strother, 1999, pp. 21–22). There was considerable debate in travel writing as to whether the latter was a natural phenomenon – thus indicative of 'Hottentots' being a different species – or a manipulation of the body dictated by cultural norms, either to enhance a woman's desirability or to ensure her chastity.[7]

The presumption that there would be an audience for the spectacle of such stereotypes surely motivated Alexander Dunlop's interest in bringing Sarah to Europe for exhibition. Clifton Crais and Pamela Scully comment upon how during her employment as Hendrik Cesars's servant, Sarah was also encouraged to 'show herself' to European patients at Cape Town's military hospital. The specifics of this exhibition are not recorded, but Crais and Scully interpret her interaction with Western men in this context as being motivated by colonial desire for 'exotic' women (Crais and Scully, 2009, pp. 50–51). Dunlop's work as a doctor in the same area brought him into contact with Sarah: he 'no doubt watched the sailors' titillation and wondered at the possibilities of showing Sara Baartman not to hundreds of sickly people but to thousands of people with money in their pockets' (Crais, 2009, p. 54). In addition, Dunlop's travels across the globe meant he was well-versed in the trade for and exhibition of exotic artefacts – the paraphernalia of empire – in European cities (Holmes, 2007, p. 46). It was under these terms which Sarah's exhibition in London was initially to be couched: on arriving in Britain with Sarah in 1810, Dunlop approached William Bullock who owned the Liverpool Museum on 22 Piccadilly, London. This museum prided itself on an extensive collection of 'Natural and Foreign Curiosities', which, in Rachel Holmes's phrasing, 'exemplified the hoarding instincts of imperialism' (Holmes, 2007, 58). Dunlop attempted to persuade Bullock to buy the rights to Sarah's exhibition along with a giraffe skin; significantly, Bullock accepted the skin, but declined Sarah, stating that 'such an exhibition would not meet the countenance of the public' (Strother, 1999, p. 47). It seems that Bullock's ethnographic displays did not extend to live human exhibits at this point in his career;[8] 'he was a museum director, not the keeper of a freak show' (Holmes, 2007, p. 59).

Nevertheless, the boundary between ethnographic display and the more general exhibition of extraordinary bodies – the freak shows – was not clearly defined, for Piccadilly was an area of London which housed Bullock's museum and numerous other displays of human curiosities and 'wonders'. Indeed, Dunlop and Cesars ultimately secured the address of 225 Piccadilly for Sarah's exhibition, very close to the site of Bullock's ostensibly more educational institution (Holmes, 2007, p. 61). Z. S. Strother has argued that Baartman's presentation departed from the performances of 'freaks' in the sense that the latter were exhibited on the grounds of their 'uniqueness' and 'individuality', whereas ethnographic 'types' were supposed to emphasise the 'typical' characteristics of a whole group of people (Strother, 1999, p. 25). However, such a perspective belies the extent to which the presentation of freak show performers would regularly invoke national and racial identities as a framing discourse for the bodies on display. Strother also fails to recognise that freak show presentation does tend to generalise 'otherness', as Rosemarie Garland-Thomson explains:

> at the same time that enfreakment elaborately foregrounds specific bodily eccentricities, it also collapses all those differences into a 'freakery', a single amorphous category of corporeal otherness. By constituting the freak as an icon of generalised embodied deviance, the exhibitions also simultaneously reinscribed gender, race, sexual aberrance, ethnicity, and disability as inextricable yet particular exclusionary systems legitimated by bodily variation – all represented by the single multivalent figure of the freak.
>
> (Garland-Thomson, 1996, p. 10)

In this context, Sarah's exhibition evidently did represent the blurring of a boundary between freakery and ethnographic display, a conflation which would become more pronounced as the century progressed.[9]

Considering her on-stage appearance and choreography can aid in understanding something more of the implications of this synthesis. Sarah was costumed in a fine, flesh-coloured garment which hugged her skin, giving the illusion of nakedness whilst actually covering her body. She was adorned with numerous necklaces, bracelets and fringes, and a decorated 'apron' of leather which covered her genitalia, but alluded to the imagined length of her labia (Holmes, 2007, pp. 63–64). Her background setting included paintings of African landscapes; she played South African instruments and danced 'in the manner of her country' (Holmes, 2007, pp. 60–61). Although these trappings seemed to suggest her 'authenticity' as a 'natural' ethnographic specimen, they are the accoutrements of performance; the construction of colonial 'otherness' for a Western audience which bore little resemblance to Sarah's everyday clothes or experiences.[10] She was overtly racialized and sexualised, invoking the signifiers of colonial discourse on the 'Hottentot' people, but this was performative, stylised, positively burlesque. In short, the mode of presenting Sarah offers a striking resemblance to the construction of freakery as detailed in the Introduction. Of course, this is not to suggest that such performance did not perpetuate deeply troubling ideologies of race and gender. But, as my analysis of the ballad *The Hottentot Venus* and the French play of the same name will demonstrate, there is some evidence to suggest that Sarah's contemporary audiences did perceive her as a performer rather than a 'natural' or 'authentic' specimen of the Hottentot people.

By her own consent? A question of agency

What is interesting for my purposes is the extent to which the textual debates around Sarah's 'consent' in her exhibition did invoke a distinction between freak show performance and racialized display/exploitation, disingenuous though this might have been. For a real source of concern was about whether Sarah was actually an enslaved woman being coerced into exhibition. In October 1810, Zachary Macaulay, a high-profile abolitionist and secretary of the African Institute, visited one of Sarah's performances, which he later stated was to learn 'under what circumstances she came to England and whether she made a public spectacle of her own free will and consent or whether she was compelled to exhibit herself and desirous of returning to her own country' (Strother, 1999, p. 43). His ensuing account offers a complicated mix of outrage and prurience. Macaulay details how she was:

> [...] clothed in a dress resembling her complexion which is very dark and her dress was so tight that her shapes above and the enormous size of her posterior parts are as visible as if the said female were naked and the dress is evidently intended to give the appearance of her being undressed.
>
> (Strother, 1999, p. 43)

He complains repeatedly about the emphasis which is placed on Sarah's body – the suggestion of her nudity – yet ironically fulfils the role of being just another audience member marvelling at her bodily otherness by remarking upon the 'enormity' of her bottom; he subsequently refers to her 'extraordinary shape' (Strother, 1999, p. 43). Why does he feel the need to highlight the 'darkness' of her complexion? This detail feeds into the detail of her near-nakedness, running the risk of reiterating the stereotype of the savage sexuality of black women that he ostensibly critiques. Presumably, Macaulay's intention is to underscore that her skin is the site of her oppression: she is a black woman, and so therefore her agency must be questionable. This theme of 'reading' the meaning of her body is continued as he describes 'that the said female by her looks gave evident signs of mortification and misery at her degraded situation in being made a spectacle for the derision of bystanders without power of resistance' (Strother, 1999, p. 44). Macaulay might not be expressing 'derision' at the spectacle of the Hottentot Venus, but he does place a heavy interpretative weight upon her body here, imposing his own narrative voice upon her 'looks'. He does not relate any attempt to actually communicate personally with Sarah at this stage, but returns a few days later in the company of two other members of the African Institute: Thomas Gisborne Babington and Peter Van Wageninge, the latter of whom spoke Dutch. This facilitates the questioning of Sarah; she is asked about her family, her happiness, whether she wants to return home, 'but said female would not answer any of such questions' (Strother, 1999, p. 45).

How should we interpret this refusal to speak? Macaulay's statement informs us that Cesars is present at the time of this questioning, and continues to issue commands to her to perform. We learn as well that there are 'many other spectators in the room at the time' (Strother, 1999, p. 45). Sarah seems condemned to the role as silent spectacle, which appears far from the rethinkings of nineteenth-century freak shows as potential sites of dialogue and exchange as detailed in the Introduction. However, there is another way of interpreting Macaulay's narrative, as he and his companions do not take account of the influence their presence might have upon the events of this particular performance. He relates: 'during the time they were present the said female at one time appeared very morose and sullen and retired into the little recess of the stage' (Strother, 1999, p. 45). Doubtlessly Macaulay's expression – 'during the time they were present' – is intended to suggest that this might be a regular occurrence, but it might also inadvertently reveal that she is behaving differently due to having an especially interrogative audience. Indeed, could it not be that Macaulay *et al* are placing her under particular pressure at this event, barking questions at her alongside Cesars's belligerent instructions? Inevitably, there is no way of answering these speculations; the gaps in Sarah's story will have to wait to be filled by neo-Victorian re-memberings. But my analysis does expose Macaulay as lacking in self-awareness and inclined towards imposing his own constructions upon Sarah's body, compounding her victim status even as he seeks to contest this. Already, it seems that interpreting the performance and volition of the 'Hottentot Venus' is a precarious business; the audience will see what they want to, they will bring their own agendas to the show, and read her as they see fit.

Chronologically speaking, Macaulay's visits to Sarah's performances were punctuated by a flurry of angry letters to the *Morning Chronicle*, in which he repeatedly questioned her consent in performing. Dunlop/Cesars responded indignantly, with one missive enquiring: 'has she [Sarah] not as good a right to exhibit herself as an Irish giant, or a dwarf?' (Crais and Scully, 2009, p. 91).[11] Her 'managers' obviously had vested interests in terming Sarah as 'exhibiting herself', but this ascription of agency, placing her on a continuum with other freak show performers, is telling. For the author of this letter to suggest that Sarah is comparable to other physical curiosities on display in Piccadilly at this time in 'choosing' to perform rests on the assumption that the newspaper's readership does not find anything debateable about the agency of 'freaks' and that they should view 'the Hottentot Venus' in the same light. In spite of these protestations, Macaulay convinced the court of the King's Bench that they should further investigate Sarah's potential enslavement, and the attorney general submitted that judges should assemble further information on Sarah's situation.[12] Depositions from a variety of people involved with the exhibition of 'the Hottentot Venus' were collected, including the above statements from Macaulay, Babington and Van Wageninge, William Bullock, and, most importantly, from Sarah herself.

On 27 November 1810, Sarah was visited at her rooms by a legal representative for Macaulay, a legal representative for Dunlop and Cesars, the Coroner of the Court, and two Dutch-speaking men; according to the note attached to the sworn deposition, Dunlop was not present, but this is contested by other accounts.[13] Her statement repeats the phrase 'she came with/by her own consent' twice in close succession (Strother, 1999, p. 41); Sarah's 'choice' in her current situation was a crucial factor in establishing her freedom – her status as a performer rather than a slave. She expresses her like of England, insists that she 'is kindly treated and has every thing she wants', and that 'she is perfectly happy in her own situation'. Her only complaint was that her current 'dress was too cold', but that she had been promised warmer clothes by Cesars (Strother, 1999, p. 41). She seemingly made it clear that she had 'no desire whatever of returning to her own country' (Strother, 1999, p. 41). The conviction of her statement is somewhat undermined by the closing remarks of the transcriber:

> To the various questions we put to her whether if she chose at any time to discontinue her person from being exhibited, she might do so, we could not draw a satisfactory answer from her – She understands very little of the Agreement she produced to us – The time of Examination lasted for about three hours.
>
> (Strother, 1999, p. 41)

Yet again, it appears that Sarah refused to speak fully when given the opportunity, and her apparent lack of understanding of the terms of her contract is worrying. Given that the interview lasted for a considerable amount of time, the written document is alarmingly short: 35 lines, as it is reproduced by Z. S. Strother. What other conversation might have taken place which was not recorded? What has been missed from this purported opportunity to hear Sarah's side of the story? The way in which Crais and Scully frame Sarah's account in their biography is significant, for they note that the deposition is a paraphrase and a translation from the Dutch. Furthermore, considering the possibility that her manager was present, we cannot know what pressure she might have been under: 'Even here, we see Sara Baartman at a remove, through the lens of Europe. The context in which she produced this account of her life, as well as the huge absences in the archival record, confound our ability to know her' (Crais and Scully, 2009, p. 99). Their gloss is poignant; we learn very little from this deposition, other than that Sarah, even in her own account, is subject to obscurity and narrative construction. She is always authored, never in control of her own story. It is this historical lacunae which makes Sarah Baartman such a tantalising prospect for neo-Victorianism, invested as the genre often is in re-voicing the silences of the nineteenth century. Yet, as the later section of this chapter will argue, neo-Victorian re-memberings of Sarah do not seek to offer a finite account of her 'consent' or 'agency' in performances or life, but tend to perpetuate the ambivalence of her narrative.

Performing Venus: two nineteenth-century versions of Sarah

However, Sarah's deposition was enough evidence for the King's Bench to end their investigation; Sarah was 'free' (whatever that meant) to continue in her performances. Interestingly, contemporary reactions to the case did not overly trouble themselves as to the validity of this ruling, which becomes apparent when studying a popular ballad published the year after the investigation: *The Hottentot Venus: A New Song* (1811). It describes London as a 'puppet show, where curious sights are seen', detailing: 'There are giants, dwarfs, and singing birds, which all are but a hum, / Compar'd to Venus on the stage, exhibiting her *bum*' (Eckstein, 2010, p. 180; original emphasis). Again, Sarah's exhibition is explicitly aligned with other freak show performers; the fascination she holds for her audiences is in her physical difference, reiterated by the bawdy reference to her bottom. Despite the recent public debates she is restored to the position of being in control of her own performance; she is in charge of the exhibition of her 'bum', no one else. Then again, if London is a 'puppet show', then are the performers which inhabit its stage thus positioned as mere objects to be manipulated for the entertainment for the audiences? Perhaps the ambivalence about Sarah's agency has not been quite resolved. Nevertheless, the popularity of her show is also contextualised against references to recent theatrical productions:

> Poor Penley with great Marmion has long since tir'd the town,
> And Denmark's prince he's now brought on, in hopes it may go down;
> Bu what are princes, warriors, chiefs? Why they're not worth a groat,
> They must all yield to that damn'd jade, the *Female Hottentot*
>
> (Eckstein, 2010, p. 181; original emphasis)

'Penley' is a reference to the theatre manager of the New Theatre in London, where adaptations of Shakespeare's plays had recently been shown (Eckstein, 2010, p. 182). The location of Sarah alongside Shakespearean actors is satirical, but also underscores her role as a performer: an actor of a part. More specifically, the 'Female Hottentot' is placed on a continuum with a theatrical *characters*. Her comparison to Hamlet – 'Denmark's prince' is surely ironic, yet perhaps inadvertently reveals some recognition of 'the Hottentot Venus' as a fictional creation: a persona for the stage, rather than reflective of the real woman. Furthermore, the suggestion that Sarah's show might prove more popular than Shakespeare has subversive implications; the works of that bastion of English culture cannot compete with a female upstart from the colonies. But it is in the gendering of Sarah's performance that more dubious connotations creep in. The word 'jade', although delivered in a comedic context, speaks of the sexualised overtones of her presentation. In this formulation, she is tantamount to a prostitute.

A reading of this ballad which might empower Sarah is potentially undermined by the references made to her performances in the setting of London's ethnographic attractions:

> His fam'd museum *Bullock* boasts, with Leopardallis skin
> From Africa, which he's got stuff'd to gull the people in;
> Of Nature's great phenomenon imported from that shore.
> To Britain's Isle, the *Hottentot* above them all must soar.
>
> (Eckhart, 2010, p. 180)

Alluding to Dunlop's initial bid to have Sarah exhibited at the Liverpool Museum, the reference to Bullock and his animal artefacts from the colonies positions the 'Hottentot Venus' alongside the bestial, inanimate trophies of empire such as the giraffe skin. She is compared to a 'Natural phenomenon'; essentialised as outside of culture and civilisation. However, it is still worth being attuned to the use of the word 'gull' with regards to Bullock's presentation of his exhibits, as it implies that the authenticity of such displays is questionable. The provenance of these 'natural phenomenon' might actually prove to be artificial. Ethnographic display, in this formulation, is subject to fraud, and thus the 'Hottentot Venus' is similarly aligned with such hoaxes. Perhaps, therefore, Sarah's contemporary audience were more inclined to see her exhibition as a performance of a role rather than a 'genuine' example of colonial savagery.

These themes of performance and artifice coalesce in the final textual representation of Sarah dating from her life time that this chapter explores: *The Hottentot Venus, or Hatred of Frenchwomen*. This 'one-act vaudeville' was written by Théaulon, Dartois, and Braiser, and first performed in November 1814, several months after Sarah first arrived to be exhibited in Paris. However, Sarah herself does not appear as a character onstage. The plot centres on the romantic inclinations of Adolph, a man whose unluckiness in love has made him averse to French women. His uncle, the Baron, is ostensibly a well-travelled man with colonial property (he refers to his 'American possessions' at one stage (Sharpley-Whiting, 1999, p. 132), and it is he who suggests to Adolph that a 'Hottentot' woman might be a more suitable object of his affections. However, the Baroness's niece, Amelia, is in love with Adolph and the women conspire to fool him: Amelia disguises herself as the 'Hottentot Venus' and tricks him into marriage. Fortunately for Amelia, Adolph recognises the error of his misguided affections when shown a picture of the Venus. The stage directions dictate that 'everyone cries out in fright' at the proffered illustration of Sarah, and the Chorus glosses Adolph's reaction: 'With such a face / She cannot be a Venus' (Sharpley-Whiting, 1999, p. 161). Order is thus restored, and the superior attractions of French women – and the French nation – are celebrated.

This production does point towards the popularity of Sarah's exhibition in Paris, but it is hardly surprising that recent critics have deemed the play highly derogatory in terms of its representation of racial otherness, figured via Sarah. Robin Mitchell, for instance, argues that the play's conclusion demonstrates that 'Blackness as an ideology became a marker of ugliness and sexual deviance, and importantly, allowed white women a role in the definition of race and nation' (Mitchell, 2010, p. 40). Sharpley-Whiting's analysis perceives the play as reaffirming racial hierarchies and reducing Sarah to 'the "enormous butt" of a joke' (Sharpley-Whiting, 2010, p. 34). While the play is certainly ideologically suspect in a variety of ways, I want to offer a slightly more complicated interpretation of its messages. Although it seems to impose oppressive representations of race and gender upon Sarah, it also demonstrates that such traditional constructions can be rather unstable, and easily undermined as well.

The Baron presents himself as literally a man of the world, imparting his experience of 'exotic' women such as 'Native American' and 'Hottentot' girls who are championed as 'the prettiest'. Indeed, seeking out a suitable wife for Adolph becomes a colonial enterprise: 'I promise to search for the woman you want, even if I have to scour the four corners of the globe' (Sharpley-Whiting, 1999, p. 132). The conquering of land and the conquering of women is easily conflated in his mind. However, the veracity of his imperialist experience is quickly undermined when he is presented with 'Liliskaa', Amelia's performance of a 'Hottentot Venus'. When Adolph declares his love for her, Amelia laughs. Wounded by her derision, Adolph questions his uncle: 'Why does she laugh at my tenderness?', to which the Baron responds: 'It's the custom of her country! They always laugh at their suitors there' (Sharpley-Whiting, 1999, p. 150). The Baron's bluster is made transparent by the audience's knowledge of Amelia's trick: the colonising sexual adventurer is exposed as a fraud. This theme is continued when the Baron addresses 'Liliskaa' in a mock 'savage' language, and she responds in kind:

> Baron (aside): I am going to make up another language. (Aloud) Kaf Kaof, roc mac tring koul magniac magnioc ros rif krou tring.
>
> Amelia (responding to him) Orf nec rolouf your zouf camatof ordief zic mac tring.
>
> Baron (embarrassed): Yes.
>
> Adolph: Yes, my dear uncle, what is she saying to you?
>
> Baron: (stupefied) (aside) How in the heck do I know? I don't even know this language (Aloud) She says that she approves of your love or something like that.
>
> Adolph: I was sure of it.
>
> (Sharpley-Whiting, 1999, p. 152)

Who is the joke upon in this exchange? In the Baron's patronising world view, 'foreign' languages are nonsense, easily aped by superior Western men. However, Amelia responds to him on his own terms, making him look foolish and undermining his colonial authority.

Amelia is certainly an astute woman; on visiting her aunt at the château and noting the quasi-gothic trappings of the setting and circumstances, she comments: 'In truth, this all resembles a chapter from a novel' (Sharpley-Whiting, 1999, p. 128); she then cautions the Baroness: 'I very much want to be a heroine of a novel, but I must forewarn you that I love freedom' (Sharpley-Whiting, 1999, p. 128). We see here that a connection is formed between being fictionalised and loss of agency, a pertinent parallel to the fictionalisation of Sarah within the play. One of the great ironies of *The Hottentot Venus* is that Sarah Baartman only appears as a representation, the portrait which inspires such horror in Adolph. The assembled throng's remarks on the picture ('With such a face / She cannot be a Venus') seem to reiterate the most oppressive ideologies about the 'ugliness' of 'savage' women, yet the illustration is not necessarily accurate, considering the caricatures of Sarah that were circulated in her lifetime. Again, the 'Hottentot Venus' is only ever seen at a remove, via the colonial gaze. Sharpley-Whiting's analysis of this scene highlights this tendency: 'Bartmann's symbolic presence acts like a mirror, legitimising existing notions of the superiority of France and the inferiority of the Other' (Sharpley-Whiting, 1999, p. 37). Yet if we return to the reflective imagery I detailed regarding freakery in the Introduction, is it not that the characters' repulsion is towards a 'monster' of their own imagining? It is the European projection of the 'other' that is ugly, not the 'real' woman. Sarah is rendered voiceless by the play, a mere fictional image, and thus Amelia's self-conscious resistance towards fictionalisation still does underscore her relative power. That Amelia can perform 'blackness' well enough to convince colonising men positions race as a trait to be appropriated and exploited for laughs. In such a formulation, Amelia is herself a colonising force upon Sarah's identity. However, as my analysis of the ballad about 'the Hottentot Venus' suggested above, there is evidence dating from Sarah's contemporary moment which implies that her own audiences could have interpreted her own exhibition as a performance of 'race' as well. Nevertheless, it is important to acknowledge that that Sarah does not appear in this play as a subject in control of her performance, but only ever as an object for appropriation.

Perhaps it is in the character of Fanchette, Amelia's friend, that a more complex crossing of boundaries between race is depicted. Another suitor of Amelia, Chevalier, refers to Fanchette as a 'savage' in jest. Fanchette reacts angrily: 'What did you call me, savage? Understand this, mister, I am no more savage than another'. He then attempts to pacify her: 'Ah, ah, ah! Calm down, my dear child! You are too pretty to be a savage. Word of honor, it would be a shame for us!' (Sharpley-Whiting, 1999, p. 143) The appellation of 'savage' is here a term to be repudiated, but it takes on another significance when Fanchette meets Amelia in disguise: 'This is the savage; I am sure of it. But she looks like everybody else' (Sharpley-Whiting, 1999, p. 157). She elaborates on this sense of recognition in a song:

> And you are a savage, I see,
> All in fact like me.
> They say, between us,
> That in your country they eat men;
> But in your eyes, miss, I read not a trace of cruelty.
> And you will eat them, I can see that,
> Just like me.
>
> (Sharpley-Whiting, 1999, p. 158)

The easier interpretation of this scene would be that Fanchette is able to perceive the 'authentic' (attractive, kind) French woman beneath the 'savage' disguise, and so this moment of (mis)recognition might serve to reconsolidate the boundaries between European and 'other' women. However, Fanchette does appear to be genuinely fooled by Amelia's costuming. Furthermore, she invokes stereotypes of 'Hottentot' savagery – cannibalism – and translates this into a metaphor for her own (presumably sexual) consumption of men. Her tone is confiding ('between us'), which suggests that she does seek some sense of engagement with the racial 'other'. At the same time, this is an instance of moulding the 'savage' woman to suit European concerns, an identification which, although sympathetic, dramatizes Rachel Adam's cautionary comments about 'obliterating [the] personhood' of the subject on display in the freak show (Adams, 2001, p. 31). Fanchette wishes to make the 'Hottentot Venus' speak for her sense of frustration and animosity towards men. Although she remarks, 'What a shame that you don't talk', she continues: 'it's a great comfort that the heavens above have deprived you and not me, for in your place I would die from unhappiness' (Sharpley-Whiting, 1999, p. 158). Although she ostensibly reaches towards dialogue, she also treats the spectacle of racial 'otherness' as a comforting reference point for her own privilege, reiterating the boundaries between them. Amelia suddenly responds: 'That would be fitting', to which Fanchette becomes incoherent; the stage directions tell us that she '*screams, and tries to save herself*' (Sharpley-Whiting, 1999, p. 158; original emphasis). Perhaps the timing of Amelia's interjection is telling;

Fanchette is chastised when she attempts to assert her superiority. Again, it is European presumptions about 'savages' which are the source of comedy here, not actually the colonial 'others' in and of themselves.

The messages of the play are deeply ambivalent. Whilst there is no meaningful agency allowed for Sarah Baartman – she is reduced to a cipher, a mere icon – *The Hottentot Venus, or Hatred of French Women* also dramatizes the problematic aspects of the racial and gendered discourses which frame the construction of Sarah as the 'other'. Colonising men are rendered absurd, racial difference is depicted as a malleable performance, and French women are revealed as 'man-eaters'. I would argue that the image of Sarah is not really the 'butt' of the play's jokes, but instead it is the fanciful meanings attached to her which are exposed as ridiculous. The carnivalesque inversions of race and gender are restored to order at the conclusion of the play, with a nationalistic song which implores the audience 'Do not abandon France' (Sharpley-Whiting, 1999, pp. 162–64), but boundaries have been transgressed, and appearances have been shown to be deceiving. None of this makes the 'real' Sarah Baartman any clearer, but it says something provocative about the dangers of 'othering', identification, and fictionalisation, themes which will return in neo-Victorian representations of Sarah's life.

The politics of posthumous exhibition: Neo-Victorian haunting and remembering

The ways in which Sarah was (mis)represented in texts dating from her life time are obviously contentious, and we have seen that her exhibition as a freak show performer raised questions about agency and 'choice' that are not easily answered. However, her exhibition in death has been even more controversial. Georges Cuvier, the French naturalist and zoologist who would dissect Sarah after her death and who was initially responsible for the exhibition of her remains at the Muséum d'Histoire Naturelle, had a particular interest in classifying and categorising every aspect of the natural world, humans included. He was introduced to Sarah during her final years in Paris, and organised her visit to the Muséum to be studied. His actual aim was to uncover the secret of the 'Hottentot' woman's genitalia, which he apparently believed might connect Sarah's people to more primitive species, to position her as a sort of 'missing link' between humans and apes. Under the scrutiny of assembled scientists and artists, he attempted to persuade her to disrobe to reveal her genitalia, to no avail.[14] Not to be deterred, he secured her corpse after her death and performed a dissection after making a cast of her body. It is this act, and her continued exhibition as a specimen in the museum after her death, which ends the debates about Sarah's agency in exhibition: she gave no consent to this use of her body, and was turned into a passive object of scrutiny and spectacle. Alice Domurat Dreger identifies the ethical issues surrounding the possession and continued display of historical freak show performers in medical museums, which impact upon how the medical profession perceives living people with unusual anatomies: 'It says that such people do not have an equal say in their fate, that they can be readily exhibited to the public as symbols of nature's freakery or medicine's miracles, whether or not they wish to be' (Dreger, 2004, p. 138). Such an argument is surely relevant to Sarah's posthumous exhibition as well, and the messages it gave to audiences about race, 'deformity' and science.

The introduction to this chapter considered Diana Ferrus's poem calling for Sarah's body to 'come home' to be buried as invoking images of her not being at rest yet, as an unquiet spirit due to her continued corporeal presence beyond death. The metaphor of 'haunting' – of Sarah as a ghost – has been regularly invoked in textual reimaginings of Sarah: even Crais and Scully's biography is subtitled: 'A Ghost Story'. Haunting and spectrality have emerged as key themes in neo-Victorian criticism, with these tropes invoked to conceptualise neo-Victorianism's voicing of the dead as a form of mediumship, the spectral revisiting of marginalised historical subjects as the return of the repressed (with clear reference to Freud's *unheimlich*), or the phantom as a way of dealing with 'bearing witness' to a traumatic past, amongst other usages.[15] Importantly for thinking about Sarah's afterlife, haunting has also been a significant notion in postcolonialism's dealing with historical legacies of racial power imbalances and exploitation. Michael F. O'Riley acknowledges the ambivalence contained within this usage: 'The haunting of the colonial frequently turns on what is undoubtedly a well-intentioned desire to relate to the Other, the silenced, and the hidden, but it also reveals a more problematic inability to situate resistance, and mobilize memory for such purposes' (O'Riley, 2007, n.p.). The ghost is an ambivalent signifier: it is between boundaries, not quite absent, but never fully present; ephemeral; reminding us of the continuation of the past in the present, but not fully part of the social and cultural realm to effect permanent change.

The relationship of the ghost to memories of a traumatic history becomes relevant to Toni Morrison's neo-Victorian novel, *Beloved* (1987), a text which deals with both personal trauma and broader racial exploitation and abuse in relation to slavery in North America. Sethe, a woman based on the historical figure of Margaret Garner who killed her daughter to avoid her being raised as a slave, deploys the notion of 'rememory' to explain the return of the past:

> 'If a house burns down, it's gone, but the place – the picture of it – stays, and not just in my rememory, but out there, in the world. What I remember is a picture floating around out there outside my head. I mean, even if I don't think it, even if I die, the picture of what I did, or knew, or saw is still out there. Right in the place where it happened [...] It's when you bump into a rememory that belongs to somebody else. Where I was before I came here, that place is real. It's never going away. Even if the whole farm – every tree and grass blade of it dies. The picture is still there and what's more, if you go there – you who never was there – if you go there and stand in the place where it was, Denver, you can't never go there. Never. Because even though it's all over – over and done with – it's going to always be there waiting for you. That's how come I had to get all my children out. No matter what'.
>
> (Morrison, 1997, pp. 35–36)

In the context of *Beloved*, haunting 'rememories' have thus been interpreted as a process of bridging the boundaries between self and other; reconstructed memories that are both individual but also shared between people united by past trauma (in this case, North American slavery).[16] However, in Sethe's terms, rememory is when memories are made material. This becomes poignant in the case of Beloved, the ghost of the child she has murdered who becomes resolutely more fleshy as the narrative progresses. And so we are returned to Kate Mitchell's theory of re-membering as explained in the Introduction, a feature of neo-Victorianism in which the ambiguous boundary between memory and the materiality of bodies is invoked. Additionally, we must not forget the sexualised connotations of re-membering. Considering the emphasis placed on Sarah's genitalia in her life and death, how does neo-Victorianism re-member (make flesh) her 'ghost' without a prurient focus on her body which ensured her dismemberment at the hands of Cuvier in the first place? Is Sarah's textual re-memberment perilously close to her exhibition as a racially marked medical specimen, or, indeed, a freak show performer? Put another way, can she be re-membered with subject with agency, or is she a perpetual victim? How does neo-Victorianism consume Sarah Baartman? I want to turn now to Suzan-Lori Parks's play *Venus* to explore how these themes become manifest.

Culpable consumption: Suzan-Lori Parks's *Venus*

The list of 'The Roles' at the beginning of the play suggests that each actor, excepting 'The Negro Resurrectionist', will play several parts. For instance, 'Miss Saartjie Baartman' will also perform as 'The Girl' and 'later The Hottentot Venus'. The role of 'The Man' will also be performed by the same actor playing 'The Baron Docteur', and 'The Chorus' will perform in several different contexts as well: as 'the 8 Human Wonders', 'the Spectators', 'the Court', and the 'Anatomists'. Of course, there might be practical reasons for why there is this sharing of roles: it means that the play can be performed by fewer actors. However, such casting does hold further symbolic resonance as well. Regarding Sarah, it suggests that she has various personae: she is not defined by her role as the 'Hottentot'. Yet, by forming a continuum between the performance of 'the Hottentot Venus' and the roles of 'The Girl' and 'Saartjie', it also implies that Sarah Baartman cannot be fixed to one 'authentic' identity. All of these stages in her life or facets of her personality can thus be conceptualised as a form of performance. It raises the question as to who is the 'real' Sarah Baartman, to which the play does not offer a finite answer. It emphasises her profound unknowability – the uncertainty which clouds so many of the details of her life, but also resists fixing her in a particular identity, a profound challenge to the 'fixing' of Sarah as a specimen of racist science for much of the nineteenth and twentieth century.[17] To have 'The Man' also playing 'The Baron Docteur', a fictionalisation of Cuvier,[18] also suggests that the 'Docteur' represents a broader sense of patriarchal authority which cuts across specific names and identities; the combination of predatorial lust and prurience that he exhibits towards Sarah is thus universalised to 'men' in general. The malleability of 'The Chorus' has more complex implications: they are 'freaks' who are displayed (exploited?) alongside Sarah, but also fulfil the part of the audience to her various exhibitions throughout the play, and the 'Anatomists' who conspire to procure her body. Therefore, this casting indicates that the roles of 'oppressed' and 'oppressor' are changeable and can become blurred.

This ambivalence serves as an introduction to an important theme throughout the play, for there are various moments when Sarah is clearly represented as participating in and being complicit with her own exploitation. This aspect of *Venus* has led to condemnatory responses from some commentators, with Jean Young offering an especially searing critique of the play based on the way in which: 'Parks depicts [Sarah] as a sovereign, consenting individual with the freedom and agency to trade in her human dignity for the promise of material gain' (Young, 1999, p. 699). In fact, Parks has made no secret of this impulse in her representation of Sarah. As she explains in an interview quoted by Sara L. Warner, Parks 'could have written a 2 hour saga with Venus being the victim. But she's multi-faceted. She's vain, beautiful, intelligent and, yes, complicit' (Warner, 2008, p. 197). The problem with imbuing Sarah with agency – with 'choosing' her own exploitation – for critics such as Young resides in the ways in which such a representation might apportion blame upon her, reiterating the conclusions of the King's Bench from her own lifetime in which Sarah was ultimately positioned as a performer and therefore, presumably, fair game for use and abuse. But is it not equally as problematic, albeit in different ways, to construct Sarah as a complete 'victim'? As suggested by my analysis of Ferrus's poem at the beginning of this chapter, how productive is it to think of Sarah as wholly passive? Imbuing Sarah with some degree of agency does not exonerate the patriarchal and racist discourses which have framed her in life and death, but, as Parks's remarks imply, offer her a psychological complexity which in itself is a form of tribute and respect, closer to a 'real' person than the construction of Sarah as an icon of silent suffering ever could offer. Having said this, there are times when the play also stops short of offering too much explanation as to Sarah's attitudes towards events and motivations behind her actions. This tentativeness, I argue, is a refusal to offer 'easy' answers to questions about Sarah's life, and a strategy of resistance against trying to appropriate her memory to speak for our contemporary anxieties about her 'choices'.

The play negotiates this apportioning of 'blame' in relation to Sarah's 'choices' by indicating that the audience is also complicit in Sarah's role as a spectacle. The framing of the first scene has overt links to a freak show, in which The Negro Resurrectionist fulfils the role of a sort of barker, introducing the exhibit. His comments culminate in the following lines which are spoken by 'All' (which presumably includes 'The Venus' as well): 'THE VENUS HOTTENTOT/THE ONLY LIVING CREATURE OF HER KIND IN THE WORLD/AND ONLY ONE STEP UHWAY FROM YOU RIGHT NOW/COME SEE THE HOT MISS HOTTENTOT/STEP IN STEP IN' (Parks, 1997, p. 7; original emphasis). We as the audience are being addressed here, and the play format to re-tell Sarah's story is evocative in this respect, for it engages with a mode of visual, staged story-telling which forms clear parallels with the freak show conventions of exhibition in the first place. In the instructions to 'COME SEE' and 'STEP IN STEP IN' legitimates the audience's interest in looking at The Venus, but also locates such spectatorship as on a continuum with her initial exhibition in her life time: we have, albeit unwittingly, come to see a freak show. As the coming chapters will demonstrate, neo-Victorian representations of freak shows frequently do offer metatextual moments of reflection/engagement, where the reader/audience is made self-conscious about their own role as paying consumer of freakery and must thus negotiate their own ethical position with regards to the re-membering of performers.[19] Of course, the name of the character speaking these lines is important as well; we are witnessing a return from the dead, a reanimation of a corpse, which comes uncomfortably close to the historical Sarah's afterlife as a museum 'exhibit'.

Another aspect of *Venus* which serves to make us self-conscious about our role as spectators is the play-within-a-play strand which is woven through the narrative. This is a production entitled '*For the Love of Venus*' and the story is a rewriting of *The Hottentot Venus, or Hatred of French Women*. Our first introduction to this comes in Scene 29, and the stage directions state: 'A play on a stage. The Baron Docteur is the only person in the audience. Perhaps he sits in a chair. It's almost as if he's watching TV. The Venus stands off to the side. She watches The Baron Docteur' (Parks, 1997, p. 25). Karen Ruth Kornweibel has argued that this scene reiterates once again the audience's complicity in Sarah's exhibition; a parallel is formed between the Baron's 'voyeurism' and the 'everyday' spectatorship of television/play viewing (Kornweibel, 2009, p. 77). The difference, of course, is that watching television is usually done in the privacy of one's own home; the audience of play (or, indeed, a freak show) both see and are seen. One of the issues with representations of extraordinary bodies in contemporary television documentaries is that audiences of such programmes are protected from direct engagement with the subjects of the show: unlike the nineteenth-century freak show, they are free to stare without interaction. In this scene, however, the Baron is not afforded such privacy, for not only do we as the audience have the opportunity to gauge his reactions, but he also comes under 'Venus's' scrutiny as well. Private viewing is never truly concealed in the world of *Venus*, and we all must take responsibility for the way we look. To have the Baron (and Sarah) witness this reimagined version of a play dating from her lifetime might suggest the formative influence that fictional representation of historical figures can actually have. Sarah (or 'Venus'), as in the original, does not appear in the play, but we witness The-Bride-to-Be's (the role of Amelia in the nineteenth-century play) revelation of her true identity at the play's conclusion, to which 'The Young Man', according to the stage directions, 'gives her a red heart box of chocolates'. After the curtain falls, 'The Baron Docteur applauds' (Parks, 1997, p. 154). The Baron Docteur's approval of this denouement – in which conventional romance with a 'civilized' woman triumphs over the 'primitive' allure of Hottentot sexuality – is telling, for his own rejection of Sarah in their sexual relationship is validated by this performance. So while Parks's reinterpretation of the original play does make a point about the role of artistic representation in shaping the treatment of Sarah in her life, it does not engage with the ambivalent politics of the first play which ridicule Western society's projection of desire onto the figure of the 'Hottentot' woman. In this instance, perhaps *Venus* actually oversimplifies the complexity of the discourses surrounding Sarah in her own life time.

Another juncture where the play deals with textual constructions of Sarah in her own lifetime is in the Court room scene, entitled 'The Venus Hottentot Before the Law'. The legal debates of 1810 surrounding whether Sarah was exhibited under her own volition are thus framed as if she herself is on trial; at one point she is led 'to a jail cell' (Parks, 1997, p. 62). The interrogation of Sarah as to her agency – originally couched in terms of care and concern – is exposed as a vilification of her 'choices'. Importantly, however, the Venus's only comment in these first two sections of the trial scene is '*Habeas Corpus*. Literally: "You should have the body" for submitting. Any of several common-law writs issued to bring the body before the court or the judge' (Parks, 1997, p. 65). It was the writ of habeas corpus, meaning that a 'prisoner' might be released from unlawful detention, which Macaulay brought before the King's Bench in 1810, operating under the argument that Sarah was being kept prisoner by her managers illegally and against her will. Parks's Venus's relation of the literal definition of the term is richly ironic, considering not only the emphasis on Sarah's body in her exhibition in life and death, but also the debates over who 'has' her body (who 'owns' her body) in her afterlife as well. The matter of her consent is addressed in her trial, but only at a distance: The Negro Resurrectionist's song, based on the words of another anonymous ballad circulated around the time of the debates over her freedom,[20] concludes that her exhibition ''twas done with full consent/of the fair Hottentot' (Parks, 1997, p. 63). This is just one example of the play's deployment of various contemporary texts about Sarah, and it is notable that when given the opportunity to answer the question of her 'consent', this neo-Victorian re-membering refers back to such documents, which offer no concrete conclusions. The opportunity to imagine Sarah's 'consent' back in to the historical record is deferred, displaced yet again, a theme which is also apparent in Barbara

Chase-Riboud's novel discussed below. When 'The Venus' is directly questioned in court, she first states: 'The Venus Hottentot/is unavailable for comment' (Parks, 1997, p. 74), an echo of Sarah's 'unsatisfactory' responses when asked whether she wanted to continue with her exhibition. The Chorus of the Court reacts angrily: 'Don't push us, Girl! / We could lock you up for life! Answer this: / Are you here of yr own free will / or are you under some restraint?' (Parks, 1997, p. 75). Significantly, therefore, the line of questioning of Sarah – supposedly for her benefit – in itself becomes a form of coercion, forming a poignant parallel with the potentially intimidating aspects of Macaulay's questioning of Sarah I analysed earlier. Her ultimate answer is simple, yet still evasive: 'Im here to make a mint' (Parks, 1997, p. 75). Parks's 'Venus' is motivated by money, but still will not say whether she 'chooses' this life. There is a comparable deferral of explanation in Barbara Chase-Riboud's novel, and this theme will be explored in further detail in the section below.

It is in the context of the play's representation of science that the concept of 're-membering' is explicitly invoked. Scene 16, 'Intermission', bears the subtitle 'Several Years from Now: In the Anatomical Theatre of Tübingen: The Dis(-re-)memberment of the Venus Hottentot' (Parks, 1997, p. 91), and a large part of the dialogue is quotations from Cuvier's autopsy report, spoken by The Baron Docteur. The ambiguity of the temporal setting of the scene suggests the ongoing cultural significance of the racist and sexist attitudes which are being spouted; the 'memory' of Sarah lives on via her dismembered body, but to dis(re)member also implies that such memories are false or inaccurate. The veracity of the Baron Docteur's proclamations and his 'scientific', patriarchal authority is thus undermined. The closeness of the terms 're-member'/dis-remember should give us pause for thought, however; if neo-Victorianism can symbolically put nineteenth-century fragments of bodies/lives back together via text, then it can also take them apart again as well, or offer false or misleading re-memberings. Tellingly, we as the audience also play a part in the dis(re)membering before us; the stage directions at the beginning of the scene read as follows: 'Scene 16 runs during the Intermission. House lights should come up and the audience should be encouraged to walk out of the theatre, take their intermission break, and then return. The Baron Docteur stands at a podium. He reads from his notebook' (Parks, 1997, p. 91). What is the significance of the audience being encouraged to be absent for part of this scene? It might suggest that the Baron's pronouncements on Sarah's body are to be ignored or evaded, are not worthy of full audience intention. But this in itself would be a questionable strategy of disrememberment, considering how influential Cuvier's (mis)reading of Sarah's body proved to be. Instead, is it that the audience's lack of attention here is part of the drama itself? In the freak show exhibition which frames the opening of the play, we are arrested, made to participate. In this medical exhibition, we are 'encouraged' to be passive, disengaged, taking a 'break': put another way, the scene represents the potential for the audience to forget Sarah, rather than re-member her. In this context, it is the medical exhibition of 'The Venus' which is most damning in Parks's play. Re-membering via the neo-Victorian freak show might be precarious, confrontational, and sometimes painful, but failure to engage with Sarah's memory would be worse.

There is another dimension to the re-membering of Sarah which goes beyond the medical and freak show exhibition of her body; she is also reimagined as a sexual subject, and she has a relationship with The Baron. Jean Young's commentary on their love scenes is critical, arguing that they 'creat[e] the illusion that Baartman was a free and liberated woman who enjoyed her status as sex object and/or was in complete denial of such status altogether' (Young, 1997, p. 703). Some aspects of the sex scenes do reiterate stereotypes of 'Hottentot' hypersexuality, for 'The Venus' is demanding in her instructions to her lover: 'Touch me / down here [...] That feels good. / Now touch me here.' (Parkes, 1997, p. 104). She is literally sleeping with the enemy, and has seemingly internalised the fetishisation of her genitalia in her need to be touched 'down there'. This hardly speaks of sexual liberation, for it is as if 'The Venus' has become a prisoner within her own iconography, her desire always mediated by her fictional persona. She has become consumed with/by her own image. It is whilst The Venus and The Baron are in bed that the thematic connection between Sarah's body, sexuality, and chocolate becomes apparent. She compares herself to the sweets: 'Do you think I look like / one of these little chocolate Brussels infants?' She then tries '*Capezzoli di Venere.* / The nipples of Venus. Mmmmm. My favorite' (Parks, 1997, p. 105). She identifies with the chocolates, which she also ingests. The motif of the cannibalistic 'Hottentot' is thus invoked, with poignant symbolic force: Venus is complicit in her own 'consumption', as a freak show performer, as a sexual icon, as a medical specimen. And yet so are we as her audience.

Hottentot Hauntings: Barbara Chase-Riboud's *Hottentot Venus*

Susan-Lori Parks's play opens with the information that 'thuh Venus Hottentot iz dead' (Parks, 1997, p. 3). Nevertheless, The Venus is still on stage at this time, and whilst her spoken words are limited, she does have a presence: it is via her 'afterlife' that the audience first meet her. Barbara Chase-Riboud's novel, *Hottentot Venus*, begins with a similar premise: Sarah narrates a first-person account of her death and so is figured as a ghost returned to tell her story. Although there are other narrative voices at work in the novel, hers is the most dominant, and so from the outset the novel appears to promise a more 'authentic' testimony on her life, attitudes and perceptions. The reader initially presumes that Sarah will be knowable, and that this version of 'The Hottentot Venus' can be clearly positioned within the strand of neo-Victorian fiction which offers a 'voice' to the marginalised and silenced of the nineteenth century. However, as Marie-Luise Kohlke's reading of the novel has argued, this 'spectral mode simultaneously attests to and calls into doubt the "authenticity" of "her" confessional narrative' (Kohlke, 2013, p. 5). She elaborates further:

> Constructing Baartman as a subject speaking from a *non-subject* position as a ghost, her (after)life-story colludes in her dehumanisation and absolute Othering by foregrounding those same processes via her vivid reliving of the persistent traumatic identity thefts she was subjected to in life.
>
> (Kohlke, 2013, p. 13)

While Sarah appears to be re-membering her own life, her spectral status means that she is disassociated and detached from her body. On one hand, this might be interpreted as offering a sense of freedom: her body, after all, has been the justification for her oppression in life. On the other, she is, as Kohlke suggests, represented as non-human. Her ghostliness speaks of her ultimate marginalisation, which bears a troubling connection with her designation as 'not human' at the hands of racist science. Having said this, it is evident in Chase-Riboud's novel that this ghostliness – the unquietness of Sarah's spirit – comes from her continued display in death. She explains:

> I remained imprisoned in my glass cage looking out at the world, as it changed with each dawn, from my transparent window, wiped clear by a cleaning lady into whose unseeing eyes I stared each day, war or peace. At first, I was upset about that, until I realized that this oversight gave me the power to haunt the Museum of Natural History [...] and to displace myself in time and space as I chose, for eternity or until my soul finally came to rest.
>
> (Chase-Riboud, 2003, p. 308)

Scientific exhibition of her body is a form of incarceration, but she also articulates haunting as a form of 'power' as well. This spectral version of Sarah does have an influence on the world around her: she vows to 'haunt to their deaths or at least accelerate their demises with [...] a maximum of torment' each of the men who were involved in her exhibition/exploitation in life and death, and relates her ghostly revenges against her former managers and the men of science with relish (Chase-Riboud, 2003, pp. 308-310). Contrary to Kohlke's reading, then, it might seem that the neo-Victorian ghost can have some agency. But clearly Sarah is unable to move on; her ghost is fixated upon the traumas of her life and experiences no 'rest' because of this.

Due to the publication date of this novel, in contrast to Parks's reimagining of Sarah, Chase-Riboud's version of 'Venus' is able to relate the circumstances of her body's repatriation and burial. Describing the attendees at her memorial ceremony garbed in the accessories that she loved in her life time she recounts: 'With a click of my tongue, I commanded a million women to rise up and bear witness to my agony by wearing red gloves in honour of Sarah Baartman. Then all was still' (Chase-Riboud, 2003, p. 317). 'Bearing witness' seems to be an expression of postcolonial and feminist recognition of Sarah's sufferings, a reparation of historical power inequalities, but Sarah herself – in her ghostly form – has witnessed much yet has remained impotent to change the course of history. She has remained silenced. Her description of her own dissection, for instance, emphasises her ability to 'bear witness' in death: 'The scalpel slid around the circumference of my skull. I screamed but no one in the hall could hear me' (Chase-Riboud, 2003, p. 280). Aside from her haunting of her abusers, she does a lot of looking on: 'I've spent two hundred years hanging from my steel hook, watching history being made by the masters of the universe; what a freak show, it has been...' (Chase-Riboud, 2003, p. 312). This might offer the opportunity for us to rethink the dynamics of Sarah's own freak show exhibition, which will be explored in more detail below: just looking does not actually achieve any material effect, and so how damaging can the gaze of an audience really be? But Sarah thus shares in the lack of agency. However, her burial is positioned as giving her a voice – the 'click' of her own language – yet this is rapidly extinguished: 'Then all was still'. The final sentence of the novel thus has a double meaning in relation to Sarah's haunting: has she found the 'stillness' of peace in death? Or is it that nothing much has changed; the power inequalities of race and gender which ensured her life and death as a spectacle are 'still' in existence? The conclusion of this story of 'Hottentot' haunting is therefore deeply ambivalent, problematizing the extent to which Sarah Baartman can ever be given reparation or justice, especially by neo-Victorian representation.

My above analysis of Parks's play suggested that *Venus* was wary of offering straightforward answers to the quandaries of Sarah's 'choice' or agency in terms of her exhibition during life. The generic expectations of a first-person narration, as in Chase-Riboud's text, might mean that the novel lends itself to a more conclusive explanation for Sarah's decisions. In the first part of the novel, where Sarah tells the reader of her death, she explains how her friend Alice has purposefully left her apartment door unlocked, leading Sarah to reflect on why she did not take this opportunity: 'I endured it for money, or so I believed. Money which equaled freedom and independence, or so I believed. But why I really endured it, I do not know. Just as I didn't know why I still remained inert and lifeless in my bath when the door to escape was open' (Chase-Riboud, 2003, p. 9). Her reasoning – financial gain – initially seems straightforward, yet this is consistently undermined by her qualifying statement 'or so I believed'. Sarah ultimately cannot answer the question as to why she continued with her life of exhibition. Why, when given the opportunity to reimagine Sarah's life, would both Parks and Chase-Riboud leave this burning uncertainty unresolved? As I intimated in my reading of *Venus,* perhaps this self-conscious absence demonstrates a sense of resistance to 'read' Sarah completely, to put her on trial in the same way as Macaulay sought to do. In *The Hottentot Venus*, Sarah is questioned by Robert – a mixed-race associate of Macaulay's, who was the son of a slave but now involved in the abolitionist movement. We have his narrative perspective on their interviews:

> The Venus might *think* she was a *free* agent, but I knew better. She was being used and misused as a freakish other, a subhuman symbol of sex and degradation. Venus was only a dirty limerick, a filthy eye-rolling voyeuristic joke. She was unimportant to the abolitionist movement, to civil rights and to human rights. She was nothing political.
>
> (Chase-Riboud, 2003, p. 122; original emphasis)

Robert's statement exposes his disapproval of Sarah. Although he and Macaulay ostensibly seek to 'free' her, they will only help her to the extent that she supports their agenda. They essentially use her for their own gains, in an ironic parallel of the 'use' of Sarah's body by Cesars and Dunlop. Her own perspective on her agency is summarily dismissed;

her 'choices' are denied by the politically-minded abolitionist men who 'know better', and if she refuses to say what they want to hear she is deemed 'unimportant' and 'nothing'.

Most pointedly, Chase-Riboud's novel rewrites the scene of Sarah Baartman's interview on 27 November 1810. Her recorded responses – she has 'no complaints' – are punctuated by Sarah's thoughts on her situation; the absences from the historical record are addressed, to an extent, with Sarah's reflections on her duping at the hands of Dunlop (in the novel, he has suggested that they will be married when she has earned enough money for a bride's dowry through her performances) and her imagining of 'death' if she had to go back to South Africa, her perception that the 'posse of white men' would 'make a fool' of her if they knew that she believed she would marry Dunlop (Chase-Riboud, 2003, p. 131). She repeatedly tells her interviewer: 'Just because I consent to this life doesn't mean I chose it', to which Robert responds: 'You haven't understood a word I've said, have you?' (Chase-Riboud, 2003, p. 134). The irony here is that he cannot understand her either. She replies:

> I don't care to understand you, I said.
> But I thought this: Your ideas are the only important thing to you. Not me myself. For example, you do not even speak my language, so who are you to talk of *my* history, *my* ideals, *my* representatives, *my* duty to allow you to save me.
>
> (Chase-Riboud, 2003, p. 134; original emphasis)

The marked disjuncture between Sarah's saying and thinking highlights the inadequacy of her recorded testimony, but whilst some gaps in the historical record are filled by Chase-Riboud, Sarah's final angry thought can be interpreted as a metatextual rebuke to the reader (and the author) of this neo-Victorian text as well. We don't speak Sarah's language either: we are uncertain of her history and her ideals, and to impose this upon her will only reiterate the appropriation at the hands of well-meaning people that she experienced in her lifetime. A thought-provoking echo is thus offered in relation to more recent perspectives on Sarah, for do debates surrounding her 'choice' or 'agency' put her on trial in a comparable way? The question 'how could she choose this?' runs the risk of being framed as an accusation: in this formulation, Sarah is either a perpetual victim, or woefully deluded. To refuse to answer the quandary of her agency leaves multiple possibilities in play; leaving some details unresolved can give dignity to Sarah as a real historical figure, as it resists wholly appropriating her life to 'speak for' contemporary political agendas.[21]

Although the novel might question the intentions of those who wish to 'save' Sarah from her life as an exhibition, there is no character cast in a more sinister light than Cuvier, the scientist who will ultimately dissect her corpse. Sarah first meets him briefly at a Parisian ball, but it is at the Museum where she has been invited to be studied as an ethnographic specimen where she gains a profound insight into his intentions towards her:

> The unblinking gaze of the doctor was as cold as ice and inspected me as if I had just arrived in a crate [...] It was the cold stare of a cobra, paralyzing with fear before striking [...] Oh Lord, this man's a murderer, I thought. I kept my eyes lowered [...] This was not the Parisian mob but God himself.
>
> (Chase-Riboud, 2003, p. 222)

Cuvier is evidently deploying the 'medical gaze' here (Foucault, 1973), a way of looking which, as Rosemarie Garland-Thomson identifies, is 'highly impersonal [...] and asymmetrical' in terms of power relationships (Garland-Thomson, 2009, p. 28). A distinction is made between the stares of the freak show audience, and the medical gaze: both are exploitative, and yet it is the doctor's gaze which is truly dehumanising for both parties – he treats her like an animal, something which might have 'arrived in a crate' yet he is also bestial; the sinister snake who will try to tempt her to reveal her body and who will symbolically feast on her remains, 'devouring' her in the chilling dissection scene towards the end of the novel (Chase-Riboud, 2003, pp. 277–78). Although it is the 'Hottentot' people who were supposed to be cannibals, it is the white, Western doctor who seeks to consume her; a cobra kills its prey for food, after all. He is a harbinger of death for Sarah – a 'murderer' – and takes a sexualised pleasure in the dismemberment of her body: 'The great Chain of Being. The great Chain of Being! The great Chain of Being, he cried out as he ejaculated, his hand deep in my entrails. He was stuttering like a Hottentot' (Chase-Riboud, 2003, p. 282). He becomes the savage 'stutterer' in his primal, brutal gratification at wallowing in her corpse. The trope of the privileged, supposedly respectable medical man who is exposed as incompetent, corrupt or even monstrous, as indicated in the Introduction, will be a recurring theme throughout this book, and Cuvier is certainly depicted in this vein of 'medical sensationalism' (Rieger, 2014, pp. 153–64). Ann Heilmann and Mark Llewellyn note that

Chase-Riboud's representation of Cuvier has 'more than a touch of Jack the Ripper' (Heilmann and Llewellyn, 2010, p. 127) and as Chapter 5 will explore in further detail, the theme of the doctor as sexualised murderer comes to fruition in the imaginings of Jack the Ripper which frequently accompany neo-Victorian versions of Joseph Merrick. And what of the comparison between Cuvier and 'God himself'? This exposes the way in which Cuvier comes to hold the strongest influence over Sarah's life – and death. It is his preservation of her body – and his racist analysis of her remains – that will dominate the reception of the 'Hottentot' people throughout the Victorian era and into the twentieth century.

At the conclusion of the scene of Sarah's dissection, her narrative voice recites a litany of names of famous Western philosophers, scientists and commentators, and proclaims: 'You are no gentlemen. This is no freak show. I am on display without compensation or compassion' (Chase-Riboud, 2003, p. 285). Marie-Luise Kohlke's analysis of this sentiment in relation to the rest of the novel is critical: 'but it is just that – a freak show that puts postmodern subjectivity and its appetite for relived suffering and degradation squarely centre stage' (Kohlke, 2013, p. 15). This is a pertinent remark, considering the way in which the reader of the text does become part of a metatextual audience for Sarah's re-membered exhibition in both freak show and scientific contexts. However, this perspective does not take account of the ways in which the freak show is not depicted in wholly negative terms in *Hottentot Venus*. In fact, Sarah's comment on the lack of 'compensation or compassion' in her posthumous display actually implies that it this absence which distinguishes scientific exhibition from the freak show, thus suggesting that the latter does contain some potential for redeeming qualities. For sure, many of the reimagined scenes of Sarah's performances invoke the most exploitative and oppressive components of freak show presentation. On her appearances in France, Sarah comments that the audience wanted to see 'a heaving, stomping, undulating, living Venus, with beastly breasts, beastly hips, beastly eyes and above all a beastly face that held no beauty for them. I was the glue of common contempt and rejection that held them all together' (Chase-Riboud, 2003, p. 5). In these terms, the freak show functions as reiterating the boundaries between self (the audience) and 'other' (the performer); as in some of the accounts of the construction of freakery discussed in the Introduction, Sarah's body signifies as all that is abject, non-human, and abnormal, serving to unite the audience on the grounds of their 'normality'.

Interestingly, we are offered some insight into audiences' perceptions of Sarah, which in part reiterate her own appraisal of the nineteenth-century freak show dynamic, but which also lead us to interrogate our own interest in reading about her exhibition. The novel contains the imagined narrative voice of Jane Austen who is contemplating her attendance at one of 'the Hottentot Venus's' performances.[22] Her letter to her sister, Cassandra, speaks of Sarah's 'dignity and humanness' in contrast to the behaviour of the audience, who 'acted like a bunch of baboons' (Chase-Riboud, 2003, p. 157). This sense of empathy towards her 'feminine vulnerability we all are burdened with in the face of a masculine society' is swiftly undermined, however, by her remarks upon her 'ugliness' (Chase-Riboud, 2003, p. 158). After the letter, there is a section which appears to be Jane's more private reflection, not addressed to any audience other than the reader:

> What had I really felt, standing there in the crowd with Mary, witnessing this cruel humiliation of one of my sex, but a secret, snivelling joy at my own safety and invulnerability... wasn't that why I loved freak shows? She, the Venus, was the Other, I was me, Jane, safe within the confines of my privileged provincial white world. I could never be she. As long as I did nothing to trespass it.
>
> (Chase-Riboud, 2003, p. 159)

Although Jane's commentary does suggest that same dubious pleasure of 'normality' in relation to the 'freakishness' of the performer which Sarah herself perceives in the audiences which come to see her, it also belies the security of this hierarchical division. For nineteenth-century women to be 'the other' is a matter of failing to adhere to gendered norms and values; in 'trespassing', any women, regardless of race, might be freakish. Nevertheless, Jane's use of the word 'trespass' also connotes some 'sin' on the part of Sarah; she has put herself beyond the pale in some way, and this 'decision' has led to her 'monstrosity' in the eyes of her audiences. This is what is at stake in re-membering Sarah as a subject with agency: it runs perilously close to imagining that she got what she deserved. Furthermore, there are metatextual avenues of reflection here as well, as Marie-Luise Kohlke comments with regards to this representation of Austen: 'Chase-Riboud's narrative politics Other her reader who, like nineteenth-century paying customers or Cuvier's audience, consume the spectacle of Baartman's dehumanisation staged for their complicit "delectation" [...], instruction, and self-affirmation' (Kohlke, 2013, p. 14). In a comparable way to the breaking down of boundaries between the 'freak show' onstage and the distance of the audience in Parks's play, such a reading implicates the reader of *Hottentot Venus* in

Sarah's posthumous exploitation. Importantly, however, the parallel which is drawn between narrative construction of freakery (Austen's letter) and authorial reflection upon this represents Chase-Riboud's self-consciousness about her role in these narrative politics as well. Although the author of *Hottentot Venus* as a black American woman writing in the twenty-first century is far from Austen in many ways, a continuum is drawn between them in the sense of interrogating the way in which a writer might offer a textual representation of a freak show performer for the consumption of others, but have a 'private' view that is rather more revealing. Via the appropriation of Austen's 'private' voice, Chase-Riboud almost writes herself into the novel, expressing anxiety about her motivations in re-membering the spectacle of Sarah.

Nevertheless, the novel does also offer another perspective on the nineteenth-century freak show, in relation to what it might offer the people who performed under these circumstances. In terms of actual records of Sarah Baartman's life, it becomes rather more difficult to trace her movements and experiences between the years of Summer 1811 until August 1814; notably, she was baptised in Manchester in December 1811, and there are newspaper notices of her appearances in Ireland (April 1812) and Suffolk (October 1812), yet there are otherwise large gaps which frustrate the attempts of biographers to account for her life. Writing on these absences, Crais and Scully remark:

> Ironically, as the Hottentot Venus became less popular, and as Sara Baartman haunts rather than inhabits the historical record, Sara might well have found a greater sense of community in England as she traveled the circuits of pleasure fairs [...] Sara Baartman would have lived among a community of performers [...] Lost to history, she might have found friends.
>
> (Crais and Scully, 2009, pp. 111–12)

It is in relation to the potential for Sarah's experiences in provincial freak shows that Chase-Riboud's novel does take up the challenge of rewriting her history, as she imagines Sarah meeting a woman, Alice, and her disabled brother, Victor, who is then constructed as 'The Turtle Boy' in the travelling show. Victor is deemed to be a 'made freak', his hunched back enhanced by a turtle-shell attached to his back, and adorned with make-up and a prosthetic nose (Chase-Riboud, 2003, p. 177). The distinctions drawn by the freak show promoter between the 'natural-born freak, a made freak and a fake freak' are actually collapsed when it comes to his description of Victor's 'fine, monstrous birth' at the hands of his costuming and presentation: all of the 'freaks' which Sarah discusses, herself included, go through this process of construction and fictionalisation, regardless of their 'natural' attributes. She strongly identifies with the other performers she meets in Piccadilly and on the road:

> I learned they all had real names like mine: Caroline Camancini, the thirty-inch fairy, Anna Swann, the albino, John Randian, the human torso, Lorenzo Dunnett, the man with the revolving head, Sigmund Sully, the skeleton man, Paul Desmule, the armless man who hurled knives at human targets, Grace McDaniels, the mule-faced woman, Dolly Dimples, the fat lady, Joseph/Josephine Herring, the double-sexed man. They had all added noble or military titles to their names: Caroline was princess, Adolph was captain, Paul was marquis, Sigmund was lord, the dwarfs were all generals. There was Baron Little Fingers, Prince Ludwig, Duchess Leona, Baroness Anna. Everyone had three names: a Khoekhoe name, an English name and a fake title. Just like me...
>
> (Chase-Riboud, 2003, p. 161)

Sarah's account dramatizes two process of constructing freakery as defined by Robert Bogdan, the 'exotic' and the 'aggrandized' mode of presentation:

> In the exotic mode the emphasis was on how different and, in many cases, inferior the person on exhibit was. With the aggrandized mode the presentation emphasized how, with the exception of the particular physical, mental, or behavioural condition, the freak was an upstanding, high-status person with talents of a conventional and socially prestigious nature.
>
> (Bodgan, 1988, p. 108)

The 'princesses', 'captains', 'marquis', generals' and 'lords' are obviously fulfilling the expectations of aggrandised freakery, whereas Sarah's 'savage' presentation accords with the 'exotic' mode. Yet, in Sarah's perception, these boundaries are blurred: they are all 'exotic' (like her) with their approximation of a Khoikhoi name; they are all 'aggrandized' with their fake titles.

This sense of solidarity leads her to understanding their shared experience of 'otherness' in relation to her own experiences: 'We were all exiles: blacks in the kingdom of whites' (Chase-Riboud, 2003, p. 162).

Despite her own sense of isolation, and her often unpleasant experiences of interaction with her audiences, her fellow performers offer Sarah solace and a collective identity which transcends her racial 'difference'. The connection formed between 'blackness' and 'freakery' is surely contentious from a modern perspective, but considering the way in which Sarah is exhibited on account of her bodily difference (which includes her skin colour), this analogy is hardly surprising. There is another, perhaps even more problematic, dimension to *Hottentot Venus*'s re-membering of nineteenth-century freak show performers aside from Sarah, though, as some of the names listed above are historically inaccurate and anachronistic: Anna Swan, as Chapter 3 will detail, was a woman of height billed as a giantess, born later in the century than Sarah Baartman's days of performing (1846). Grace McDaniels was indeed billed as 'the mule-faced woman' due to her facial deformities, but she was born in 1888 and lived into the twentieth century, touring freak shows until her death in 1958.[23] In effect, the novel stages a collapsing of the history of the freak show into Baartman's own cultural moment. It could be that this telescoping of performers suggests a timeless quality about freak show dynamics, the sense of historical repetition that constructs freakish identity. But, more troublingly, perhaps disregarding the historical detail of such performers lives actually runs counter to the novel's palpable need to reappropriate the memory of one freak show performer, which is done at the expense of others. The novel, potentially inadvertently, dramatizes the ease with which freak show performers might be (mis)re-membered, with ambivalent ideological consequences.

The final incarnation of Chase-Riboud's re-membering of Sarah Baartman that I want to consider comes from her frank account of how her large bottom was cultivated, and the process of the elongation of her labia. In the part of the novel set in South Africa, she describes how she is considered to be 'a marriageable and desirable virgin' due to her physical appearance. Importantly, this draws attention to the difference in cultural norms with regards to beauty – the very features which are considered repulsive to Western eyes are lauded and cultivated in her own culture. And this emphasis on the shaping of Sarah's body is significant. She describes how her bottom is 'massaged with butter and secret swelling ointments until they sprang a foot from the curve of my spine':

> My shape became my reason for being and that of my guardian. My shape became me and I became my shape. [...] But the crowning glory of our beauty was our sex, now hidden under the elaborate

> beaded apron all maidens had to wear. My aunt began to cultivate its size and shape for it was the ultimate symbol of my femininity, my sexuality, my worth as a bride, much more so than my virginity. My aunt was charged with this treatment and she applied herself diligently. She knew it was my only chance in life: a husband.
>
> (Chase-Riboud, 2003, p. 21)

Refusing the essentialist ideologies of the 'Hottentot' women's 'natural' difference from European norms of beauty circulated in historical ethnographic texts, the novel suggests that Khoikhoi women's bodies were literally and symbolically constructed by cultural norms and expectations. Sarah's (by Western standards) unusual body is not 'natural', but fashioned to suit her culture's ideals, exposing the patriarchal demands upon her body even as a 'free' woman in South Africa. Tellingly, a continuum is thus highlighted between the 'real' woman and the 'Hottentot Venus', for as an exhibit Baartman's body also became her raison d'être. Furthermore, the novel offers a detailed description of the process of elongating her labia – stones are inserted into her flesh to lengthen the skin surrounding her vagina. While this emphasis on the body being constructed seems to thwart the essentialist understandings of the body as natural and fixed, there are also troubling elements in this information being included in the text. Might this narrative attention to Baartman's genitalia also replicate the nineteenth-century fascination with her body, and pander to giving a neo-Victorian audience access to Baartman's 'otherness'? How different is this from the Western audience's and doctors' fascination with her 'apron' in her own moment? This is not easily resolved, but functions as a pertinent example of the way in which neo-Victorianism might inadvertently invoke the more prurient aspects of the freak show, even as they appear to be critiqued.

Conclusion

Sarah Baartman is an important case study for exploring the ideologies and ethics surrounding textual constructions of freakery, cultural afterlives, and neo-Victorian re-memberings. Her stage persona and cultural reception in her own life time was situated at a complicated boundary between ethnographic specimen of the supposedly 'natural' world and freak show performer. Interestingly, the two nineteenth-century texts discussed – *The Hottentot Venus: A New Song* and *The Hottentot Venus, or Hatred of Frenchwomen* – are inclined towards understanding her racialized identity as a form of performance, self-consciously constructed. The debacle surrounding her exhibition in Britain placed particular emphasis on the quandary of her agency – as evidenced by Macaulay's and Baartman's own statements – and the level of consent or 'choice' that she exercised in being exhibited was never wholly resolved. This is a key theme which becomes manifest in neo-Victorian depictions of Sarah. Suzan-Lori Parks's play *Venus* has been criticized for depicting Baartman as complicit in her own exploitation. Similarly, Barbara Chase-Riboud's novel *Hottentot Venus* offers no easy answers to why Sarah continued to perform despite considerable abuse and denigration. However, both resist fixing her in a static role as a victim or a fool, allowing multiple possibilities for her perception of her life which dignify her with emotional and psychological complexity.

Sarah's presentation as 'the Hottentot Venus' meant that she was always already mythologised, with connotations of 'primitive' sexuality and a stage-name which ironically signalled her aberration from the Western ideals of feminine beauty. The dangers of such fictionalisation are made comically apparent in *The Hottentot Venus, or Hatred of Frenchwomen.* Sarah's reputation surpasses her identity as a 'real' woman, yet the colonial fears and fantasies which shape her image make fools of the people who invest too heavily in myths of 'Hottentot' sexuality. Unsurprisingly, issues of sexuality are also central to the neo-Victorian representations of Baartman. Parks's play imagines her as a desiring, sexualised subject, but also as having internalised the stereotypes which have defined her performances. Chase-Riboud's novel is inclined to perceive Sarah as a sexual victim at the hands of patriarchal and colonial science, which undermines medical authority and casts her posthumous dismemberment as a sexual assault. However, the text also struggles with the ethical issues at stake in re-membering Sarah. It invokes the neo-Victorian trope of haunting in an attempt to negotiate the difficulty in giving flesh to the past, but *Hottentot Venus* also cannot resist re-membering Sarah's genitalia which comes perilously close to the prurience of the freak show.

Nevertheless, both neo-Victorian texts also demonstrate a certain amount of self-consciousness about their relationship to the nineteenth-century freak show, and also make their audiences/readers aware of our ambivalent engagement with Sarah's continued exhibition after her death. But these (re)constructions of the freak show pale in comparison to the exploitation which the neo-Victorian versions of Sarah experience at the hands of science. Both texts feature Cuvier as the most heinous abuser of Baartman: admittedly, the Baron in Parks's play does seem to experience a sense of guilt about his use of Sarah, but Chase-Riboud's Cuvier is perverse, cruel, and ultimately monstrous. This demonization of science exposes the sexist and colonial ideologies which undercut its supposed objectivity, and indicate that the neo-Victorian freak show might offer – albeit limited – opportunities for redressing historical power inequalities. But perhaps this damning representation of the posthumous objectification and exhibition of Sarah Baartman also reveals neo-Victorianism's desire to distance itself from certain forms of re-memberment over others. The metatheatrical and metatextual elements of Parks's play and Chase-Riboud's novel provoke us to interrogate our own interest in the continued 'consumption' of Sarah's body as a form of entertainment and education. The myth of 'Hottentot' cannibalism is reimagined as Sarah's contemporaries 'feasting' on her body via their desires. And yet, as Marie-Luise Kohlke has argued, we also become complicit in this process, as neo-Victorian biofiction can become 'a vampiric and cannibalistic enterprise' (Kohlke, 2013, p. 13). A continuum is formed between us and the audiences who came to see Sarah perform, but, more troubling, also between us and the professionals who dismembered her, and the audiences who viewed her remains in the Parisian museums. There are aspects of the cultural afterlife of Sarah Baartman which surely leave a sour taste in our mouths.

2

Separation Anxieties: Sex, Death, and Chang and Eng Bunker

Chang and Eng were the 'original' Siamese Twins,[1] born in Siam (which is now known as Thailand) in 1811. The brothers were xiphopagus conjoined twins, connected at the sternum by a small band of cartilage. In 1829, a British merchant named Robert Hunter 'discovered' the brothers and paid their mother to allow him to take the boys abroad to be exhibited in a series of freak shows. After successfully breaking the oppressive terms of their contract, Chang and Eng became their own managers yet continued to perform as 'curiosities'. The brothers were extremely successful and famous in their day; it is, of course, from them that the term name 'Siamese twins' originates. Whilst touring America, they met and married two sisters – Chang to Adelaide Yates, and Eng to Sarah Anne Yates, and took the Americanised surname 'Bunker'.[2] The couples settled initially in one large house in North Carolina, farming their plantation and owning several slaves. They subsequently organised two households – Chang would live with his wife and family for one half of the week, and then the brothers would move on to Eng's home. Chang fathered 10 children, and Eng fathered 11. The brothers died in 1874; Chang expiring in his sleep and Eng, awaking to find his brother dead, following him several hours later.

These are the basic facts of Chang and Eng's life, but certain aspects of their lives have, perhaps unsurprisingly, been the cause of much commentary and debate. In his landmark study on the cultural and psychological meanings of 'freaks', Leslie Fielder reflects upon the autopsy report of the brothers, in which Dr Harrison Allen speculates that Eng 'died, in all probability, in a state of syncope induced by fright' (Allen, 1875, p. 40):

> the phrase 'died of fright' resonates in my mind, evoking the terror of lifelong mutual dependency. In their relationship I feel caricatured symbiotic relations more familiar to me – not sealed in the flesh, like theirs, but quite as inescapable: parents and children, unjoined siblings, lovers, husbands and wives [...] both live always with the threat of that ultimate disparity which will occur when one begins to die, and finally – the other still living – is dead.
>
> (Fielder, 1981, p. 218)

Fielder's remarks encapsulate several key issues which inform the cultural afterlife of Chang and Eng and, indeed, the discursive construction of conjoinment more broadly. Firstly, he invokes the challenge which conjoined twins pose to the boundaries between self and other. Elizabeth Grosz writes of the ways in which conjoined twins 'occupy the impossible middle ground' between 'one being and another' (Grosz, 1996, p. 57) and for Fielder such lack of individuation becomes the horror of dependency, which Alice Domurat Dreger articulates as 'especially challenging' in Western culture which 'equates individualism with independence, and interdependence with weakness' (Dreger, 2004, p. 31). However, what is interesting about Fielder's response is his recognition of the 'dependency' of conjoinment as not being limited to the very specific experience of being a conjoined twin. For Fielder, Chang and Eng function as a 'caricature' of filial and emotional bonds more broadly. Chang and Eng's unusual body is here appropriated as an allegory for constructions of personal and social identity beyond their immediate circumstances. Such a strategy which might appear to contest the construction of the 'freak' as the extreme other by which 'normal' identity is defined. Nevertheless, as Clare Barker suggests, to use unusual bodies as an allegory has also been perceived as intensely derogatory from a disability studies perspective, which has emphasised 'the alienating or stigmatizing effects of metaphorical representation' (Barker, 2011, p. 15).[3]

Fielder's examples of relationships of dependency – parents and children, lovers, husbands and wives – implicitly raise questions about Chang and Eng's 'relations' in another sense, which are at the forefront of interpretations of their bodies and lives. For, in popular and critical accounts of Chang and Eng, it is surely their marriage and parenthood which has generated the most speculation. As Alice Domurat Dreger has noted, discourses on conjoined twins are often concerned with issues of their sexual activity (Dreger, 2004, p. 62), and in Chang and Eng's lifetime, there was a great deal of anxiety generated by their marriage, and their large number of children. Furthermore, despite Fielder's recognition that all emotional relationships of dependency are threatened by the prospect of 'one half' of a partnership dying, his musings are still contextualised by imagining how Eng must have felt on waking and discovering his brother dead beside him. The ultimate 'terror' of conjoinment is the prospect of being left behind, attached to a corpse, the 'fright' which purportedly killed Eng.

This chapter will explore the ways in which these central preoccupations of thinking about conjoinment – the ways to make meanings from the example of the conjoined body, the anxieties surrounding conjoined sexuality, the horror of conjoined mortality – become manifest in both nineteenth-century and neo-Victorian texts about Chang and Eng. The textual representations of the twins dating from the nineteenth century discussed are Mark Twain's article 'Personal Habits of the Siamese Twins' (1869) and his short story *Those Extraordinary Twins* (1894), and the reports on the autopsy of the twins written by Harrison Allen and William B. Pancoast (both published in 1875). Twain's article is fixated on the tension between connection and separateness in relation to the twins' personal habits and 'morality'; the process of the brothers' courtship of the Yates sisters is of particular concern, and the tone of the piece oscillates between idealistic romance and suggestive speculation. My analysis of his short story will emphasise Twain's violent medical metaphors for thinking about the process of authorship, the text's critique of freak show discourses yet simultaneous invocation of such modes of representation, and the ways in which the lives of his twins are haunted by the prospect of death. Furthermore, I argue that the autopsy reports crystallise the tension between the 'normalisation' and 'othering' of the twins which occurs in Twain's fictions; both Allen and Pancoast's reports repeatedly invoke morally-charged evaluations of the twins' lives even as they offer a 'scientific' account of their remains. In short, sex, death, and the prospect of separation become central tropes even in these first textual 'afterlives' of the brothers. Using the themes raised by these nineteenth-century accounts as a context, my reading of Darin Strauss's *Chang and Eng* (2000) and Mark Slouka's *God's Fool* (2002) will explore the extent to which these neo-Victorian versions of Chang and Eng are able to challenge such discourses. Strauss's text, though seeking to individuate the twins, struggles to transcend the framing devices of the freak show; ultimately, the brothers' sex lives are represented in a voyeuristic, othering, and misogynistic light. *God's Fool* offers a more complex vision of conjoined sexuality, life and death. My analysis of the text will suggest that it offers routes for metatextual reflection on the role of the reader in neo-Victorian fiction depicting extraordinary bodies, and will consider the politics of the broadened understanding of 'connections' which Slouka deploys.

Mark Twain on conjoinment: Violent authorship and confused identity

Scholarship on the life and work of Mark Twain has identified a recurring preoccupation with twins, doppelgängers and doubles,[4] and the lives of Chang and Eng – and the metaphorical uses to which their bodies might be put – occur in several of his texts. The first I want to consider is a piece entitled 'Personal Habits of the Siamese Twins', which was published in *Packard's Monthly* in August 1869. Considering the twins' previous years of touring North America and Europe, and their highly-publicised marriage to the Yates sisters in 1843, by this stage Chang and Eng were household names for Twain's American readership. The article's humour, blending historical fact with fictional embellishment, focuses mainly upon the quandary of the twins' differences in the face of their anatomical proximity. Twain contrasts Chang's Catholicism with Eng's Baptist faith, Eng's energetic disposition in the face of Chang's lethargy, but most significant are their political differences: 'During the War they were strong partisans, and both fought gallantly all through the great struggle – Eng on the Union side and Chang on the Confederate' (Twain, 1869, n.p.). In this context, Chang and Eng's billing as 'the United Brothers' takes on particular significance;[5] the motif of separation within a united 'body' allegorises the struggles of North America during the Civil War.[6]

As my reading of Slouka's novel below will demonstrate, the brothers' experience of the American Civil War, specifically with regards to racial difference, is an important facet of their representation in neo-Victorian texts. But prior to his remarks on the war, Twain's article introduces a more integral theme in the notion of narrating the lives of the twins. Twain posits that he wants to write about 'certain curious details of various kinds concerning them, which, belonging only to their private life, have never crept into print', continuing to explain that: 'knowing the Twins intimately, I feel that I am peculiarly well qualified for the task I have taken upon myself' (Twain, 1869, n.p.). The article is thus couched in terms of revelation and confession; the emphasis on their 'private life' offers a tantalising suggestion of personal details made public, with a hint of salaciousness. Twain's claim to 'know the twins intimately' and attendant invocation of authority is ironic, for his confident disclosures are 'peculiar' due to the fact that he has not actually met the twins.[7] This trope of narrative disclosure will return in neo-Victorian narrations of Chang and Eng's life, yet Twain's incongruous self-assurance suggests that the connection between narrative disclosure and knowledge will always be problematic.

Fuelling the insinuation that sordid details of the twins' lives will be revealed, Twain dwells upon the challenges that conjoinment poses to the brother's romantic prospects:

> Both fell in love with the same girl. Each tried to steal clandestine interviews with her, but at the critical moment the other would always turn up. By-and-bye, Eng saw, with distraction, that Chang had won the girl's affections; and from that day forth, he had to bear with the agony of being a witness to all their dainty billing and cooing. But, with a magnanimity that did him infinite credit, he succumbed to his fate, and gave countenance and encouragement to a state of things that bade fair to sunder his generous heartstrings. He sat from seven every evening until two in the morning listening to the fond foolishness of the two lovers, and to the concussion of hundreds of squandered kisses – for the privilege of sharing only one of which he would have given his right hand.
>
> (Twain, 1869, n.p.)

Twain's imagining of the perils of conjoined desire raises several important points. Conjoinment is both sameness and separateness; the twins are subject to comparable emotional impulses and yet struggle for individuation in romantic possessiveness. Furthermore, in this formulation conjoined sexual expression must always necessarily have an audience, albeit unwilling; the fictionalised Eng is always a third party, the most extreme version of a cuckolded lover. Alice Domurat Dreger has suggested that conjoined sexuality inspires anxiety and fascination because it challenges notions of privacy, and transgresses various boundaries of 'normal' desire: incest, queerness, group sex (Dreger, 2012, n.p.). Such crossing of boundaries becomes apparent in the ambiguity of Eng's desire to 'share' one of the kisses. Presumably this refers to kissing the girl, and yet has additional connotations when his proximity to his brother means that so many of their experiences are necessarily shared. Therefore, Eng's envy might be due to the desire for heterosexual contact with his beloved, but also hints at the 'shared' sexuality of conjoinment. The terminology used to articulate Eng's experience of his brother's romance is also notable. The 'sundering' of his heartstrings associates separation with emotional pain, a provocative metaphor considering the way in which separation is routinely offered as the only 'proper' resolution for conjoined identity and desire (Dreger, 2004, pp. 43–44). And yet Eng's wish to participate in the kisses between Eng and the girl is expressed in the vocabulary of amputation; he would 'give his right hand' for this opportunity. Twain is thus deploying ambivalent vocabulary to explore conjoined sexuality, paradoxically locating such experience between the desire for union *and* separateness.

The identity of the 'girl' in this romantic tableau is suggested by the subsequent remark that 'By-and-Bye Eng fell in love with his sister-in-law's sister, and married her, and since that day they have all lived together, night and day, in a exceeding sociability which is touching and beautiful to behold and which is a scathing rebuke to our boasted civilisation' (Twain, 1869, n.p.). Following the historical facts of the Bunkers' marital arrangement, Chang's beau is Adelaide and Eng's is her sister, Sarah. Twain's apparent celebration of the Bunkers' marital arrangements as an ideal vision of unity and cooperation ostensibly chastises prurient speculation of the time about this arrangement as morally dubious. However, their domestic space is still positioned as outside 'civilisation' which draws attention to the brothers' status as ethnic others.[8] The authenticity of Eng's emotional feelings is placed under scrutiny towards the end of the article. Recounting the ways in which Chang's body is affected when his brother drinks alcohol,[9] Twain explains that 'Chang's moral principles were unsullied, his conscience clear; and so all just men were forced to confess that he was not morally, but only physically drunk' (Twain, 1869, n.p.). This vexed boundary between the moral and physical is imbued with additional implications in Twain's explanation of the 'sympathy' between the brothers: 'The sympathy existing between these two brothers is so close and so refined that the feelings, the impulses, the emotions of the one are instantly experienced by the other [...] We have already seen with what happy facility they both fell in love with the same girl' (Twain, 1869, n.p.) In this context, Eng's desire for 'the girl' (Adelaide) is a result of his brother's passion, and yet surely such passion flows both ways, and hints at adulterous impulses from both brothers towards their respective sisters-in-law? However, if Twain can claim to make a distinction between being morally and physically intoxicated by alcohol, between consciously deciding to get drunk and just experiencing the physical affects, then does this also imply that any 'physical' manifestation of desire which actually comes from the other brother's intentions is similarly pardoned from moral censure? Such possibilities are further complicated by Twain's farcical conclusion: 'There is a moral in these solemn writings – or, at least, a warning in these solemn morals; one or the other. No matter, it is somehow. Let us heed it; let us profit it' (Twain, 1869, n.p.). Any 'moral' or 'serious' message in the article is thus undermined, and, by extension, perhaps the prospect that we can pass judgement on the twins – unique as their circumstances are – is also problematized. Whether this implies that the situation of conjoined sexuality is beyond moralising, or, indeed, beyond taking seriously, is not easily answered.

Twain's other significant treatment of conjoined twins comes in his short story, *Those Extraordinary Twins*. In his foreword to the text he explains:

> I had seen a picture of a youthful Italian 'freak' – or 'freaks' – which was – or which were – on exhibition in our cities – a combination consisting of two heads and four arms joined to a single body and a single pair of legs – and I thought I would write an extravagantly fantastic little story with this freak of nature for hero – or heroes.
>
> (Twain, 2009, p. 150)

As Robert A. Wiggins suggests, Twain's description of the twins' body and their nationality suggests an alternative source to Chang and Eng; the Tocci twins. Giacomo and Giovanni Batista Tocci, born in Italy in 1877, were dicephalus conjoined twins, having separate upper bodies and arms, but being fused below the waist. They were exhibited in Europe during the 1880s, and toured United States in 1891, and thus in some ways offer a more convincing inspiration for the story than the Bunkers.[10] However, as Cynthia Wu has argued, it is difficult to ignore Twain's previous interest in Chang and Eng when considering his representation of conjoinment in *Those Extraordinary Twins*, particularly when there are some striking parallels between the experiences of his fictional twins and the biographical details of Chang and Eng.[11] Aside from these factual resonances, I suggest that Twain's story is a productive source for thinking about the cultural afterlife of Chang and Eng as it engages with issues of conjoinment – and how such embodiment might be narrated – which are central to the ethics of exhibition, identity and authorship which become apparent in neo-Victorian appropriations of Chang and Eng's lives.

Twain's initial aim was to write a novel about the lives of conjoined twins, but found that the other characters of the tale were becoming too dominant, and he struggled to manage his material: 'it was not one story, but two stories tangled together; and they obstructed and interrupted each other at every turn and created no end of confusion and annoyance. I could not offer the book for publication, for I was afraid it would unseat the reader's reason' (Twain, 2009, p. 149). The story itself takes on the qualities of the disorderly bodies to which it refers, which highlights the ways in which bodies – extraordinary or otherwise – can be understood as discursive constructions. Furthermore, such a tangled 'body' of text is conceptualised as having potentially pernicious effects upon the consumer of such stories; the representation of an unusual body will corrupt the reader's mind. As we shall see in Chapter 5's discussion of Joseph Merrick, the potential for freak shows to trouble public morals was an important aspect of his construction as a 'deviant' body in the eyes of Fredrick Treves. In the context of Twain's stories, a strange parallel is formed between the supposedly dangerous effects which the display of 'freaks' might have upon a 'normal' audience and the way in which a 'monstrous' story might influence a readership.[12] If in Twain's framing texts have the potential to become freakish, then he also suggests that the author might be in a position to tame such an unruly body: 'I pulled one of the stories out by the roots, and left the other one – a kind of literary Caesarean operation' (Twain, 2009, p. 150). Famously, of course, this second story was to become the novel *Pudd'nhead Wilson* (1894) and in his additional remarks on the alterations to his original tale he explains that the conjoined twins of *Wilson* were divided: 'I took those twins apart and made two separate men of them' (Twain, 2009, p. 152).[13] His vocabulary is suggestive; the author is placed in the position of surgeon to the freakish text in the sense that he has the power to deliver the unruly story and also to enact the medical dream of separating – and therefore normalising – conjoined twins. As I shall discuss in further detail below, medical discourse surrounding Chang and Eng repeatedly dwelled on the possibility of their separation, even after their deaths.

Interestingly, however, this process of separation was not a clean cut. Nancy Fredricks' analysis of *Pudd'nhead Wilson* demonstrates the ways in which the presence of conjoinment 'haunts' the representation of the twins in the novel (Fredricks, 1989, p. 485). Catharine O'Connell, also commenting on the ways in which Twain has seemingly failed to rewrite the twins as wholly separate subjects, suggests that a better metaphor for the 'surgical' procedure of the texts' composition: 'would be the (unsuccessful) separation of conjoined twins' (O'Connell, 2002, p. 101). This image of the author as a failed surgeon attempting to eradicate an 'abnormal' body and yet failing has thought-provoking consequences, for what might he produce instead? Can authorial intervention actually make an unusual body even more 'freakish'? In the explanation of one brother, Angelo, about their earlier life before coming to the small town, he tells the group how 'he and Luigi had to travel with a freak-show during two years and suffer semi-starvation' (Twain, 2009, p. 166). This experience is couched in terms of ill-treatment, exploitation and coercion and therefore is seemingly a damning portrayal of freak show dynamics. However, there are moments when the text does actually deploy the modes and language of freak show presentation to represent the twins. The brothers introduce themselves as 'Count Luigi and Angelo Capello' (Twain, 2009, p. 154), an appellation which coheres with Robert Bogdan's assessment of nineteenth-century freak show discourse as an 'aggrandized' mode of performance (Bogdan, 1988, p. 108). In this light, we can see that the text simultaneously refuses and invokes the culture of the freak show; albeit uneasy with freakery's exploitative elements, the text still struggles to find alternative methods of representation.

The brothers ultimately achieve a certain amount of respect in the local community, but when Luigi is appointed as a town official the confusion over what role Angelo his brother should take leads to widespread chaos. The dubious solution reached by the townsfolk is that the offending twin should be lynched:

> But others said: 'No – Count Angelo is innocent; we mustn't hang him'.
>
> 'Who said anything about hanging him? We are only going to hang the other one'.
>
> 'Then that is all right – there is no objection to that'. So they hanged Luigi. And so ends the history of 'Those Extraordinary Twins'.
>
> (Twain, 2009, p. 208)

The ending is obviously absurd, but it is also ambivalent; does the history of 'Those Extraordinary Twins' end because one brother dies, or both? Considering the practicalities of their conjoinment, it is clearly the latter. The townspeople are represented as foolish for being deluded into thinking of the twins as separate subjects. In the world of the text, conjoined twins are always situated at a blurred boundary between self and other, evidenced from Twain's initial struggles over how to delineate the twins in the inspirational photograph; should they be addressed as singular, or plural? In addition, the conclusion of the short story points towards the apparent inevitability of conjoined death. One twin has died and so must the other, and although this injustice is couched in comic terms it still invokes the horror of deathly symbiosis which haunts subsequent representations of Chang and Eng.

Picking over the bones: Medical constructions of Chang and Eng

Despite the medical analogy of authorship which Twain deploys in explaining his division of two stories, the culture of medical display of unusual bodies is treated satirically in *Those Extraordinary Twins*. In a conversation between the brothers, the more religious Angelo frets over having just narrowly missed being obliged to fight a duel on the Sabbath: '"my soul would have been lost – lost"'. Luigi responds: '"Oh, don't fret, it wasn't in any danger [...] they wouldn't waste it for a little thing like that; there's a glass case all ready for it in the heavenly museum, and a pin to stick it up with"' (Twain, 2009, p. 201). The humour here, of course, is in the slippage between body and soul; although it is usually the former that will be preserved as a specimen in a medical museum, it seems that the latter is also of value as a spectacle. Luigi's pointed remark on the ways in which the 'soul' of the individual with an extraordinary body can become public property strikes a chord with the ways in which Sarah Baartman's remains were treated, and the sense of medical proprietorship which Treves feels over Joseph Merrick which will be discussed in Chapter 5. Interestingly, however, medical accounts of Chang and Eng's body after their death are still concerned with the 'morality' of the brothers' lives.

Two of the physicians who undertook the autopsy on Chang and Eng published papers based on their findings: Harrison Allen and William H. Pancoast. Acquiring the brothers' body for dissection and analysis proved to be a difficult enterprise for the medical men involved: Sarah and Adelaide were understandably reluctant to relinquish their husbands' bodies,[14] and only agreed to the autopsy on certain conditions, as detailed by Pancoast: '[the wives] gave us permission to make such a post-mortem examination as would not disfigure the cadavers, and to examine the strange band that united them, on what was called its posterior part, but in no way to deface it in front, nor to divide it asunder' (Pancoast, 1875, p. 152). Interestingly, this condition also finds its way into Allen's report in terms of his (now infamous) diagnosis of death by fright for Eng:

> With reference to the cause of death of the Siamese twins it maybe briefly said that, in consequence of the restrictions by which we

> were bound, no examinations of the brains was made. It cannot, therefore, be proved that the cause of Chang's death was a cerebral clot, although such an opinion from the suddenness of death [...] is tenable. Eng died, in all probability, in a state of syncope induced by fright – a view which the over-distended bladder and the retraction of the right testicle would appear to corroborate.
>
> (Allen, 1875, p. 40)

Cynthia Wu's analysis of this statement is significant, as she observes that earlier in Allen's report he noted that it was Eng's left testicle that had retracted: 'While this discrepancy may have been a mere copyediting error, it contributes to the haze of ambiguity surrounding Eng's death. The official cause of death that was recorded appears to reflect anxieties held by the normatively bodied when forced to confront the concept of interdependency' (Wu, 2012, p. 54). She subsequently discusses the ways in which the 'death by fright' conclusion has entered into the popular imagination when considering anxieties about conjoinment, also mentioning Leslie Fielder's dismay at this prospect (Wu, 2012, pp. 54–55). Pointedly, such detail also suggests that 're-membering' is not just the privilege of neo-Victorianism; the emphasis on the ways in which the genitalia of subjects with extraordinary bodies might offer an insight into their emotional or psychological experiences is evidently a theme in nineteenth-century medicine as well, as Chapter 5 will consider in relation to Fredrick Treves's oft-quoted statement on the relative 'normality' of Joseph Merrick's penis.

I am also interested in the palpable irritation which Allen's report expresses towards the brothers' wives; they are 'bound' by the restrictions of Sarah and Adelaide, implying that such feminised matters as personal, emotional connections are actually getting in the way of scientific knowledge. Of course, Allen's choice of words is loaded in the context of conjoinment. The wives are a burden, in much the same way as the dead brother is a burden to the living, and in the scientific imagination we see that separation is the key to success whereas connections are always restrictions. There is thus a certain irony in the way in which the brothers' marital and family circumstances also keep getting in the way of the expression of 'objective' scientific assessment in both reports. Allen begins his report with a summary of the twins' marriage, children and living arrangements (Allen, 1875, pp. 3–4). Pancoast's commentary is more substantial. Entitled 'Report on the Surgical Considerations in Regard to the Propriety of an Operation for the Separation of Eng and Chang Bunker, Commonly Known as the Siamese Twins', the term 'propriety' resonates throughout Pancoast's report, with its loaded implications of both ethical and moral decency. He suggests that the reason for the autopsy was to confirm whether the twins could have actually been separated during their lifetime and was thus to 'gratify a desire very widely entertained' (Pancoast, 1875, p. 150). The notion of the autopsy being for gratification of desire offers some interesting avenues of speculation. If the twins and their wives were regularly accused of immorality during their married lives, then the public interest in finding out whether their unusual domestic situation was avoidable suggests a rather prurient fascination on behalf of the wider population. Indeed, has the complex web of desire and gratification which attends conjoined sexuality in the public imagination actually spread to implicate the 'normal' moral majority?

Pancoast explicitly tackles the matter of the marital bed of conjoined twins by explaining a system of 'alternate mastery' which the twins developed:

> they had agreed that each should in turn control the action of the other. Thus Eng would for one week be complete master; they would live for that time at Eng's house, and Chang would submit his will and desires completely to those of Eng, and vice versa. Though it seems most immoral and shocking that the two should occupy the same marital couch with the wife of one, yet so thorough was this understanding of alternate mastery, that, as I was told by one of the widows, there never had been any improper relations between the wives and the brothers.
>
> (pp. 156–57)

The slippery concepts of both 'desire' and the 'improper' are raised again here, and more specifically aligned with the realm of the sexual. Pancoast's tone wavers between high moral approbation for the couples' dedication to preserving standards of propriety in the face of adversity, and a slightly gossipy disclosure of how many people might have been in bed together at one time. In seeking to normalise the twins, Pancoast cannot resist hinting at the salacious possibilities of their bedroom activities. His approval at the twins' adaptation to their situation is somewhat undermined by his final recommendation that, if at all possible, conjoined twins should be separated:

> even if both perished, the risk might be justified; the moral sense of the community, at least in a Christian country, would then not be shocked by the unnatural complication which otherwise would arise,

> and did arise in the case of the Siamese twins, proving the cause of so much criticism – a criticism severe and unjust.
>
> (Pancoast, 1875, p. 166–67)

Although Pancoast appears to suggest that the twins managed their lives very well, it is the opinion of the broader community to which medicine must pander. This seems an incongruous conclusion from a medical man with the confidence of Pancoast, and perhaps might lead us to question whether he is entirely convinced by the wives' claims of decency. His remark about the superior moral sense of a 'Christian' country brings the twins' ethnicity into sharp focus and covertly casts aspersions on their own standards, even as such criticism is dismissed as 'unjust'. In Pancoast's final assessment, death becomes preferable to the disruptive force which conjoined sexuality might exercise upon a community. In addition to re-membering being a theme of nineteenth-century medical discourse on unusual anatomies, then, it is apparent that physicians such as Pancoast were also susceptible to indulging in some aspects of 'medical sensationalism' as discussed in this book's Introduction.

From the accounts of Twain, Allen and Pancoast, it is apparent that the themes of sex and death loom large in nineteenth-century representations of Chang and Eng. In addition, Twain's texts offer an ambivalent account of the gaze in relation to both freak show and medical models of exhibiting bodies. It is significant that such anxieties are maintained in twentieth-century accounts of the twins' lives. For example, Irving and Amy Wallace's biography of Chang and Eng initially appears inclined to be cautious about offering any information about how the brothers and their wives might have negotiated their sex lives: 'There exists little actual information as to the twins' sexual practices, and any answers to the persisting questions must therefore be largely speculative' (Wallace and Wallace, 1978, p. 181). Remarkably, however, the next several pages of the biography are dedicated to such speculation, with Wallace and Wallace going so far as to suggest various sexual positions which might have been most effective to getting the job done with the minimal physical strain to the parties involved and the least possible embarrassment for the non-participating twin (Wallace and Wallace, 1978, pp. 181–83). Absurd though this example is, it does raise several interesting issues. For in this biography – and in the nineteenth-century accounts of the twins' lives discussed above – the principal obstacle posed by their conjoinment appears to be its barrier to them having a normal sex-life. Indeed, there is no evidence to suggest that the twins were significantly 'disabled' in a physical sense by their conjoinment, as their performances frequently entailed them demonstrating acrobatic stunts.[15] Instead, Chang and Eng's 'disability' appears to be that they were prevented from leading a 'normal' sex life according to the prevailing moral standards of the day.

What is also telling about the Wallaces' account of Chang and Eng's sexual activities is that they have no qualms about devoting such scrutiny to the matter. Disregarding the lack of 'actual information', they implicitly imagine themselves as witnesses to the private sexual activity of the brothers. As the twins spent a considerable amount of their lives performing under the public gaze in American and European freak shows, it is almost as if there should be no barrier to us not being privy to all aspects of their lives – we are the paying customers who have bought the biography, after all, and are therefore entitled to the full story. And as their remarks above demonstrate, if the 'actual information' about these sexual practices has not been preserved then invention becomes permissible. In the Wallaces' imagination, the twins' bedrooms become just another forum for exhibition. It is this difficult boundary between fact and imagination with regards to Chang and Eng's sexual activities with which neo-Victorianism must engage. Concerns about the ways in which the neo-Victorian fascination with nineteenth-century sexuality might become 'the new Orientalism' (Kohlke, 2008, p. 352) become heightened in the case of Chang and Eng as historical subjects hailing from the Far East. And, of course, the opportunities for prurient exploitation are compounded by their physical difference: might neo-Victorian re-memberings of Chang and Eng become, in an expression quoted by Robert Bogdan in relation to the freak show, a 'pornography of disability'?[16] Bearing in mind the ways in which power relationships of sexuality, disability and race intersect in representations of Chang and Eng, I will now turn to two neo-Victorian novels which take the Bunker brothers as their subject: Darin Strauss's *Chang and Eng* (2000) and Mark Slouka's *God's Fool* (2002).

Disabling sexuality: Darin Strauss's *Chang and Eng*

Strauss's novel features Eng as the first-person narrator throughout the main body of the text, but his story is framed by a Prologue and Epilogue written mainly in the third person. The Prologue begins with Eng waking to find his brother's body 'cold' against his: '*Eng is alone. The smell is asphyxiating*' (Strauss, 2000, p. 10). As in the neo-Victorian versions of Sarah Baartman discussed in Chapter 1, to begin a narrative with the death of the subject has complex implications. Considering that Chang and Eng's fame is founded on the exhibition of their body, the deterioration of such a body might ostensibly imply that the text's focus will be offering an insight beyond the corporeal. However, as indicated in my Introduction, and explored further in relation to Sarah Baartman in the previous chapter, a freak show performer's career was not over when they died; the exhibition of extraordinary bodies after death has been a particularly troubling aspect of the cultural afterlife of many nineteenth-century subjects. Furthermore, to begin the story of Eng with the death of his brother reiterates the projected terror at the prospect of conjoined death which becomes apparent in Allen's autopsy report. It is a truism to suggest that death will come to all of us, yet the experience of living whilst physically attached to a corpse, accompanied by the probability that one's own death is imminent, is the preserve of twins such as Chang and Eng. The physical experience of such a state is made explicit by the narrative voice; invoking the sense of smell, the above description reduces Chang and Eng to the realm of the bodily otherness and abjection from the outset. This otherness is reiterated by the external third-person narration describing the scene; the tone is impersonal and objective rather than emotive and subjective. With Eng's dawning recognition that his brother has died, and that he will shortly be dead as well, the narrative voice states: '*Eng's life full of leering faces, slander, and unlikely love begins to recede [...] he is seized by memory, it being the wondrous strange hand pulling him back to the fading shores of his past*' (Strauss, 2000, p. 10; original emphasis). It is Eng's experience of having an extraordinary body that will shape his narrative, and it is the tale of his 'unlikely love' that will shape this text. Furthermore, this quotation also suggests that Strauss's re-imagining of Eng's life will be conscious of the twins' life as a spectacle; the 'leering' faces – with attendant connotations of a look of sexual interest and desire – will figure prominently in the novel.

On the subject of the gaze of their audiences, Eng's account of their experience as freak show performers is repeatedly couched in terms of degradation. He describes their life as an exhibition as: 'Going from exhibit hall to exhibit hall in a cage, a thousand nights spent smiling while such words as "horrible" and "disgusting" made their way above the din and into our ears' (Strauss, 2000, p. 56). The trappings of the brothers' act – display in a cage – emphasizes the limitations placed on their body, and their agency. They are trapped within the accoutrements of freakery, and vulnerable to the insulting words of their audience, a re-membering of the nineteenth-century freak show that is far from the opportunities for constructive interaction between audience and performer which I suggested, via Nadja Durbach's arguments, in the Introduction (Durbach, 2010, p. 9). However, there is a marked difference between Eng's and Chang's respective attitudes towards exhibition within the novel. Eng relates Chang's waving at the crowds as they entered the town, Wilkesboro, where they will shortly meet the Yates sisters:

> It was this sort of pandering showmanship that I hated, and strove to avoid for most of my career. (Like most everybody, I am proud of certain accomplishments: that we never participated in, nor were in any way associated with, an American circus; my predilection for reading, which saved me from the manner of immigrant speech that Chang never lost).
>
> (Strauss, 2000, p. 17)

On a certain level, Strauss's decision to offer just Eng's narrative perspective marks a development from the struggles of nineteenth-century commentators such as Twain to accord conjoined twins with independent subjectivity and might be interpreted as a strategy of 'normalisation' of Eng's experiences. Such an impulse surely informs this description of the brothers' differing attitudes towards 'showmanship'. However, this desire for individuation raises further ideological concerns. Chang's willingness to perform is conflated with his comparable lack of education to Eng within this novel, which in turn is associated with Chang being marked as racially other. As Holly E. Martin observes: 'Strauss asserts the notion that Chang was lacking in intelligence throughout the novel by writing Chang's speech in broken, pidgin English, even sometimes substituting the letter "l" for the letter "r" in a stereotypical depiction of Chang's language' (Martin, 2011, pp. 384–85). Therefore, to embrace public exhibition is aligned with being uneducated and racially different, ironically reiterating the strains of orientalist derogation in Twain's and Pancoast's texts. Yet perhaps Strauss's emphasis on the disabling – rather than enabling – aspects of such exhibition suggests that this novel will be sensitive to the ethical quandaries of Victorian freak shows, and will not seek to replicate such discourses.

Nevertheless, I argue that with regards to the representation of the twins' sex lives – the driving force of this narrative – this is not quite the case. In the early stages of his relationship with Sarah, Eng remarks: 'Rather than a flood of passion, love came to me as a curious and distant spectacle' (Strauss, 2000, p. 66). Love for a Siamese twin is aligned with the discourse of the freak show – 'curiosity', 'spectacle'. It would seem that Eng has internalised his role as freak show performer to such an extent that this will also mark his experience of private passion. In the run-up to the brothers' marriage, Eng explains how the brothers plan to deal with the challenges of the wedding night:

> This is the method Chang and I decided upon, and told the newspapers about: Whenever one of us needed privacy with his wife, the other was to become 'insensate' for the next hour, to become unconscious, allowing each twin to enjoy his wife in seclusion. Though our situation seemed immoral and shocking to the outside world, it was through what we called an 'alternative mastery' that we would be certain to remain pure [...] In this way we would avoid allegations of improper relations between our wives and ourselves.
>
> (Strauss, 2000, p. 160)

There are striking textual echoes between Eng's explanation and Pancoast's description of how the twins avoided their marital arrangements being viewed as 'immoral and shocking' quoted above. Such resonance gives pause for thought, as Strauss's Eng thus becomes a mouth-piece for medical authority and social propriety.

However, the 're-membered' reality of the sex scenes in Strauss's novel are very different; the experience of three in a bed does not allow for being 'insensate', and Strauss's depiction of the twins' sex life 're-members' what is probably the ultimate fear/fantasy of prurient speculation when it comes to conjoined twin sexuality: Eng is sexually attracted to his brother's wife. The couples decide that Chang and Adelaide will have the first opportunity to consummate their marriage, and as the three of them proceed to bed, Eng refers to 'the main bedroom and the riddles therein' (Strauss, 2000, p. 164). This turn of phrase implies that the way in which they are going to make their sex-life work is a mystery for the twins as well. In this moment, there is a sense of identification between Eng and the novel's readership, for the marriage bed of conjoined twins is also a 'riddle' for him. Such an acknowledgement might promise that the scene we are about to witness will challenge the 'otherness' of the twins; how to have sex when joined to another person also baffles Eng, perhaps reassuring the reader of our narrator's 'normalcy'.

Such promise – and any aspirations of privacy – are quickly dispelled, when Adelaide herself cannot seem to ignore Eng: 'My brother's wife glanced at me, then her eyes darted away. She seemed to be talking to both of us' (Strauss, 2000, p. 165). Eng does attempt to follow the brothers' plan, yet this is abruptly thwarted by the bodily experience of his brother having sex: 'I closed my eyes – the method Chang and I had decided upon – to become "mindless" for the next hour. But with each bounce or jolt or kick of Adelaide's leg, my eyes opened instinctively, as if against my will' (Strauss, 2000, p. 165). We see that the division between mind and body does not work; the fleshy reality of sex intrudes on mental willpower and Eng becomes an unwilling participant in the experience. Due to the narrative structure of the novel, we do not have Chang's perspective on the sex between Eng and Sarah, but there is an implication that he too is experiencing sexual pleasure: 'My brother's eyes were closed, but he wore an inexplicable and bothersome smile' (Strauss, 2000, p. 170). Furthermore, 'as I flipped all of us over, my brother moaned as if he'd been kicked or slapped inadvertently. But Chang could not have been, because all of Sarah's hands and feet were touching mine' (Strauss, 2000, p. 170). Aside from pandering to the rumours of sexual immorality that dogged the twins throughout their lives, this representation also suggests that the marriage bed of conjoined twins has queer connotations; the twins are necessarily entwined in their sexual pleasure. Incongruously, such permutations of desire are hinted at in the ambiguity of Twain's description of Eng's desire to 'share' in his brother's kisses with his lover (Twain, 1869, n.p.).

Although Adelaide and Eng never actually have sex, as the relationship between them develops they do intentionally hold hands whilst she copulates with Chang. The subtle and torturous process of courtship between Eng and Adelaide culminates in Eng kissing his brother's wife as Chang lies in a post-coital sleep. Shortly after this, the household which is shared by the brothers, wives and their children mysteriously catches fire; in the novel, it is this disaster which motivates the building of another family home where the families can be separated. After this division Eng and Adelaide do not share any further clandestine intimacies. In this sense, Strauss's novel reiterates the dominant discourse of separation of twins being equated with sexual normalcy, which is still implicit in accounts of present-day surgical separations of conjoined twins. Analysing medical and media accounts of separation surgery, Alice Domurat Dreger observes:

> [...] one gets the sense that many adults seem to fear a conjoined child will grow up to be loved sexually almost as much as they fear a conjoined child will *not* grow up to be loved sexually. Regardless of which fear looms larger, sexual anxiety forms a prominent and convoluted theme in medical and media narratives of conjoinment and separation.
>
> (Dreger, 2004, p. 62)

Chang and Eng could not be surgically separated during their lifetime, and yet in Strauss's novel the parting of the wives and families stands in for the literal separation that would fully 'normalise' the twins' sex lives. The fact that the twins' sex life is still not fully separate seems to trail off in the novel, as if domestic 'normalcy' ensures more moral – and, implicitly, heteronormative – sexual arrangements.

However, towards the very end of the novel, the spectre of past indiscretions returns to haunt Eng. To make money after the Civil War the brothers briefly revisit their career as freak show performers. The indignity of this further round of exploitation places a further strain on their relationship and the novel depicts a fierce argument between the twins which culminates in a vicious brawl. In the hurtful words that are exchanged, Chang suddenly reveals his knowledge of Eng's relationship with Adelaide: '"I know everything. Idiot, I knew, I knew, I knew [...] You five inches from me all the time [...] You not think I would have eyes to see everything?"' (Strauss, 2000, p. 339). We should note Chang's emphasis on sight in this revelation; the spectacle of conjoined sexuality prevents privacy for anyone in their crowded bed. In this turn of phrase, the novel seems to echo the necessity of gazing on the twins' sexual activities implied by the Wallaces' account I offered earlier. Strauss's account of the brothers' sexuality is still informed by the discourse of the spectacle, the trappings of the Victorian freak show. Furthermore, Chang also indicates that it was he that lit the fire which destroyed the family home: 'You kill the home in your way [....] I light fire' (Strauss, 2000, p. 340). It is the complications of conjoined sexuality which literally and symbolically destroy their family home, the illusion of American normalcy they have desperately tried to construct. The morning after the fight and Chang's confession it is revealed that Chang has had a stroke – he becomes physically disabled and, necessarily, Eng is also physically impaired. The logic of this conclusion is ethically troubling, for it suggests that the brothers' disability has ultimately come from sexual transgression, and its attendant consequences.

There is another spectre of transgressive sexuality haunting Strauss's novel; miscegenation. In the early stages of Eng's courtship with Sarah, she discloses that her family's reputation has been tainted by a sexual assault she was subjected to by a male slave:

> Of course it had been against her will, she said, and only once, by a slave, that horrible slave, and she talked of how her brother Jefferson had stumbled upon them in the woods. And of the subsequent trial, and of the hanging, which had been such an event for Wilkesboro

> that the school had been closed for the day. Children had been encouraged to watch.
>
> (Strauss, 2000, p. 114)

Raising the stereotype of black men as a sexual threat to white women,[17] the novel thus positions Sarah's interest in marrying Eng, despite his own relative racial otherness and bodily difference, as being justified by such an experience. As Cynthia Wu explains: 'The question of why two middle-class women would wed a set of Asian conjoined men is explained by invoking an even more unspeakable sexual transgression – a white woman's sexual involvement with black men' (Wu, 2012, p. 139). The punishment of miscegenation has also been made a spectacle in the town; a public event for family consumption, which has an uncomfortable parallel to the 'visibility' of the twins' sex lives in terms of the ever-present audience of the non-participating brother, and the broader spectacle of the racially marked body which both a lynching and the twins' freak show experiences share.

Eng later overhears a conversation between the sisters which implies that this was actually consensual sex: 'I was overcome by shock, then rage [...] Had my wife lied to me about the slave?'(Strauss, 2000, p. 210). Sarah is thus not a victim, and her sexual transgression has led to the death of an innocent man. In the act of making love to his wife, Eng describes 'her throat arched as if yielding to the hangman' (Strauss, 2000, p. 171). Although this image comes before Eng's knowledge of Sarah's consent in her prior sexual experience, it implies Sarah's guilt and also that sex with Eng becomes a substitute for the punishment she has avoided. This might be interpreted as a moment of connection between Eng and the executed slave; both men, marked as racially other, have been manipulated by her white middle-class privilege. Nevertheless, such fleeting suggestions of male solidarity come loaded with misogyny; Sarah's body becomes marked as sexually deviant and, when coupled with Adelaide's seeming lust for conjoined sexual transgression, returns to the nineteenth-century construction of conjoined sexuality as 'improper'.

Alternative connections: Mark Slouka's *God's Fool*

Slouka's novel, published several years after *Chang and Eng*, offers an interesting counterpoint to Strauss's text in various ways. It literally gives Chang's side of the brothers' story – a first-person narrative from his perspective – and Slouka's version of Chang's voice bears no trace of the stilted English which makes Strauss's representation so problematic. In contrast to Strauss's novel and the nineteenth-century texts, *God's Fool* treats the prospect of conjoined death as an opportunity for reflection upon the process of making narrative rather than an occasion for horror. Chang recounts a period when the twins are living in poverty in London:

> I remember wondering – almost dispassionately, as though it were someone else – which one of us would wake to find the other dead [...] Boil it down and it comes to this: Death is a conjugation. The *I* dies. The narrative of your life, newly orphaned, is picked up by a third person. *I lay my head on the table by the iron gas-pipe, and slept/He died Tuesday afternoon in a lodging house off Black-horse yard.*
>
> (Slouka, 2002, p. 180; original emphasis)

Slouka's version of Chang recognises that bodily experience is structured like a language, and his use of the grammatical term 'conjugation' is interesting, having a resonance with 'conjugal', suggesting the brother's union, and also, presumably, their union in death. However, to reduce death to the level of linguistics indicates the inadequacy of language to communicate this experience and, ironically, the impossibility of conceptualising it in any other way. Death is just a concept in the mind of a conjoined twin, just as much as it is for any other human, dispelling the extreme otherness of conjoined mortality and providing a pertinent critique of the slippage between first and third person narration in the Prologue to Strauss's *Chang and Eng*.

In another contrast with *Chang and Eng*, the marital relationships between the brothers and their wives do not take centre stage in Slouka's novel. In Cynthia Wu's terms: '*God's Fool* presents the reader with a scant and matter-of-fact description of sex, dispelling it as a nonissue' (Wu, 2012, p. 139). For example, Strauss's imagining of tangled limbs and desires gives way to sex between Chang and Adelaide as routine and unspectacular. Chang describes the couple's reaction after their son, Samuel, dies: 'Addy came to our bed that week, but though we pleased each other, sweating in the darkness, neither of us took much comfort in the thing. It was a weapon, nothing more – something to wield against the grief – and both of us knew it' (Slouka, 2002, p. 24). Although Chang's explanation of their love-making indicates the tensions in his and Adelaide's relationship, the phrase that their sexual encounter is 'nothing more' has thought-provoking implications. Their sex life is not extraordinary, not an occasion for transgression or speculation, and, remarkably given the context, resolutely does not involve his brother. In terms of their married sex lives, Slouka's version of Chang and Eng has offered a practical and mundane answer to the question which Alice Domurat Dreger poses: 'So what *do* conjoined twins do about sex? So far as I can ascertain, they do what most people do: seek out a lover, find a little privacy, and do the deed, understanding it to be a one-on-one affair' (Dreger, 2004, p. 49). So the concept of 'nothing more' also serves to thwart the fantasy of conjoined sexuality as a group event, denying the economy of exhibition which the Wallaces and Strauss cannot think beyond.

Yet Wu's commentary on the novel does not take into account of the other representations of desire and sexuality, outside of Chang and Eng's domestic space, which are depicted in the text. Slouka's novel re-members a relationship between the brothers and a woman which has been relegated to a footnote in their histories. According to Wallace and Wallace, in their years of touring Europe Chang and Eng did have female admirers, and they briefly recount the story of one:

> Her full name is not known to history. Her first name was Sophia. She was young and beautiful, and was a member of London society. She met the united twins and, as a pamphlet of the period reported, 'by some unaccountable caprice, fell violently in love with both'. Sophia pursued the twins, wrote poetry to them, and published her verse. She loved them as one, not either one separately – perhaps the perversity of it had some sexual appeal to her.
>
> (Wallace and Wallace, 1978, p. 89)

The Wallaces biography does not make much of this 'romance'; Sophia becomes just another occasion for dramatizing the 'perversity' of conjoined twins' sexuality. Taking up the challenge of representing a woman who has been lost to history, *God's Fool* furnishes Sophia with the surname 'Marchant' and relocates her to Paris where she meets the brothers at a soirée.

Chang tells of a routine that the brothers have contrived to amuse the other guests at this event:

> We had stumbled onto the idea quite accidently when, at the beginning of the evening, a young woman had offered my brother her hand and I, unaware, had reached for it first. The group laughed at this apparent competition between us, and as our host took us around [...] we quite naturally, and almost unconsciously, expanded

> on our early success. Feigning innocence, pretending to be unaware of what all the laughter could be about, I would now snatch at any feminine hand that came our way and bring it to my lips, murmuring 'enchanté', my eyes closed as if – like a Hottentot at a symphony – I found it all simply too intoxicating, too wonderful, while my brother, playing the role of the frustrated second, would shake his head and mumble imprecations or, better still, pretend to jerk me slightly just as my lips were about to touch the soft white skin of my latest enchantress.
>
> (Slouka, 2002, p. 117)

Of course, this ostensible sexual rivalry between the brothers offers a parallel with Twain's description of their romantic competitiveness in 'Personal Habits of the Siamese Twins'. The crucial difference is the brothers' self-conscious performance of this role. It is their conjoinment which makes the 'joke' possible – the concept of either twin being a viable romantic figure is ridiculous to their audience, considering their physical condition – and yet Chang colludes with this strategy of exhibition. In this scene, the twins dramatize the quandary of agency in relation to freak show performance. Critics such as Robert Bogdan have allowed for the possibility that subjects with extraordinary bodies could achieve economic and personal autonomy by utilising freak show modes of presentation to their own advantage,[18] whereas David Gerber has argued that the agency of performers is always compromised by the lack of other options available to people with unusual anatomies in the era of the freak show.[19] By using the phrase 'almost unconsciously' to describe the brothers' pandering to their audience's expectations, Slouka's rendering of this scene leaves both possibilities in play, recognising the ambivalent concepts of choice and will when it comes to acting out a role that the brothers have not chosen for themselves. Chang's reference to the 'Hottentot' is also telling. The private parties in Paris which the brothers attend are the same circuit of exhibition which Sarah Baartman was subjected to earlier in the nineteenth century. Chang's citation of Baartman's stage name suggests that he recognises that his performance of refinement only marks the brothers as more savage and racially other.

However, on meeting Sophia, such performances are rendered obsolete. She addresses the brothers as her intellectual equal, and they strike up a friendship which sees Chang and Eng regularly visiting her apartment. It is important to note that this relationship is between Chang and Sophia rather than the three. Chang explains:

> [...] we excluded [Eng] as brutally as lovers in their first fire have always eclipsed those around them [...] He had nowhere to go. Neither did we. I knew what was happening, and I didn't care [...] For years, given our different natures, we had been as easy with one another as men could be [...] Oh, I understood how he felt – at times it was though I would tear myself in two – and yet, I repeat, I didn't care.
> (Slouka, 2002, pp. 137–38)

This description of Sophia and Chang's relationship demonstrates the ways in which the couple obtain privacy regardless of Eng's presence. Yet this need for privacy becomes an act of violence towards Eng; he is 'brutally' excluded, and Chang's desire for Sophia inspires the wish for separation, 'I would tear myself in two'. Such a conceptualisation represents Sophia as a threat to the brothers' bodily integrity, and might seem to hint at Dreger's delineation of separation as the only viable resolution for conjoined sexuality (Dreger, 2004, pp. 43–44). However, this can also be read as an alternative view of conjoinment in the sense that Sophia almost begins to replace Eng in terms of Chang's emotional need for connection. This slippage has queer connotations, but also points towards Dreger's recognition of the possibility 'that people who are conjoined obtain from their twins something akin to the stalwart companionship, understanding, and unconditional love many others find primarily though committed romantic partnership' (Dreger, 2002, p. 49). And yet this connection is clearly disturbed by Sophia, perhaps positioning female sexuality as a disruptive force.

Chang and Sophia's blossoming relationship is abruptly halted by the brothers' managers, who feel that the negative publicity it is receiving will damage their career. Their chaperone, Dumat, attempts to explain to Chang that his desire for female companionship is natural yet Sophia's interest in him is not:

> [...] 'members of the fairer sex [...] not only share your thoughts but, in some circumstances, under certain peculiar conditions, turn what is natural and wholesome into something twisted and rank. In these cases, the seed, if I may, instead of emerging from corruption, instead of leaving its base origin and blossoming, in the fullness of time, into the love sanctioned by God and man alike, grows morbid and rots'.
> (Slouka, 2002, p. 148)

Dumat's use of natural images to explain women's 'proper' sexual desire positions any deviation from this as unnatural, an abomination. The vocabulary he uses suggests deformity; in short, it is Sophia's desire for Chang that is monstrous. The brothers flee from Dumat's condemnation, but hear him read from 'Monsieur Hugo':

> 'If you won't listen to me [...] then at least listen to Monsieur Hugo, who lets her speak for herself [...] "I love you [...] not only because you are deformed, but because you are low [...] A lover despised, mocked, grotesque, hideous [...] exposed to laughter on that pillory called the stage [...] has an extraordinary attraction to me. It is a taste of the fruit of hell [...] I am in love with a nightmare. You are the incarnation of infernal mirth"'.
>
> (Slouka, 2002, p. 150)

The words which Dumat quotes are from Victor Hugo's novel *The Man who Laughs*, published in 1869. They are spoken by Josiana, a woman who is sexually attracted to the disfigured Gwynplaine due to his deformity. A strange collapsing of history is enacted here; the brothers' tour of Paris is in the 1830s, over thirty years before the publication of Hugo's text. Is this because the sexual allure of freakery is supposedly timeless? Or, does Dumat's quotation from Hugo instead represent the ways in which unusual bodies are shaped by texts in the past, present, and future? As Chang dwells on Dumat's comments, the words of Hugo shape his interpretation of his relationship with Sophia:

> 'A lover despised, mocked, grotesque...' I had known the pillory of the stage. Did I believe that Sophia Marchant had loved me because I was hideous? [...] 'I am in love with a nightmare'. Could I say with absolute certainty that somewhere deep in her inmost soul she was not drawn to me the way fingers are drawn to a scab, or eyes to a wound? 'You are the incarnation of infernal mirth'. I could not.
>
> (Slouka, 2002, pp. 152–53)

Chang's reaction dramatizes compellingly the ways in which texts can warp perceptions of extraordinary bodies and, indeed, the subject's own perception of his body. The construction of freakery – and extraordinary bodies as objects of perverse sexual attraction – might be fictional, yet has a profound effect upon Chang's ability to form relationships and perceive himself as a viable sexual subject. The novel's self-consciousness about such discursive power offers an important avenue for metatextual reflection upon the ideological consequences of neo-Victorian representations of freakery. The ways in which bodies are written about – for education, but also for entertainment – have the potential to shape an individual's experience of their own body and desires.

Slouka's novel imagines a sexual encounter between the twins and a prostitute during their time in Paris, which – despite speculation from some biographers – does not have basis in historical fact.[20] On wandering into the city's red light district, the brothers are accosted by a prostitute and lose their virginity. The text describes this scene in some detail, and in contrast to the depiction of Chang's marital relations, the woman has sex with both brothers. Chang is shocked by her forwardness, and afterwards realises that she has told the other woman in the brothel and they have come to watch: 'Yet again we had been seen as nothing more than freaks on a stage' (Slouka, 2002, p. 159). Chang's remark goes some way towards shifting the context of the graphic depiction of this sex scene. The reader is overtly positioned in the voyeuristic congregation of spectators in the brothel and Chang's recognition that bearing witness to this sexual encounter is no better than being the audience at a freak show serves as a metatextual rebuke to us as well. But he subsequently reflects on his initial reaction:

> Do I blame us for the pleasure we took that evening? No, I do not. Life offered itself, and knowing that, for such as ourselves, another opportunity might never come, we took it. Do I blame her for tainting it? For wanting us because we were the way we were? Because the fact of our doubleness excited her? [...] Would that I had known then what I do now: that the heart is large, large – enough to house all manner of contradictions [...] We were what we were, after all. How absurd, it seems to me now, to want to be desired for something you're not! Or to blame someone for wanting you for what you are, when all the world over generations of men and women have lived and died dreaming of precisely that.
>
> (Slouka, 2002, pp. 158–59)

We see that this unnamed woman is essentially the realisation of the hints at Sophia's passion. Chang's acceptance of his bodily difference, and the interest which it might hold for others, implicitly absolves Sophia of 'perversity' and, in a sense, become a normalizing, even 'universalizing' strategy of understanding conjoined sexuality (Garland-Thomson, 2006, p. 259). Yet does such a move simultaneously absolve the reader's potential interest in learning more about the sexuality of conjoined twins? Is such a justification desirable, considering the ethical issues raised by Slouka as a 'singleton'[21] author writing as a nineteenth-century conjoined twin?

Slouka does not overtly address these questions in relation to the twins' sexuality, but perhaps does respond to them in an alternative context, which is similarly ethically fraught. Cynthia Wu has discussed the Bunkers' ownership of slaves in the context of assimilation in to a certain version of middle-class white identity in nineteenth-century America's Deep South,[22] and for a contemporary audience the brothers' use of the labour of enslaved people on their farms is surely one of the most unpalatable aspects of their lives. *God's Fool* does not balk at representing this form of exploitation, imaging a scene where Chang brings home Lewis, a black man they have purchased:

> [...] he refused to even glance my way, but just sat there, his head lolling slightly on his neck with every jolt and roll of the wagon, staring out across those hot Virginia fields as if acknowledging my presence wasn't worth the effort required to turn his head [...]: I stared at him, willing him to turn [...] And suddenly I knew, with absolute certainty, that he would never turn so long as I wanted him to [...] His pride – if that was what it was – infuriated me. It seemed almost contrary to nature, like a mole chattering at a mastiff, or a rabbit showing its teeth. Yet there was something fascinating in it as well. Trapped by circumstance, a slave for life, he would defend his collection of invisible dignities to death.
>
> (Slouka, 2002, p. 15)

Considering his own experiences as a spectacle, Chang's emphasis on the power of the gaze is telling. Rosemarie Garland-Thomson, writing on the variety of ways of 'staring', identifies that gazing can be a 'manifestation of dominance', particularly in relation to racism (Garland-Thomson, 2009, pp. 41–42). While Chang has experienced oppressive looks due to his unusual body and his own ethnicity, this has apparently taught him little about the oppression of invoking power inequalities. He attempts to assert his relative authority over Lewis, yet the latter declines to accord Chang this role by refusing to return his look. In this context, Chang realises that meeting the gaze – or stare – can be a form of recognition and that Lewis's repudiation of his 'master's' power is a strategy of resistance. Chang's angry response is to deploy the discourse of the 'natural' order in relation to race, which seemingly reiterates his assumption of superiority over this man, yet also suggests a connection between his own experience of conjoinment and slavery.

This point of identification between conjoinment and slavery is subsequently made explicit:

> If the majority of blacks bore their burden with relative equanimity, it seemed to me, perhaps it was because they instinctively recognised the necessity of their situation. We were all slaves to something, after all – to time, to love. Perhaps the reason Barnum's crowds had never tired of coming to stare was because our 'band of union' [...] had made visible a universal condition.
>
> (Slouka, 2002, p. 21)

In a challenge to thinking of conjoined twins as the ultimate other and figures of horror and/or pity that need to be 'fixed' by medicine, Alice Domurat Dreger has argued that it might be more productive to recognise the ways in which conjoinment has similarities with other, more routine, human relationships:

> [There is] value [in] putting aside what seems perpetually obvious – how different being conjoined must be from being a singleton – to think about the less obvious: how being conjoined is *like* other human experiences [...] considering how conjoinment is like other experiences opens a window of sympathy that may allow singletons to take seriously the positive claims people who are conjoined make about themselves and their physical situations.
>
> (Dreger, 2004, p. 19)

As a political strategy for rethinking attitudes towards extraordinary bodies this is surely valuable. And yet Chang's recognition of the ways in which conjoinment might be applied to other experiences perhaps exposes the limitations of such a perspective. He constructs a continuum between enslavement, temporal ties, emotional bonds, and finally, conjoinment, apparently universalising aspects of conjoinment and simultaneously normalising the oppression and exploitation of slavery.

His casual delineation of slavery as 'inevitable' of course demonstrates his own historically specific prejudices and failings, yet also dramatizes a broader inadequacy in thinking that points of identification with extraordinary bodies will always be progressive, as the Introduction's discussion of Rachel Adams's understanding of freak show audience's identification with the performers as 'obliterating [...] personhood' indicated (Adams, 2001, p. 31). To deploy *Neo-Victorian Freakery's* opening metaphor of the mirror, Chang wishes to see aspects of his own identity reflected back in the situation of the enslaved people that he encounters, but the chain of connection he establishes is callous in the extreme. On the other hand, perhaps it is this fierce need for identification that is at the heart of the struggles some critics have engaged in to understand the Bunkers' acceptance of and participation in slavery. For example, this becomes evident in Leslie Fielder's gloss: 'It is for me the most astonishing fact about their astonishing lives; though the accounts I have read do not pause to reflect how, holding other humans in bondage, they must have felt their own monstrous bondage mitigated or annulled' (Fielder, 1981, p. 214). In this context, what the novel's representation of Chang's ready acceptance of slavery demonstrates is a resistance to moulding the brothers' lives into a socially-acceptable, politically correct narrative which can be blithely consumed by a neo-Victorian readership. We are discouraged to identify with Chang – to deploy him as a mirror for our own preoccupations and desires – but this 'otherness' is not predicated on his unusual body, but his unpalatable racist ignorance and prejudice. Furthermore, Slouka's novel also exposes the dangers of subjecting the 'other' to metaphor. As my opening comments to this chapter indicated, disability scholars have argued that disability-as-a-metaphor invokes oppression and alienation. Perhaps what Slouka's text achieves is closer to Clare Barker's contention that deploying metaphor when thinking about exceptional bodies is not necessarily always negative: 'metaphors may be sensitively employed within progressive political narratives' (Barker, 2011, p. 20). The opportunity for self-consciousness in reading *God's Fool* comes in our recognition of the *lack* of sensitivity involved in Chang's use of metaphor, productively cautioning us from allegorizing him or others in a comparable way.

However, the brothers' use of enslaved people is stopped by the encroaching Civil War. As in Twain's article on the Bunkers, the brothers' increasing animosity towards each other is allegorised by these external circumstances: 'Eng and I lived, those first few years of the war, in a republic of our own. We didn't speak. We didn't fight' (Slouka, 2002, p. 247). Yet the war is not deployed as a sustained metaphor of the twins' conflict despite union, so much as the reason why Chang's bond with his eldest son, Christopher, is broken. Of all the relationships depicted in the text, it is Chang's connection with Christopher which is the strongest. Christopher runs away to fight in the war, and despite Chang's efforts to pursue him and return him to safety, the family receive the notice of his death. His reaction is telling: 'I had lost him – the one I couldn't, wouldn't lose – my boy, my heart' (Slouka, 2002,

p. 266). It is Christopher's death which symbolically takes Chang's heart; emotional dependency is articulated via an image of entwined, interdependent bodies. Ironically, then, it is Christopher's death that will threaten Chang's existence, rather than Eng's, refusing the inevitability of conjoined mortality which haunts the other texts discussed in this chapter. And yet the report of Christopher's death is erroneous, as the final lines of the novel see his return to his family.[23] In this sense, the 'conclusion' of Slouka's version of the twins offers a vision of life beyond death; the Bunkers' afterlife will be their shared descendants.[24]

Conclusion

This chapter has identified a collection of themes which inform the textual representations of Chang and Eng Bunker in the nineteenth century, and which have been revisited by neo-Victorian reimaginings of the brothers. In all of these texts, the bodies of Chang and Eng have had to bear a heavy metaphorical weight, whether in terms of providing an opportunity for thinking about the boundaries of subjectivity, life and death, the 'norms' of sexual behaviour, or racial identity. Mark Twain's article on the 'Siamese' twins presents the prospect of Chang and Eng as sexual subjects as both absurd and provocative. For William Pancoast, the sexual activities of conjoined twins are a threat to the moral values of broader society. Harrison Allen's account of the brothers implies that separation leads to knowledge, whereas conjoinment leads to confusion and the ultimate horror of death. Both Twain and Pancoast insinuate that conjoined sexuality is beyond civilisation and are thus unable to extrapolate the potential 'impropriety' of conjoinment from the twins' 'Siamese' identity. In all of the nineteenth-century texts Chang and Eng are constructed as resolutely 'other', condemned by their extraordinary body to a life beyond comprehension.

Twain's *Those Extraordinary Twins* places the author in the quasi-medical position of being able to separate conjoined identities, a conceptualisation which has thought-provoking resonances with the narrative structure of Strauss's *Chang and Eng*. Through the process of first-person narration, Strauss's text makes a clear distinction between the brothers and there are moments where the reader is encouraged to understand and sympathise with Eng. However, we can also view the decision to offer only one side of the conjoined twins' story as an act of narrative violence as well. For, in only giving voice to Eng, Strauss enacts an imaginary separation of the brothers. Although his narrative could be interpreted as a strategy of according individuality to the twins, it also fulfils the dream of separation which a 'singleton' society tends to perceive as the only productive resolution for conjoinment. Though we might, at times, be encouraged to identify with Eng, this process of 're-membering' cannot imagine an extraordinary body beyond the discursive matrix of the freak show: pity, the gaze, and prurient speculation. In articulating conjoined sexuality, Strauss's text positions the twins' body as awkward, uncomfortable and deviant, and, ultimately, disabled. The novel's efforts to offer Chang and Eng separate identities relies upon racial stereotypes, which also bear traces of misogyny in relation to Sarah's use of racially 'other' bodies for her own pleasure.

Whilst *Chang and Eng* turns the bedrooms of conjoined twins into freak shows, Slouka's *God's Fool* compels the reader to interrogate their own role as a spectator to conjoined sexuality. The novel allows us to think beyond separation as the only viable solution to conjoinment, demonstrating that emotional connections can be as enduring as physical bonds. However, *God's Fool* also problematizes the notion that all 'bonds' are equal. Chang's casual attitude towards slavery highlights the ethical quandaries of identification between subjects in differing contexts. Unlike the other texts discussed in this chapter, conjoined death is not the end for the Bunker brothers and it looks to their children as the carriers of the twins' cultural afterlives. This emphasis on future generations is crucial; what versions of the past do we want to perpetuate? What aspects of history might we want to rewrite? *God's Fool* makes explicit the ways in which texts – fictional or otherwise – shape our understandings of bodies, metatextually recognising its own responsibility as a representation of the brothers and provoking the reader to scrutinise the way that she might look upon others as well.

3

Excessively Feminine? Anna Swan, Gendering Giantesses, and the Genre of the 'True Life Story' Pamphlet

Fevvers, the fabulous winged protagonist of Angela Carter's *Nights at the Circus* (1984), is a woman of generous proportions. In his interview with this freak show performer turned trapeze artist, Jack Walser repeatedly invokes the vocabulary of largeness, noting her 'vast, blue, indecorous eyes' and her 'six inches of false lash' (Carter, 1985, p. 7). Walser views Fevvers as a 'marvellous giantess' (Carter, 1985, p. 42), and he experiences a certain sexual attraction to her size: 'God! She could easily crush him to death in her huge arms, although he was a big man [...] A seismic erotic disturbance convulsed him' (Carter, 1985, p. 52). In this formulation, the erotic frisson of a big woman comes from the potential she has to reverse gendered expectations. Despite his own manly size, Walser might be made vulnerable and passive in her arms. However, her magnitude also leads him to question her gender identity in a more derisive way: 'Her face, in its Brobdingnagian symmetry, might have been hacked from wood and brightly painted up by those artists who build carnival ladies for fairgrounds or figureheads for sailing ships. It flickered through his mind: Is she really a man?' (Carter, 1985, p. 35). The allusion to the fictional giants of Jonathan Swift's *Gulliver's Travels* (1726) and the alignment of Fevvers with a sculpture – one which might feature at a 'fairground', nonetheless – call into question the 'authenticity' of her gender identity. Giantesses such as Fevvers might generate gender trouble,[1] but this does not liberate her from the regulatory system of heteronormative gender as invoked by Walser; within this economy, bigness is not a feminine characteristic and therefore must signify as masculine. Nevertheless, as Walser spends more time with Fevvers on the circus's Russian tour, he comes to recognise that the multiple sites of her indeterminacy – her dubious narratives, her drag-esque performances of gender, the perpetual quandary of the authenticity of her wings – might actually fulfil an important function. If her wings were to be exposed as real:

> She would no longer be an extraordinary woman, no more the Greatest *Aerialiste* in the world but – a freak. Marvellous, indeed, but a marvellous monster, an exemplary being denied the human privilege of flesh and blood, always the object of the observer, never the subject of sympathy, an alien creature forever estranged. She owes it to herself to remain a woman, he thought [...] As a symbolic woman, she has meaning, as an anomaly, none.
>
> (Carter, 1985, p. 161)

In Walser's terms, freakishness – or monstrosity – is not compatible with humanity, let alone femininity. As long as Fevvers maintains some claim on 'womanhood', however extraordinary, she can still signify as human, yet to trouble gender too far is to enter into the realms of the freakish.[2]

And yet Walser's confident separation of the boundaries between monstrosity and 'normative' gender is not easy to maintain. According to Margrit Shildrick:

> Monsters clearly cannot exist apart from 'normal' bodies, but at the same time they are excessive to the binary, uncontained by any fixed category of exclusion. Like women, they refuse to stay in place: they change shape, they combine elements which should remain separate; in short they are labile. In the same way that the feminine has been deployed as the undecidable signifier of excess, so too the catachrestic term 'monster' both escapes binary closure and displaces simple difference. Monsters signify not the oppositional other safely fenced off within its own boundaries, but the otherness of possible worlds, or possible versions of ourselves, not yet realised.
>
> (Shildrick, 2002, p. 129)

As the previous chapters of *Neo-Victorian Freakery* have already demonstrated, the definition of 'monstrosity' (or 'freakery') depends upon the construction of 'normality' at a specific social and historical moment. In a comparable way to the binary construction of femininity/masculinity, 'normal' bodies cannot exist without the monstrous 'other'. More specifically, however, monstrosity becomes entwined with femininity due to the mutual association with *excess*: that which refuses finite quantification, is liable to be unruly, the surfeit which threatens boundaries. For Shildrick, this connection can be productive; the transgressions of the division between self and other (normal/freakish, masculine/feminine) can suggest new forms of subjectivity, of what it means to be human. And the notion of 'excess' straining against the confines of gendered expectations is particularly pertinent to the figure of the gigantic woman.

The focus of this chapter is Anna Swan, who was born in Nova Scotia, Canada, in 1846, to Scottish immigrant parents of average height. She grew rapidly from childhood, reaching her adult height of just under 8 feet. She was exhibited as a 'giantess' by P. T. Barnum in his 'American Museum' in New York during the 1860s and spent time touring Europe. She married another 'giant', Martin Van Buren Bates, in London during 1871, and the couple received a wedding gift from Queen Victoria. The Bates settled on a farm in Seville, Ohio and planned to retire from show business and raise a family. Anna gave birth to two children; a stillborn girl, in 1872, and a boy in 1879. After a protracted labour, her son only lived several hours after birth. The couple made a brief return to touring, but would return to their farm where Anna died in 1888.[3] This chapter begins by studying several nineteenth-century accounts of Anna's life. The first will be the anonymous 'true life story' pamphlet, *The Nova Scotia Giantess, Miss Anna H. Swan, A Brief Account of her Birth and History*, which was published during her life time.[4] My reading of this text will emphasize the tension between Anna's physical dimensions and her construction as a feminine, 'lady-like' subject. The pamphlet endeavours to code her persona as feminine in contrast to a corporeal size which would be traditionally associated with masculine power and dominance. The text struggles with this balancing act, exposing anxieties about 'big women' who might use their stature to achieve status and wealth in a man's world. Indeed, other writings about Anna dating from the nineteenth century discussed in this chapter – particularly Edward S. Wood's *Giants and Dwarves* (1868)– display a comparable impulse to contain the 'excess' of a giantess's body, whether through pseudo-scientific theorising or retelling incidents from her life to emphasize her feminine vulnerability.

My opening reading of Fevvers as a 'marvellous giantess' (albeit subject to enfreakment in the eyes of Walser) offers a context for the key themes which emerge in the neo-Victorian novels based on Anna: the ways in which giantesses might challenge normative gender expectations; the potential for erotic objectification/sexual exploitation of 'big' women; and the fraught continuum between freakery and femininity. As other critics have argued, there are some compelling points of connection between Carter's *Nights at the Circus* and Susan Swan's[5]

The Biggest Modern Woman of the World (1983).[6] Both are multi-voiced, postmodern narratives, and both offer a feminist reappropriation of 'bigness'. As a development of prior criticism, which has tended towards interpreting the various, often conflicting narrative voices of Swan's novel as a postmodern challenge to 'traditional' history,[7] my interpretation of the text emphasizes its often ambivalent relationship to the genre of the 'true life story' pamphlet. I highlight how being a 'giantess' becomes a symbol of agency, power and strength for women, but also the extent to which this fictionalised version of Anna is still subject to nineteenth-century expectations of patriarchal subservience and the oppression of women's sexuality. Bigger is not always better for Anna's lovers, and her perceived threat to masculine dominance leads her to be belittled in a variety of ways. Furthermore, the novel's representation of Anna's child-bearing places the responsibility – and blame – for the production of 'freakish' offspring with the mother, a troubling reiteration of the theory of 'maternal impression' which often informed the exhibition of performers in the nineteenth-century freak show.

Stacy Carlson's *Among the Wonderful* (2011) reimagines the performers and workers at P. T. Barnum's American Museum and self-consciously engages with the ways in which texts about freak show performers might be simultaneously empowering and exploitative. Carlson's text has a dual narrative structure: sections of the novel are told from the perspective of Emile Guillaudeu, a taxidermist at John Scudder's museum which has been taken over by Barnum. The other significant narrative voice is Ana Swift, who is clearly a fictionalised version of Anna Swan due to her status as a 'giantess' in the museum and her Canadian nationality. Comparable preoccupations with gender and sexuality with regards to giantesses emerge, but also notable is Ana's attempt to take control of her textual destiny by composing her own 'True Life History'. She achieves some degree of self-expression and autonomy in this process, but the gendered power struggle for ownership of her story after her death offers a salutary metatextual reflection on the ethical dilemmas of neo-Victorian reimagining of freak show performers.

The trouble with big women: Nineteenth-century representations of Anna Swan

As the Introduction noted, Rosemarie Garland-Thomson has argued that 'true life story' pamphlets, documents which were often available to purchase to accompany the exhibition of performers, were an integral component of the construction of 'freakery' in the nineteenth century. Such texts regularly fabricated fantastical stories about the performer's early life and accomplishments and thus transgressed the boundary between 'fact' and 'fiction' in the representation of extraordinary bodies (Garland-Thomson, 1996, pp. 5–7). Some commentators on the Victorian freak show have tended towards dismissing the value of such documents with regards to uncovering the 'truth' of performers' lives and experiences, for these pamphlets were frequently written by the performers' managers (Fielder, 1981, p. 271). While Matthew Sweet offers a 'defence' of the nineteenth-century freak show in his book *Inventing the Victorians*, he struggles to see the value of these 'biographies', remarking that they demonstrate how the 'voices' of performers 'were often enthusiastically silenced by their managers, who liked to drum up custom by generating exotic – and bogus – narratives around their stars' (Sweet, 2001, p. 153). Fielder and Sweet are surely right to question the veracity of these texts, yet Robert Bogdan offers an important counter-argument to justify the worth of 'true life stories' for freakery studies:

> At first glance these materials appear useless. They are so contrived, so obviously produced merely to win customers' attention that they can be easily dismissed as lies. But fraud is central to the freak show, and lies make good data – that is, if one knows that they are lies and if deception is the subject of investigation. After all, misrepresentation is integral to the manufacture of freaks.
>
> (Bogdan, 1988, p. 11)

Although these pamphlets do contain notable inaccuracies and blatant fabrication, they thus also can function as an important resource for analysis of the discursive construction of individual performers' personae, as well as demonstrating the trappings and techniques of freakery more broadly. Furthermore, as Bogdan highlights, although the first-person narrative voice of the actual performer might often be conspicuously absent, the 'true life story' documents are multi-voiced texts, offering newspaper accounts of performer's public appearances, 'medical' testimony and audience testimony, alongside the performer's 'biography' and sometimes also travelogue-esque account of their exhibitions (Bogdan, 1988, pp. 19–20). Significantly, the formation of the performer's personae is therefore sometimes rather uneven: analysis of 'true life stories' can expose inconsistencies, ideological anxieties, and unexpected tensions in the construction of nineteenth-century freakery, which are ripe for reappropriation by neo-Victorianism. Bearing this in mind, the anonymously written *The Nova Scotia Giantess* which focuses on the life and career of Anna Swan offers some useful contexts for thinking about key themes in the fashioning of her identity which are subsequently reimagined in neo-Victorian fiction.

As suggested in the pamphlet's title, we are initially introduced to Anna as a hailing from Canada, and some of her parents' family history is also offered. Her father, an immigrant from Scotland, is described as purchasing a farm 'to cultivate the virgin land of which he had possessed himself'. He is characterised as follows: 'Mr. Swan was a man of quite ordinary stature, though of fine physique. He was but five feet six inches in height, and weighed but a hundred and forty pounds; still he was of more than ordinary physical power; unyielding, determined, and muscular, he was just the man for a new country' (*Nova Scotia*, 1894, p. 7). The vocabulary deployed to describe his immigration to Canada invokes a familiar gendered trope of the colonised land as feminised: the 'virgin land' being taken 'possession' of alludes to the settlers in this 'new' country as a virile, masculinised force. In this vein, it is also interesting that Mr. Swan is represented as possessing traits associated with potent masculinity. While his own average height and weight is noted, his 'manly' features are also asserted, perhaps implying that his masculinity is not to be considered compromised by his daughter's 'bigness'.

Anna is depicted as attractive and well-proportioned: 'in all her growth she was remarkable for her symmetry and equal development' (*Nova Scotia*, 1894, p. 10). As both Robert Bogdan and Nadja Durbach have identified in different contexts, the frequent invocation of the 'regularity' of the performers in their promotion, aside from their one remarkable physical trait, operates as a reassuring function to the audiences who attend the shows; they will not be placed in the position of having to witness an aesthetically displeasing or 'sick' spectacle, and thus the general 'respectability' of the exhibition is consolidated (Bogdan, 1988, p. 277; Durbach, 2010, pp. 26–27). However, in the case of a *female* performer such as Anna, such reassurance surely becomes particularly loaded: if women have traditionally been judged by their physical appearance, then such descriptions become bound up with gendered expectations about how women should appear in society as well. Indeed, the appeal which Anna might have for male audiences is hinted at in the description of her dealings with young men whilst she was being schooled in a local town:

> There were plenty of young sparks about Pictou, tall, strapping, young Nova Scotians, who, seeing a handsome girl like Anna, of the

> same height as themselves, took it for granted she was more than eleven years of age, and found means, as young men will even in our days, to convey love notes to her, and urge her to indulge in flirtations. Without stopping to enquire whether Anna's heart did, or did not, beat quicker on these occasions, her governesses testify that she invariably brought these *billet doux* unopened, and placed them in their hands; and when she returned to her loving parents, at the age of fifteen years, Anna was heart-whole, and was a loving, obedient, and very accomplished daughter.
>
> (*Nova Scotia*, 1894, pp. 10–11)

Anna is depicted as vulnerable to sexual attention due to her size: she appears older than her actual years, and therefore as fair game for romantically-inclined youths. However, this narrative of her reaction to these advances emphasizes her conformity to nineteenth-century expectations of female chastity: the reference to her being 'heart-whole' suggests devotion to her parents, and also that her heart has not been broken by precocious romantic entanglements. But the notion of 'wholeness' with regards to contact with the opposite sex might also be interpreted as alluding to virginity; she is 'intact', as it were, impermeable to potential sexual contact. She is dutiful, 'accomplished' and respectful of her elders. In short, Anna is represented as knowing her place, and as not being inclined towards transgression, even when given the opportunity. However, given such a virtuous construction of the young giantess's character, it is slightly ominous that this anecdote is shortly followed by this proclamation: 'Miss Anna H. Swan is, by very long odds, the most magnificent female example of the human race who has ever lived on the terrestrial globe, from the time that our unfortunate mother Eve was driven out of that beautiful garden' (*Nova Scotia*, 1894, p. 11). Such a rapid reference to the consequences of female disobedience and insubordination to patriarchal expectations – the 'unfortunate' Eve, who most certainly wasn't inclined to obey orders and exercise appropriate deference – seems rather pointed. It operates as a cautionary note to young women who might not behave as well as Anna purportedly did, but additionally offers a vague admonition to Anna herself: she is a shining example of femininity, but she must continue to be so, lest she 'fall' like Eve. Apparently, she does resist such temptations. The potential sexual allure of Anna is also mentioned in an account of her adult tours; whilst journeying back East, she stops off at Salt Lake City and offers: 'a private reception to the numerous wives and children of the Mormon prophet. At a subsequent interview,

Brigham Young used his utmost endeavours to induce Miss Swan to become a resident of Utah, but she preferred returning to a Christian land' (*Nova Scotia*, 1894, p. 15). That Brigham Young himself – the founder of Salt Lake City, leader of the Latter Day Saint movement, and practicing polygamist – requests Anna's residence in the community offers a compelling allusion to her sexual attractiveness and, again, her sense of propriety in spurning such advances.

There are, however, references to the ways in which Anna's size does trouble the gendered expectations upon nineteenth-century women. The pamphlet gives a version of events from the evening of the fire at P. T. Barnum's American Museum in July 1865:

> In this fire Miss Swan lost the whole of her valuable wardrobe, and almost a fortune in jewels, the value of which was greatly enhanced in her own view from the fact they were presents from all the most eminent men on the American Continent. Thoughtless for the moment of her own property, Miss Swan, during the conflagration, worked, not like twenty women, but more like twenty men, to assist in saving human life; and it is a fact, well known in New York, that she was the last person to leave the building.
>
> (*Nova Scotia*, 1894, p. 12)

Anna's experience of loss in the fire is defined via her feminine accoutrements. Furthermore, there is a passing hint to a sense of feminine vanity here as well: 'in her own view' she values her possessions as they are gifts from male admirers – we again are reminded of her attractiveness to men. However, there is an overt cross-gendered representation of her efforts in the fire: to work 'like twenty men' implies masculine characteristics such as physical strength and bravery rather than the presumably less effectual contribution that even 'twenty' women might make. Interestingly, this narrative omits one of the more sensational aspects of Anna's experience of this fire at the Museum: as the account from *The New York Tribune* below indicates, Anna's size prevented her earlier escape and she was hoisted down by the firemen at the scene in front of an assembled throng. Why should such detail be passed over here? In this context, I suspect that such emphasis on her vulnerability – her being placed in the archetypal feminine role of the damsel in distress – would compromise the heroic, masculine construction of her persona at this textual moment, which makes the other accounts discussed below even more notable for their desire to confine her to a more traditionally feminine position.

Edward S. Wood's book *Giants and Dwarves* is one such narrative. This study – part pseudo-medical account, part survey of mythology and literature, part biographical compendium of notable freak show performers – is self-conscious about its generic instability. In the book's preface, Wood initially seems apologetic about his use of 'professional' publicity material from freak shows and exhibitions. However, he also suggests in reference to this material: 'The Author feels very much like a showman who is opening a caravan full of wonders, some if not all of which he hopes may interest each one of the enlightened public who may honour him by "walking up"' (Wood, 1868, p. iv). For Wood, the freak show pamphlets do appear to add veracity to his own textual accounts and, in addition, he recognises the ways in which his role as author of such a text implicates him in the dynamics of exhibition and display; the author is positioned in the role of a freak show proprietor, yet this is not exploitative, but 'enlightening' and educational. Such a perspective is to be interrogated in the neo-Victorian version of Anna's life in Stacy Carlson's novel discussed below.

However, the specific depiction of the fire on 13 July 1865 at Barnum's museum is important in relation to the gendering of Anna. Wood describes the scene as follows: 'She was found at the head of the stairs in a swooning condition from the smoke, and was with difficulty got out of the building. She lost everything that she possessed except the clothes she wore' (Wood, 1868, pp. 229–30). Her 'swoon' cannot be further removed from the resourceful contribution she makes to the fighting of the fire in the 'true life story' pamphlet. She is passive due to her unconsciousness, emphasised by her being 'found' rather than actively seeking recovery. The reason why her departure from the building was 'difficult' remains unsaid here, but leaves the reader to speculate that she was cumbersome due to her size, or obstructive of the rescue in some other way. Anna is couched as a burden: feminine in some ways, yet not quite compliant enough in others. Indeed, Wood's construction of gigantism more generally is damning. Contrary to the repeated emphasis on Anna's refinement, dignity, and intelligence in her 'true life story' pamphlet, Wood argues that 'giants are almost always characterized by mental and bodily weakness [....] Giants seldom have strength or valour commensurate with their physical proportions, but are as a rule sickly, knock-kneed, splay-footed, feeble in mind, and short-lived' (Wood, 1868, p. 109). The author does not trouble himself with offering any serious evidence – medical or otherwise – for these claims, which leads to the unsavoury conclusion that it is anecdotes of famous giants such as Anna that function as illustrations of his point. Most troublingly, such sentiments have an afterlife in twentieth-century accounts of gigantism as well: Leslie Fielder remarks of 'giants' that 'when not actually feeble-minded, they tend to be melancholy and hypochondriac, and with good reason, since they move through their brief lives crippled by the tug of gravity, which dooms their bodies sooner or later to buckle and break' (Fielder, 1981, p. 106). In addition to the ableist presumptions of such claims ('good' bodies are seemingly always strong and healthy), the notable repetition of vocabulary here testifies to the pervasiveness of nineteenth-century stereotypes of gigantism, which, as we shall see, are both reiterated and reappropriated in neo-Victorian depictions of Anna.

The final representation of Anna's experience of the Museum fire that I wish to consider comes from *The New York Tribune*, published on 14 July 1865:

> The giant girl, Anna Swan, was only rescued with the utmost difficulty. There was not a door through which her bulky frame could obtain a passage. It was likewise feared that the stairs would break down, even if she should reach them [...] as the heat grew in intensity, the perspiration rolled from her face in little brooks and rivulets, which pattered musically upon the floor. At length, as a last resort, the employees of the place procured a lofty derrick which fortunately happened to be standing near, and erected it alongside of the Museum. A portion of the wall was then broken off on each side of the window, the strong tackle was got in readiness, the tall woman was made fast to one end and swung over the heads of the people in the street, with eighteen men grasping the other extremity of the line, and lowered down from the third story, amid enthusiastic applause.[8]

As in Wood's relation of her rescue, Anna does not take an active role in the experience. She repeatedly has things done to her in the process, and, ironically considering that in some ways her frame thwarts the expectations of femininity, it is her bigness that ensures her need to be saved by men: she is made passive by her proportions. The reference to the fluids running from her body are suggestive; we are reminded of Margrit Shildrick's remarks, as quoted at the beginning of this chapter, of how monstrous/feminine bodies cannot be contained. Put another way, to use a phrase of Shildrick's from another text, the feminine body is coded as 'leaky'.[9] In this context, however, Anna's 'leakiness' is not particularly empowering or transgressive: it is a signifier of her feminised fear in the face of danger. Finally, despite the palpable seriousness of the situation – Anna clearly could have died in the fire – the rescue before the witness of the assembled crowd takes on an aspect of a performance, reiterated by the 'enthusiastic applause' of the throng. Anna's large, perspiring body becomes a spectacle: another compromise to her femininity for, as Mary Russo suggests, one of the dictates of feminine comportment is to avoid 'making a spectacle out of one's self' (Russo, 1995, p. 53). This element of entertainment in this scene is made explicit by Leslie Fielder's later commentary on Anna's rescue: he suggests that there is 'something inescapably comic in the notion of so huge a body [...] being hauled out by mechanical hoist from the burning timbers of Barnum's American Museum' (Fielder, 1981, p. 117). Crass as Fielder's comments are, they do crystallize how performers cannot always be in control of the audience's reception of their bodies, and are subject to being read – as gendered and sexualised, obedient and unruly, tragic or comic – in a variety of ways.

Sexy spieling and freakish femininity: Susan Swan's *The Biggest Modern Woman of the World*

My above use of references to Leslie Fielder's work on Anna Swan casts his commentary in a damning light. However, it is worth noting that he does acknowledge the limitations of his analysis:

> Attempting to retell her story, I am baffled by the fact that, like earlier accounts, mine does not transcend the appeal of a newspaper 'human interest' article. Nor do any of the surviving photographs of her and her husband or the tomb of their lost child suggest the true terror of her plight.
>
> (Fielder, 1981, pp. 117–18)

Here Fielder raises an important point, which is relevant to all of the performers studied in this book: how to 'retell the story' of nineteenth-century performers in a way which does justice to the nuances and complexities of their lives, without merely deploying these historical subjects as figures of entertainment and prurience? Fielder appears to suggest that the 'truth' of Anna's life might reside in the details of her marriage and child-bearing, yet both of these aspects seem to fix her within conventional roles for women: wife, and mother. As my earlier discussion of Robert Bogdan's exploration of the 'true life story' genre indicate, the claim to 'truth' that these pamphlets announce is disingenuous; they largely function as works of fiction. Nevertheless, for Bogdan, such 'misrepresentation' is, in itself, a crucial component of freak show presentation (Bogdan, 1988, p. 11). Furthermore, from a neo-Victorian perspective, this self-conscious collapsing of the boundaries between 'fact' and 'lies' (or, framed in another way, 'history' and 'fiction') is particularly suggestive in terms of neo-Victorianism's investment in questioning the traditional master narrative of history, and the genre's ideological commitment to offering alternative versions of the nineteenth century which re-centre the era's marginalised subjects. When there is a very limited 'official' historical record of certain social groups or individuals, fictionalisation becomes an important strategy for redressing historical power inequalities.[10] In this context, I want to suggest that Susan Swan's *The Biggest Modern Woman of the World* deploys aspects of freak show presentation as a narrative mode for offering Anna's perspective on her life and career, due to the possibilities it can offer for alternative versions of history and problematizing 'truth' and 'fact'. However, the extent to which this proves a liberatory strategy for the fictional Anna – or the re-membering of the historical Anna Swan – is debateable.

The opening chapter of the novel is entitled 'spieling'. This is a term which appears repeatedly throughout the novel, and is a key aspect of the tradition of freak show presentation. The 'spieler' – also known as the 'talker', 'blower', or 'barker' – was tasked with enticing an audience into a performer's exhibition, and also sometimes speaking for the performer during the act. As Robert Bogdan explains, studying the North American tradition of freak show spielers: 'Their job was to attract the crowd, to grab attention with their modulating voices and slick talk. Using exaggeration and misrepresentation, they told passersby of the wonders that waited them for the price of one thin dime' (Bogdan, 1988, p. 94). The problematic aspects of this form of presentation in terms of granting agency for the individual performers are evident: they are spoken for, represented in someone else's terms. However, Swan's Anna begins the novel by offering her own 'spiel':

> Now I am in full voice... blowing my own horn... Spieling the way I used to for P. T. Barnum, Queen Victoria, and all the normals who came to my performances after I grew up into an eight-foot giantess who toured North America and the Continent. This is my final appearance, and I promise to tell all. What really happened to the BIGGEST MODERN WOMAN OF THE WORLD in a never-before revealed autobiography which contains testimonials and documents

> by friends and associates (from their perspective) of a Victorian lady who refused to be inconsequential.
>
> (Swan, 1988, p. 2; original emphasis)

She takes ownership of her performance and self-presentation, and this is framed as a feminist strategy as well: a statement of her 'refusal' to be spoken for as a 'Victorian lady'. At the same time, Smaro Kamboureli has argued that Anna's deployment of tropes of confession – 'telling all' and 'autobiography' – are incongruous with the postmodern aspects of the novel's form. In Kamboureli's terms, this is a failure of Anna's ownership of her own story, for 'she can never exceed the carnivalesque world of freaks' due to her 'inability to possess language' outside of this freak show discourse (Kamboureli, 1991, n.p.).

Initially, Anna perceives her work at Barnum's American Museum as the construction of a distinct persona, separate from her 'private' self. She remarks: 'I had begun to understand that performance is not true exposure, and that if I acted skilfully, I could hide behind my stage presence and fear nothing' (Swan, 1988, p. 115). 'Spieling' thus becomes a form of protection, as her 'giantess' act is assumed at various points in the novel, both by the scenes she describes of her performances, but also in terms of her lapse into hyperbole and self-aggrandisement. To use the terminology of Joan Riviere and her work on gender as performance, Anna assumes 'freakishness' as a masquerade.[11] However, there are also pitfalls with this strategy, as evidenced with Anna's narration of the fires at Barnum's museum. At the scene of the first fire, Anna explains:

> I stormed out of the museum in the first fire, and met Samuel Hurd and a phalanx of firemen who tried to throw their nets and ladders on me so I put up my dukes and sent six firemen sprawling [...] the crowd cheered to see Hurd dragging on the ground as he clung to the folds of my plaid gown.
>
> (Swan, 1988, pp. 141–42)

The men assume that she will need to be rescued, but she thwarts their expectations – her bigness, in this instance, is a symbol of her superior strength and power over men, in a notable echo of the story of her experience of the more famous fire in 1865 in the 'true life story' pamphlet discussed above.

However, the retelling of her rescue in July 1865 is more complicated: 'I stole a look out from my skirt and saw the tackle knock a wall away on either side of me. [...] Fly for free enterprise, giantess! Swing for Wall Street – its bulls and its bears! And kick your heels up so the crowd can be fired by a peek at the steaming mystery of your unspeakables! (Swan, 1988, p. 143). She is evidently hiding her face in her skirts, suggesting a cowering fear which, whilst understandable given her precarious circumstances, still alludes to the feminine vulnerability emphasised in Wood's and *The New York Tribune*'s contemporary accounts. Yet her release from the building in the firemen's winch offers the opportunity for 'spieling'; here, she assumes the persona of 'giantess' and is acutely aware of the way in which her public rescue becomes a form of performance, which in turn becomes an advertisement for Barnum's museum. She is a commodity, a symbol of 'free enterprise' hovering over the financial centre which is 'Wall Street', and a sexualised spectacle, providing a titillating glimpse of her 'unspeakables' to the assembled crowd. It is moments such as this which evidence H. Wylie's reading of the novel, which claims that: 'Anna's fate in the masculinist economy of the spectacle is to be resolutely objectified' (Wylie, 2002, p. 239). Although she apparently colludes with this mode of representation by voicing her own spiel to accompany this scene, she is also exploited at the same time. Her ambivalence towards this complicity is made explicit in her description of her outpouring of emotion after the fire:

> I wept for myself and the selves I was in my growth, including the AGORAPHOBIC VICTIM who cowered as the tackle ball broke the museum wall, the VICTORIAN LADY hauled like a pachyderm over the heads in the street, the GIANT ACTRESS who smiled as she was lowered to the roaring crowds and, finally, the BIG SURVIVOR who failed to convey her waters to the fiery wimbles until the festival was over.
>
> (Swan, 1988, p. 145; original emphasis)

Her use of capitalisation to proclaim the various roles she has fulfilled in the rescue process ostensibly alludes to her 'stage presence', yet Anna also now recognises that she cannot separate these out from 'myself': these 'selves' are all part of her myriad identity; her 'freak show' persona is not her sum total, but this 'masquerade' is still a facet of her 'true' self as well.[12] In a sense, Anna has become her own 'true life history' pamphlet, fulfilling the discursive constructions of her 'giantess' identity even as she acknowledges their fictional qualities. This tension operates on a metatextual level as well, for Susan Swan's retelling of Anna's rescue encompasses the historical figure's representation in the contemporary texts discussed above, even as it hyperbolises them. This metatexutal slippage between self and text has also been noted by H. Wylie, who argues that: 'Anna [...] is a commodity in Swan's novel just as she is a commodity in [her managers'] eyes' (Wylie, 2002, p. 239). Moreover, the reader thus becomes part of the 'freak show' audience which consumes Anna's life story alongside the imagined crowds within the text; as I shall explore below, this ambivalent association is developed further in Carlson's *Among the Wonderful*.

Swan's novel has received a significant amount of critical attention for its feminist impulses in rewriting nineteenth-century expectations of femininity.[13] The fictional Anna recounts her early exhibitions in Canada, where the local farmers 'circled around to test for human skin behind my skirts, or wager on my gender. (The uneducated often doubt a woman can attain my size)' (Swan, 1988, p. 38). In an interesting parallel with Walser's perception of Fevvers in *Nights at the Circus*, largeness in a woman casts doubt not only upon her gender identity, but her very humanity: the 'test for human skin' implies that they have suspicions as to whether she is some sort of model or mannequin. It also implies sexual molestation as well. Significantly, however, this rendering of Anna is given the opportunity to summarily dismiss such confusion or abuse: these responses could only stem from ignorance. But she does not always find it so easy to disregard the pressures she is placed under to conform. On her marriage to Martin and their settling in Seville, Ohio, she writes a letter to her mother:

> I find myself cast in a new part. Anna, the entertainer, has been replaced by a wifely manipulator whose sole purpose is moderating the behaviour of her husband. I stare at this substantial female head smiling inquisitively above a torso gussied-up with wide Cluny lace and Bohemian garnets [...] Oh Momma, I am finding housewifery difficult. Why didn't you tell me it is more work than being a spieler?
> (Swan, 1988, pp. 273–74)

Despite the oppressive aspects of her life as a freak show performer, she identifies that a life 'off-stage' as a housewife is no less of an act, and that it comes with its own limitations. She experiences a sense of dissociation from her body – a split in her self-perception, as she 'stares' at her own head and body imprisoned in feminine clothing. She objectifies herself, becoming the 'manipulator' to both her husband but also her puppet-like body. Ironically, therefore, it is her attempt to be a 'normal' woman – subservient, confined in the private sphere – that makes her feel contrived and artificial. As discussed above, Kamboureli understands Anna's reliance on 'spieling' as a 'fail[ure] to distinguish between public and private discourse' (1991, n.p.), but perhaps it is more useful to recognise that it is 'private' discourse that fails Anna. Albeit dabbling with unstable identities, commercial and sexual exploitation, the world of freakery still offers more than the performance of domesticated femininity.

Furthermore, the spectre of female disobedience which haunts the characterisation of Anna in the *Nova Scotia Giantess* pamphlet – the sense that she has always conformed to social expectations, yet her size might offer opportunities for insubordination and unruliness – becomes manifest in Anna's account of her attitude towards her husband:

> I am sick of my wifely role and yet unable to behave any other way with my husband. I do not know if he or the institution of marriage provokes my behaviour. Because it's a mistake for wives like me to take on the role of civilizing their mates. Why should I be my husband's divine conscience when the job develops my character while he remains the same as before?
>
> (Swan, 1988, pp. 290–91)

Martin is made irascible by the Ohio community's suspicion of his support of the Confederacy in the Civil War, but also by his impotency (more on this shortly). Nineteenth-century codes of wifely behaviour suggest that Anna must be an edifying influence on her husband, a self-sacrificing 'Angel in the House'.[14] In this context of her career and the opportunities it has afforded her, predicated on her extraordinary body, on one hand it appears that Anna's restlessness can be attributed to her size, her excess, her sense of being too 'big' to be confined by the trappings of feminine domesticity. On the other, Anna's analysis also implies that her dissatisfaction is not just about her own failure to adhere to the norm (put another way, her 'freakishness'), but that the 'norm' itself is to blame: the expectations placed upon all women in the domestic sphere are unrealistic and inhibiting. If any woman fails to meet these impossible requisites she might be deemed obstreperous, disruptive and transgressive. It is patriarchal discourse that constructs all women who refuse to accept their lot – regardless of height – as monstrous or freakish.

In this vein, it is telling that it is when Anna has ostensibly left the world of public exhibition that she experiences the most profound challenge to her 'bigness'. Charles Stratton and Lavinia Warren, fellow performers from the American Museum, have become embroiled in peddling a quack remedy – 'Nelvana's Nordic Regulator' – which supposedly has the ability to alter height; as Charles proclaims: '"If you are tall, it will make you shorter [...] If you are too short, it will make you taller"' (Swan, 1988, p. 300). She samples it as an experiment, and it seems that she does begin to shrink, being able to walk through a door frame which was previously too small without ducking. Disconcertingly, her manager-turned-lover Apollo Ingalls seems pleased by this diminishment:

> 'Anna, think of all the afflicted women like yourself who would like to be shorter than their men. Think of the joy Nelvana's would bring to their world by removing two, three – in your case, twenty-five – inches that interferes with your femininity'. 'Apollo, I am not certain I wish to be small and insignificant,' I blurted. 'Well, I doubt if you will go down to 5'5" but something under six feet might be very nice,' he replied [...] 'Something under six feet? Apollo, I'd be puny.' Apollo laughed and began to kiss my neck. A fresh wave of dread made me feel depressed. Did Apollo mean it? His grinning face said he did [...] 'Don't you want to be one of the diminutive females our age idealizes, sweetheart?'
>
> (p. 309)

Apollo's remarks crystallise the strand of anxiety about bigness in women which run through the nineteenth-century accounts of Anna Swan: smallness is feminine and attractive, as it coheres with the expectations upon women to be vulnerable and dependent upon men. To make a giantess shrink would contain her perceived threat to masculinity. Although it is subsequently revealed that Apollo has been deceiving her, faking her shorter measurements to have the opportunity to recoup his lost money by obtaining her endorsement of the product, this plot illustrates how the regulation of Anna's height becomes a struggle with patriarchal oppression and manipulation. Her height might make her 'freakish', but to be shorter would condemn her to becoming the Victorian feminine 'ideal': 'diminutive', and ultimately with limited access to the public sphere of paid work.

Of course, this matter of size in relation to women – and men – has the potential to be interpreted in a more explicitly sexualised way. Anna speaks of her interest in men's 'hand size', and explains: 'experience has taught me there is a correlation between the size of the hand and the size of what makes a man a man. Besides, men's hands have helped to shape my life' (Swan, 1988, p. 5). Metaphorically, and somewhat ominously, her remark suggests that she might have been manipulated in her career by patriarchal powers. More literally, there is a bawdy allusion at work here, for her comment implies a correlation between hand and penis size in men. In this context, Anna's initial comments on her father's hand size offer an interesting counterpart to the presentation of her 'manly', potent patriarch in *The Nova Scotia Giantess*. She recounts how his:

> fingers were a nice fit with my four-year-old mitt. By that time I realized I wasn't an extension of my mother's body and I considered my father a physical equivalent. (It is not the lot of young giants to be awed by parent dimensions.) When I was twelve, my fingers enfolded by father's baby fist. His bantam size endeared him to me and set the precedent for my reaction to all human males. Their size makes them seem vulnerable and I confess that as a grown woman I can't meet a man smaller than myself – i.e., every man except Angus – without acting like a welcome wagon. I want to shout to all of them: SAMPLE ANNIE'S FREE EATS & TONICS! GUARANTEED TO MAKE YOU GROW.
>
> (Swan, 1988, p. 7; original emphasis)

There are some complex issues of size, gender, and sexuality at work in this quotation. It implies that Anna's size forestalls some elements of the typical Oedipal process of gender development: although she learns to separate herself from her mother, she perceives her father as an equal as a child (instead of experiencing a sense of lack/castration). If hands are already linked to genitalia, then Anna's size associates her with masculinity; men appear 'vulnerable' in relation to her, and her size thus feminises them. However, we again witness her conceptualisation of her self as a product to be consumed, which functions as a way of reassuring men who encounter her. The salacious implications of her making them 'grow' are clear; they will find her sexually attractive, which will make them 'bigger' men. Nevertheless, considering the dubious role of 'tonics' later on in the novel, such comfort and claims are cast as spurious, quack bromides for the men who might be intimidated by her.

Martin, as a giant of only slightly shorter stature than Anna, ostensibly should be able to measure up, and not be so vulnerable to feelings of sexual inadequacy. As Leslie Fielder has indicated, the exhibition of male giants would often include suggestive remarks about the subject's endowment and sexual prowess (Fielder, 1981, pp. 108–11). Unfortunately for Anna, her husband is sexually inexperienced and impotent. On their honeymoon, his genitalia is revealed to be 'a small nub of purple bobbed from the centre of Martin's enormous frame. The organ was no longer than a baby's' (Swan, 1988, p. 209). On one level, this might be interpreted as exposing the fallacy of 'true life' pamphlets and the trappings of freakery, and the ways in which textual accounts of the freak show construct unrealistic representations of actual bodies. Despite being subjected to unrealistic expectations about her own body due to freak show discourse, Anna is exposed as being just as readily duped by outlandish claims as any other audience member. However, Martin's impotency also becomes the mark of his 'disability'. Despite her being eager to represent Anna as being a feminist icon because of her height, Swan ironically replicates Wood's assertion that 'giants' are inclined to be sickly, weak and pathetic in her depiction of Anna's husband.

Yet it is not only male genitalia which is assessed via a criteria of size in the novel. As a continuation of the theme of sexual 're-membering' discussed with regards to neo-Victorian representations of Sarah Baartman in Chapter 1, Anna's vagina is a source of fascination to many who encounter her. Mary Russo's work on the 'female grotesque' is pertinent here. She explores the various cultural connections between 'excess', 'monstrosity' and the female body, and points out the association between the 'grotesque' and the vagina. The term 'grotesque' is also a reference to a cave – 'the grotto-esque'. Russo elaborates: 'As bodily metaphor, the grotesque cave tends to look like (and in the most gross metaphorical sense be identified with) the cavernous anatomical female body' (Russo, 1995, p. 1). This association is pertinent to male anxieties about Anna's size in the text, as her perceived bigness inspires men to penetrate her in an effort to quantify and conquer her 'cavernous' excess. As a girl, she is friends with a local boy with dwarfism named Hubert. In a childish 'game' gone awry, he basically rapes her with an icicle to measure her genitalia. Reflecting on this incident, Anna opines: 'Hubert's icicle had not only ruptured my maidenhead; it had punctured my belief in myself as a magic being. I was human and vulnerable – a female who, like every other female, could be penetrated in a way that no man could' (Swan, 1988, p. 35). Anna's childhood perception of her size is that it affords her strength and power; she is invulnerable and potent. This assault thus returns her to her 'proper' gender role of penetrability and helplessness: the patriarchal expectations of femininity. To use the euphemism offered in *The Nova Scotia Giantess*, Anna does not survive her formative years as 'heart-whole', and yet the boundaries between the 'freakish' and the 'normal' female body are collapsed, as, regardless of size, all women are subject to abuse and exploitation.

The text's exposure of the 'enfreakment' of women in the nineteenth century with regards to sexuality also becomes apparent in Martin's attitude towards his wife's sexual responses. After another failed love-making session, when Anna challenges her husband's lack of attentiveness to her own desires, she tells us that 'the giant looked at me as if I had three heads' (Swan, 1988, p. 297). Martin subsequently claims that he has received advice from a doctor that Anna's giant proportions mean that she cannot achieve orgasm. Of course, the spurious medical advice which has shaped Martin's opinions resonate with the more patriarchal opinions of Victorian medicine; for example, Dr William Acton's writings on female sexuality prescribed that the 'perfect ideal' of a wife and mother should be 'so pure-hearted as to be utterly ignorant of and averse to any sensual indulgence, but it unselfishly attached to the man she loves, as to be willing to give up her own wishes and feelings for his sake' (Acton, 1865, as cited in Lynda Nead, 1988, p. 19). Any sort of female sexual pleasure is therefore couched as 'abnormal'. Anna questions her husband's beliefs, reflecting: 'Was I a freak in my sexual response? Impossible' (Swan, 1988, p. 298). Her refusal to accept that her sexual desire is 'freakish' poses a resounding defiance to nineteenth-century medical opinion on behalf of all women, not just giantesses. The novel thus challenges the chastity of Anna as depicted in her historical 'true life story' pamphlet, and furthermore discounts the covert condemnation of women who might 'fall' from the impossible dictates of feminine propriety.

It is the discourse of medicine that leads to her most troubling 'exhibition' as an adult woman, continuing the trope of 'medical sensationalism' which runs throughout the examples of neo-Victorian freakery which I discuss. In an extract from a tract concerning 'Anatomical Wonders' authored by Martin, he tells of Anna's medical examination on board a ship to Europe: he has persuaded the doctor to allow him to bear clandestine witness to this event, and is hidden in a neighbouring bathroom as he watches:

> From my post I saw the doctor's face contort, and realized his arm had disappeared into the pleats of skin. First the folds swallowed his fingers and wrist and then his forearm. The man achieved penetration as far as his elbow. The patient appeared unaware of her examiner's distress. Her eyes stayed shut in serene contemplation. Naughton looked around and for a second his eyes held mine. I changed position. I was sweating in the hot little cubby-hole.
>
> (Swan, 1988, p. 172)

Naughton then summons his assistant to complete the 'internal examination' due to his larger hand size and Martin is duly presented with Anna's gynaecological measurements. This is obviously a highly disturbing scene. Martin's shifting movements and sweating suggest sexual arousal, and the meeting of the doctor's gaze suggests collusion: Martin is a voyeur, and this ostensibly 'medical' examination has connotations of a gang rape. Anna's passivity is emphasized; her shut eyes means that she does not meet the gaze of the doctors, Martin, or us as the metatextual audience. For we too are forced to collude in Anna's penetration; as in Chase-Riboud's depiction of Sarah Baartman's dissection, discussed in Chapter 1, the readership of Susan Swan's novel becomes complicit in this medically-sanctioned rape and we are made overtly aware of the ethical quandaries of such participation.

Nevertheless, there are aspects of the novel's invocation of both freak show and medical representation with regards to gender which do not seem so attuned to the ideological implications at stake. The text retells both Anna's delivery of a stillborn baby girl, and the birth of a son who died shortly afterwards. In Swan's fictionalisation, both children are the result of Anna's affair with her manager, Apollo, for Martin's impotence precludes his ability to produce 'giant' offspring. As their marriage has not been consummated, Martin is aware of his role as cuckolded husband when the first pregnancy is announced, yet is willing to claim the child as his own and is sensitive when Anna's daughter dies: 'The giant has been kind, and far more loving than I have any right to expect, doing and saying all that he can to make me feel that I have not failed although this is exactly how I do feel: female and flawed. I could aid neither myself nor my child during her birth' (Swan, 1988, p. 242). While Anna's sense of guilt is an understandable part of her grieving process for her lost daughter, her feelings of failure and inadequacy can be interpreted in an alternative way, particularly in the light of her son's subsequent birth and death. Both children are very big; the novel cites '18 pounds and 27 inches' as the size of her daughter (Swan, 1988, p. 240) whereas the boy is 23 pounds and 12 ounces – as in the case of the historical child, the largest baby ever recorded. In the case of the historical Anna Swan, there is no doubt over the child's paternity, and hence the baby's size is perhaps understandable given the dimensions of both parents.

However, by rewriting Anna's history and giving paternity to the average-sized Apollo, Swan might be considered as thwarting the feminist message of the earlier sections of the novel: the baby has inherited Anna's gigantic proportions, and implicitly, she is therefore given some burden for his size leading to a difficult birth and ultimate death. Robert Bogdan has highlighted the ways in which 'true life story' pamphlets of the nineteenth century would often attribute the birth of children with extraordinary bodies to the theory of 'maternal impression': 'the form a child took was directly related to the kind of experience the mother had' (Bogdan, 1988, p. 110). In the case of Joseph Merrick, the subject of Chapter 5, his 'elephant'-esque features were attributed to his mother being trampled by such an animal while pregnant with her son (Howell and Ford, 2001, p. 12), but the development of a child might also be affected by a whole range of external factors, from food cravings in pregnancy, to the 'fears and desires' of the mother (Adams, 2001, p. 187). It is the latter circumstances which are troubling in the case of Swan's version of Anna, for, as Rachel Adams has noted, such theories place the 'blame' for unusual anatomies with the mother: 'It was [...] a way of policing women by threatening that their crimes would become visible for all to see' (Adams, 2001, p. 187). The large child thus bears the burden of Anna's sexual infidelity and, furthermore, is also reported as having ambiguous gender characteristics: 'Dr Robinson said his sex was uncertain as he possessed an unformed male organ on his outer body and might have had female organs inside. Martin wished the death record to say "male" but the doctors refused and pencilled in "sex unknown" under the cause of death' (Swan, 1988, p. 327). There is no mention made of the child being intersex in medical accounts of the birth,[15] so why should the novel include such a detail? Bearing in mind the strain of anxiety about gender trouble which stalks nineteenth-century narratives of Anna, which is otherwise so resolutely challenged in *The Biggest Modern Woman of the World*, it seems that the novel cannot finally transcend the sense that Anna's size and sexual desires have resulted in the perpetuation of 'freakery', which is not productive for mother or child, and ends in death.

Possessing the textual corpus: Stacy Carlson's *Among the Wonderful*

The representation of Anna Swan in Stacy Carlson's *Among the Wonderful* is slightly different to Susan Swan's novel in the sense that the 'giantess' figure in the text is named Ana Swift: thus the division between historical 'fact' and 'fiction' is more clearly drawn from the outset. However, Ana's Canadian nationality, her height, and her employment at Barnum's Museum offer some overt points of connection between the historical woman and Carlson's fictional character. Nevertheless, as I shall explore in more detail below, Ana's life ends at the American Museum, as she dies in the conflagration of 1865. The chapters which are from Ana's perspective are repeatedly entitled 'She Stands Up', and 'She Stands up Again'. This phrase might suggest that Ana's narrative is a form of empowerment, as it has connotations of 'standing up and being counted', or 'making a stand' – a motif of protest, or political statement, which is reminiscent of the feminist reappropriation of 'big women' in Susan Swan's novel. Yet it is when Ana is standing that her difference from others is most apparent. The chapter titles therefore suggest from the outset that Ana's words will have a double resonance; they might be empowering, but also have the potential to become a form of spectacle, or even exploitation.

Her introductory narrative relates her journey by boat from Canada to America. Standing out on the deck she perceives the gaze of fellow passengers: 'I did not look [...] Were my hours, days, years of being gazed upon not enough to earn me a moment's privacy? [...] I perceived the eyes of the two women boring through my back. I was sure they discussed their strange luck that I should be here for them to behold' (Carlson, 2011, p. 1). She experiences their gaze as a form of penetration; a violation and an intrusion. She contemplates her mother's warnings to her about how others might understand her height:

> [...] there I was, reflected in their small, astonished faces and their delicate gasps. I straightened to my full height and cooled the rage with your words, with what you'd told me, Mother, time after time: *You are a mirror held up in front of other people, Ana, which reflects their truest selves.* But if that is so, then truly all humanity is an abomination.
>
> (Carlson, 2011, p. 2; original emphasis)

Reminiscent of the mirror-imagery discussed in this book's Introduction, we see that the extraordinary body is used a metaphor for reflecting the spectator's fears and fantasies. Ana's combination of ambivalence towards her own appearance and misanthropy – her words suggest that both she and her audiences are 'abominations' – is unsurprising considering the mirror-related abuse to which she has been subjected: she later tells us that a former manager and lover, Mr Ramsey, would have sex with her before a mirror for the gratification of paying men hiding in her bedroom (Carlson, 2011, pp. 81–83). However, in this specific scenario, the economy of exploitation is rapidly thwarted, as Ana realises that the women are pointing past her to the sight of America beyond

(Carlson, 2011, p. 2). This opening scene thus tells us that gazes can be misinterpreted and redirected: Ana will not always be a spectacle in this text, but the novel is self-conscious as to how unusual bodies might be used and abused.

As the anecdote about Mr Ramsey indicates, as with the versions of Anna represented in *The Nova Scotia Giantess* and *The Biggest Modern Woman of the World,* Carlson's Ana inspires a certain sexual fascination from the men who encounter her, yet she also arouses gender-related anxieties as well. She describes several memorable reactions from audience members at past performances:

> In Halifax I encountered a lady who, when she saw me [...], began to violently pull her own hair and did not stop until her escort shielded her from my sight. One fellow seemed to take no notice of me at all. But as he stood with the others looking into my booth he suffered a delayed reaction: He crossed his left leg tightly over his right and leaned forward, twisted as a pretzel, as if he was overcome with the need to urinate, pointing at me while his hat toppled off his head.
>
> (Carlson, 2011, pp. 59–60)

In the nineteenth century, women's hair is coded as an important signifier of femininity, and also sexuality.[16] This woman's reaction might thus be interpreted as an acting out of the menace to conventional norms of feminine beauty and desirability that the spectacle of the outsized woman poses. The man who 'twists', apparently with the 'need to urinate', locates the source of his somatic reaction to his genitalia, yet this is an emasculating response, as his gendered costume – the hat – is rendered unstable in the process. Perhaps more significantly, in both cases it is the audience members themselves who are rendered physically odd by their encounter with Ana; they are the source of ridicule and spectacle, in contrast to her weary yet stoic dignity.

However, as intimated by her (mis)interpretation of the audience's gaze at the novel's beginning, Ana remains apprehensive about the extent to which she can control the terms under which she is exhibited. As she increasingly suffers under the physical pain of her large body, she contemplates suicide, but is stopped by the thought of what might happen to her corpse:

> [...] a problem arises in the thought of my body left behind, helplessly vulnerable to unknown humiliations. The idea of someone pacing my length, scratching his head and wondering how he'll

> transport the body, and someone else lifting my cold arm to press his tiny hand to my lifeless paw, even these mild images unleash the most sublime terror in me; I could never let that happen.
>
> (Carlson, 2011, p. 226)

As the treatment of the remains of Sarah Baartman detailed in Chapter 1 makes all too apparent, the death of a freak show performer does not necessarily terminate their role as spectacle. For Ana, she imagines being made into an awkward burden in death, or still being used as a reference point for the measuring of men's bodies. Nevertheless, one of the most significant divergences between the life of Anna Swan and the character of Ana Swift is their respective fates in the American Museum fire. The above discussion of Anna Swan's rescue in 1865, told by *The New York Tribune* and reimagined by Susan Swan, both highlighted the aspect of spectacle verging on entertainment at the hoisting of Anna's body away from the building in front of the crowds. For Carlson's Ana, this is untenable: 'I looked down onto a sea of upturned faces and the wrongness of it pushed me back. A crowd, no different from standing in my booth or walking in the galleries. Would I give them the biggest spectacle of all? Would I give them this gift?' (Carlson, 2011, p. 451). Her decision is to stay in the building – tantamount to suicide – and let her body be consumed by the flames. On one hand, this seems like a depressing finale for this neo-Victorian version of Anna Swan; her subsequent glittering career, marriage, and child-bearing are effectively erased from the historical record, an act which might seem like an incongruous silencing in the light of the genre's typical commitment to recentring marginalised subjects. On the other, perhaps it reinstalls Ana as an agent of her own destiny, however tragic. There is no trace of her corpse left by the fire, despite rumours of Barnum's men searching the ashes for her bones, presumably in an attempt to continue her exhibition (Carlson, 2011, p. 457). Her role as spectacle, which has been such an ambivalent experience throughout her short life, is finally over.

Yet this is not strictly the case, for Ana has a textual afterlife both within the novel and beyond. On her employment at the museum, Ana is required to write a True Life Story, a pamphlet that will tell the audience her story much in the same vein as the historical example I analyse in the first section of this chapter. She has not brought the former versions of this to Barnum's museum and she articulates her disdain for these texts which give various ridiculous accounts of her life, including an 'early life' in the Hebrides, 'where I was apparently raised by a clan of druids whose tendency to use me as a centrepiece for cultic invocations partially accounted for my stature' (Carlson, 2011, p. 73). Also, we learn that she has featured in a version of *Jack and the Beanstalk* where she is figured as an ogress, and also when she has been cast as 'Anoo, a mighty South American Amazon' (Carlson, 2011, p. 73). The way in which Ana views these narratives is important in several ways. There are ideological implications in these texts: clearly, an unusual body has to be accounted for in some way; her body, and, implicitly, Ana, cannot just speak for itself. She later remarks: 'Without a story, however full it was of nonsense, I was just an oversized body on display' (Carlson, 2011, p. 84). Rosemarie Garland-Thomson's account of the construction of freakery argues that 'the exceptional body seems to compel explanation, inspire representation' (Garland-Thomson, 1996, p. 1), and one of the primary instruments of this 'explanation' and 'representation' is the narrative provided by the 'true life story' pamphlet which gives meaning to the extraordinary body on display. Thus, the potential agency of freak show performers becomes a matter of who tells their stories, and to what ends.

Indeed, what is notable about Ana's 'stories' is that they are always written by someone else, the various managers who have dictated the terms of her exhibition and have claimed the profits made from the spectacle of her body. At the museum, she now has the opportunity to write her own True Life story, to make her own narrative voice heard, in a motif that is reminiscent of the strand of neo-Victorian fiction which seeks to empower otherwise marginalised historical figures through granting agency via narration. However, it is important to note that Ana struggles with this enterprise: 'the prospect of writing it irritated me in the extreme; it gave me the feeling that *I* was falling for some kind of prank' (Carlson, 2011, p. 73; original emphasis). Put another way, Ana recognises that the text which she will ostensibly own could well be used against her, interpreted as a signifier of her collusion with the dynamics of freak show exploitation as opposed to an opportunity to take ownership of her history. After various false starts, what eventually emerges is a multi-voiced narrative, a text which 'swerved hopelessly back and forth in its chronology' (Carlson, 2011 p. 209) and yet which gives Ana a certain satisfaction and respite from her schedule of exhibition at the museum. She reflects on the pleasure that the text gives her: 'Writing is an imperfect alchemy [...] Words have histories that span centuries, and what does that have to do with me? On the other hand, writing is a manifestation of our pathetic, inborn determination to leave a trace of ourselves, no matter how flimsy, to persevere beyond death' (Carlson, 2011, p. 210). The novel thus implies that

Ana will have the opportunity to take control over how her life will be re-membered, but also that language necessarily does not have a sole owner – words are always inherited from a prior source, and though they might be put to use by an individual, they will also be available for further reappropriation in forums that are beyond the control of the author. Ana comes to avoid this unpredictability by keeping her History to herself: 'Compelled to record the strands of my life, I did not care that most of them did not twine together into a braid; these strands were not meant for anyone's eyes but mine' (Carlson, 2011, p. 425). Her comment on the 'eyes' is important – reading can also be conceptualised as a form a gazing, but Ana's emphasis on her text being for her eyes only underscores the way in which her writing has become representative of her agency.

Nevertheless, Ana has acknowledged the ways in which her writing might leave a legacy for future generations to know and understand her by, to 'persevere beyond death' (Carlson, 2011, p. 210), and so is moved to recover her 'True History' from her bedroom to survive her. Her choice of curator for her memory is significant; she encounters Guillaudeu worrying over the fate of the museum's collection of live and stuffed animals and implores him to take the document. Guillaudeu's initial role at the American Museum is a continuation of his post as taxidermist at John Scudder's Museum. He takes a strong professional and personal interest in natural history, and it is significant in his respect that his 'hero' is a certain Baron Georges Cuvier (Carlson, 2011, p. 9), the man who played such a seminal role in Sarah Bartmann's exploitative afterlife. However, Guillaudeu's attitude towards the Baron changes when he begins to have more interaction with the human 'ethnographic' exhibits in Barnum's Museum. Seeking information about the various tribesmen who Barnum has transported to New York, he consults Cuvier's writings about the 'races of man' and is horrified by the racist 'degradations' that he reads, which leads him to discard the book forever (Carlson, 2011, pp. 108–10). Such a reaction might initially suggest that Gullaudeu is sensitive to the ideological and ethical quandaries of treating humans as 'exhibits'. However, although Guillaudeu has had a substantial role in the novel, his encounters with Ana are very brief and he frequently refers to her as 'the giantess'; unable to perceive her as an individual woman, she is reduced to the label of her physical anomaly.

Furthermore, there is a certain irony in Ana's choice of guardian of her textual afterlife, as Guillaudeu's role as a taxidermist means that he has a history of preserving the dead to be looked at – for educational purposes, but also for entertainment. Such potential comes to a disturbing fruition at the novel's conclusion. Guillaudeu is now making a living from introducing and reciting sections of Ana's True History for profit, and also selling copies to enthusiastic audiences: 'The book already had sold so many copies that there had been a second printing. After news of it had reached New York they'd received letters from Barnum's lawyers, who claimed that Barnum owned the rights [...] Holding tightly to the leather-bound volume, Guillaudeu emerged from the wings into the bright light of the stage' (Carlson, 2011, p. 458). These final words of the novel should give us pause for thought. Ana has taken control over the narrative of her life and yet now, in her death, she has no agency over who will profit from her story. Indeed, surely such a conclusion underscores the ways in which she has become immortalised in the trappings of the freak show; exposed, exploited and sold for entertainment. The ownership of Ana's story is contested by her employer, yet the image of Guillaudeu 'holding tightly' to her text as he takes centre stage emphasizes his almost sexualized possession of her textual body.[17] Of course, the fact that Guillaudeu is now a performer means that he too will be subjected to a potentially objectifying audience gaze, but this is a faint echo of the life time of scrutiny that Ana has endured. Via her own 'true life story', Ana's anxieties about posthumous exhibition have come to fruition.

Conclusion

This chapter has argued that 'big' women – such as Anna Swan – might exceed the boundaries of normative nineteenth-century femininity, an aberration which is perceived as freakish. However, there is evidence in both Victorian and neo-Victorian narratives about Anna which suggests that femininity in itself can be constructed as 'monstrous' as well. The historical Anna's 'true life story' pamphlet works hard to establish her feminine propriety, but this is subtly undermined by the emphasis on her potential sexual attractiveness as well. In accounts of her rescue from the fire at Barnum's Museum in 1865, we see that Anna's size troubles traditional gender roles but also becomes an allegory for her 'excessive' femininity as well. As such, the texts struggle to contain Anna's 'bigness'. For Susan Swan, it is Anna's gigantism which is the symbol of her feminist potential. Furthermore, her career as a freak show performer – albeit subjecting her to sexualised scrutiny in some ways – affords her a sense of agency in the public sphere, outside of the restrictions of Victorian domestic femininity. In addition, Anna is imagined as a sexual agent, taking pleasure in her body despite patriarchal attempts to confine and control her. What *The Biggest Modern Woman of the World* indicates is that Anna, despite her size and unusual career, is in some ways not exceptional: her experiences demonstrate the ways in which women who fail to meet the (impossible) ideals of nineteenth-century feminine propriety might be subject to 'enfreakment' as well. Ironically, however, the novel does project some of the more derogatory stereotypes which feature in nineteenth-century discourses of gigantism onto the fictionalized version of Martin Bates. Another way in which Swan's text is not wholly revisionary is in its allusions to the theory of maternal impression; the unusual appearance – and ultimate death – of Anna's children seems to be a consequence of her adultery. In this instance, women's sexual transgression perpetuates freakishness, which somewhat undermines the feminist potential of the novel.

Stacy Carlson's Ana Swift, like Swan's Anna, is a figure of gendered and sexual anxiety; positioned as having the potential to be made a spectacle of against her will, but simultaneously challenge her audience's nominal gender roles. But it is *Among the Wonderful*'s engagement with the genre of the 'true life story' pamphlet which has the most significant implications for thinking about neo-Victorian's potential for audience/reader self-reflection and interrogation. The novel's representation of Guillaudeu's ownership of Anna's textual corpus after her death has crucial metatextual implications. For hasn't Carlson, like Guillaudeu, reanimated Anna Swan's life for an audience, and aren't we, as consumers of the text, also implicated in the dynamics of the neo-Victorian freak show? In a similar vein, Swan's version of Anna takes control of her own 'spieling' and thus attempts to assert some degree of ownership over her 'giantess' persona. Yet my analysis also indicates that Anna is metatextually commodified by Swan's fictionalisation, particularly as a sexual spectacle. Indeed, it is worth noting here that the descendants of the historical Anna Swan publically expressed their discomfort with Susan Swan's use of their ancestor as a fictional character.[18] This reception of the novel thus offers a pertinent example of the perils of neo-Victorian bio-fiction, as considered in the Introduction. In summary, then, it is the ending of Carlson's novel which offers the most thought-provoking parable on the ethical quandaries of re-membering freak show performers and the potential uses – and abuses – such bodies might be resubmitted to in neo-Victorian appropriations of their lives.

4

Innocence, Experience, and Childhood Dramas: Charles Stratton and Lavinia Warren

In Stacy Carlson's *Among the Wonderful*, a conversation takes place between three of the employees of P. T. Barnum's American Museum. The 'giantess' Ana Swift, the 'bearded lady' Maud Kraike, and the resident pianist Thomas Willoughby are discussing their colleague, Charles Stratton, otherwise known as General Tom Thumb. Maud articulates her discomfort with Charles's precociousness:

> 'You know who is the strangest of them all? Who gives me chills every time I think about him? [...] Tom Thumb.'
>
> 'What?' said Thomas. 'He's just a little boy!'
>
> 'He's terrifying,' Maud declared. 'Think about how young he is [...] this will be the entire scope of his life, where he looks for all types of sustenance.'
>
> 'Like Caligula in the Roman Army,' Thomas murmured [...]
>
> 'But Ana, you've experienced normal life with your family. It's in you somewhere. He won't have that, ever'.
>
> (Carlson, 2011, pp. 147–48)

There are several themes here which are significant in terms of both nineteenth-century and neo-Victorian representations of Stratton. His persona is based on a combination of worldliness and youth: first 'discovered' by Barnum aged just four years old, he was performing at the age of five, yet billed as being eleven to make his short stature even more remarkable. For Maud, this synthesis is disconcerting. In part, she perceives him to be something of a victim. His childhood has been interrupted, and she hints that this will lead to him being a damaged adult, constantly seeking the approval of his audience. However, she is not exactly sympathetic: this lack of 'normality' makes him a disturbing, 'strange' figure for those he encounters. Furthermore, although Thomas initially protests that Charles is 'just a little boy!', suggesting purity and unworldliness, his subsequent comparison of the boy to 'Caligula' is ominous. The name of this infamous Roman emperor has become a byword for despotism, insanity, and sexual deviance,[1] and to associate the young Charles with this figure undermines any assumption of childhood innocence. 'Little' boys can grow into dangerous, 'abnormal', hyper-sexualised men.

Charles Stratton and Lavinia Warren were people of short stature; referred to as 'dwarves' during their lifetimes, they were promoted and managed by Barnum and toured the world in freak shows and exhibitions. Stratton was born in Connecticut, United States in 1838. Although of average size at birth and in infancy, he stopped growing as a young child and would remain at a height of just over 3ft. He was engaged as one of Barnum's exhibits at the age of 4, and continued to work with him until his death in 1883. Billed as 'General Tom Thumb', Stratton's act generated considerable wealth and fame for both him and Barnum and led to Stratton being introduced to American presidents and politicians, and notable royals and aristocrats in Europe. Warren was born in 1841 in Middleborough, Massachusetts. After leaving a career as a school teacher, she began her stage career performing on a Mississippi show boat before subsequently being managed by Barnum. She married Stratton in a high-profile ceremony, orchestrated by Barnum, in 1863. Her sister Minnie was also a woman of short stature whose career was managed by Barnum. Although the Strattons had no children, one of Barnum's famed hoaxes involved exhibiting the couple with their 'baby' (it was later revealed that the Strattons were pictured with a succession of infants, who would be abruptly replaced once they grew too large) and then circulating reports of the child's 'death' when the ruse became too strenuous to maintain. Minnie did, however, become pregnant by her husband, but both mother and child died in childbirth in 1878. After Stratton's death, Lavinia married Count Primo Magri, an Italian man with restricted growth, and continued to work as a touring performer. She died in 1919.[2]

As numerous commentators have identified, the nineteenth century can be located as a turning point in the historical construction of the notion of 'childhood'. Through economic, legal and cultural shifts, children began to be associated with innocence, vulnerability, and being in need of protection from the adult world. But what of individuals who might be perceived as crossing the boundaries between the notion of the 'adult' and the 'child' due to their physical appearance and their ensuing treatment by society? This chapter takes nineteenth-century and neo-Victorian textual representations of Charles Stratton and his wife, Lavinia Warren, as its focus, firstly demonstrating that 'dwarfism' was constructed as troubling the increasingly regulated borders between 'the child' and 'the adult' in the nineteenth century, especially in relation to sexuality. Both Albert Smith's play *Hop O' My Thumb* (1846) and the 'true life story' pamphlet about Stratton (1863) construct him as a hyper-sexualised, 'trickster' figure, yet as also subject to being a figure of foolishness and derision. My reading of P. T. Barnum's account of his manipulation of Stratton as a child exposes themes of abuse in relation to children which also intersect with broader power inequalities of class and race. Lavinia is both infantilised and sexualised in the 'true life story' pamphlet, but emerges as a more intelligent and complex personality in her own *Autobiography of Mrs Tom Thumb* (1979)[3] and alongside her sister Minnie in Sylvester Bleeker's *General Tom Thumb's Three Year Tour Around the World* (1872). The themes of childhood, sexuality and abuse take centre stage in the neo-Victorian novels of Charles and Lavinia's lives. Jane Sullivan's *Little People* (2011) and Melanie Benjamin's *The Autobiography of Mrs Tom Thumb* (2011) remember Charles as a damaged adult due to his childhood experiences, but emphasise Lavinia's intelligence and agency. However, *Little People*'s engagement with the 'Tom Thumb Baby' hoax, and Benjamin's novel's depiction of Lavinia's belittlement of her sister Minnie expose the ways in which the exploited can become exploiters, and the problems of treating 'little people' like children. Yet the tensions between innocence and experience – and the social power relations involved in this with regards to childhood, sexuality, disability, race, and class – are not easily resolved in neo-Victorian versions of Charles and Lavinia.

Child, interrupted: Nineteenth-century constructions of childhood and dwarfism

It has become something of a truism to acknowledge that the concept of 'childhood' is historically and culturally specific, yet it is important to note that the nineteenth century was a period of significant change – and conflict – with regards to the construction of 'the child'. The Romantic ideal of the child as pure, innocent and in need of protection was highly influential, but simultaneously the Puritan view that children were fundamentally wicked and thus needed to be controlled by force was also apparent.[4] The extent to which children would be protected from the world of work – and implicitly cared for in the home in their early years – is complicated by issues of gender, class, and race, but on both sides of the Atlantic there were major legal shifts which altered attitudes towards child labour. As Karen Sánchez-Eppler identifies in the context of North America, at the beginning of the nineteenth century it was expected that children would participate in some sort of labour, but by the beginning of the twentieth century, individual states began to pass laws to limit children working (Sánchez-Eppler, 2005, pp. xvii–xviii). In Britain, a series of Acts throughout the century increasingly redefined prohibitions on children of certain ages working in dangerous jobs.[5] Yet the nineteenth-century ideal of childhood is decidedly located in the middle classes: 'The invention of childhood entailed the creation of a protracted period in which the child would ideally be protected from the difficulties and responsibilities of daily life – ultimately including the need to work' (Sánchez-Eppler, 2005, p. 152), but this was not always a possibility in households where finances were a concern. Furthermore, as both Sánchez-Eppler and Wilma King emphasise respectively, the exemption of children from the workplace did not include domestic labour and such chores were gendered in the sense that the home was the feminine sphere (Sánchez-Eppler, 2005, p. 152; King, 2011, location 189). In North America, constructions of childhood and race become even more complicated in the context of slavery. Wilma King identifies the ways in which enslaved black people tended to be infantilised, regardless of age (King, 2011, location 145), but more specifically, her study of enslaved youth in nineteenth-century America contends that such children 'had virtually no childhood because they entered the workplace early and were subjected to arbitrary authority, punishment, and separation, just as enslaved adults were' (King, 2011, location 222). The ways in which discourses gender, class, and race intersect with the construction of the Victorian child will become relevant to the representation of both Charles and Lavinia in both nineteenth-century and neo-Victorian texts.

The increasing anxiety about 'child labour' being a form of exploitation takes on a more sinister complexion in the context of sexuality in Victorian Britain. The scandal of W. T. Stead's exposé of London's trade in child prostitution affected the raising of the age of consent from 13 to 16 as part of the Criminal Law Amendment Act of 1885, which constructed childhood 'innocence' as being separate from the adult world of sexuality.[6] But the Victorian 'cult of childhood' can also be interpreted as carrying dubious impulses towards the eroticisation of youth, one of the most infamous examples being Charles Dodgson's ambiguous fascination with young girls.[7] Nevertheless, suspicions of the inherent 'badness' of children also influenced attitudes towards child sexuality; Michel Foucault, for example, explores the discursive construction of the sexualised child with regards to the regulation of masturbation (Foucault, 1998, pp. 27–30). In summary, then, nineteenth-century attitudes towards childhood represent a volatile set of ideologies concerning 'innocence' and 'experience'.

For the purposes of this chapter, the ways in which constructions of dwarfism intersects with these debates about the 'proper' boundaries and behaviours of childhood is crucial. In her philosophical exploration of the concept of 'the miniature', Susan Stewart identifies the ways in which physical smallness is associated with the realm of childhood as 'the child is in some physical sense a miniature of the adult' but also because childhood is 'limited in physical scope' (Stewart, 1993, p. 44). She discusses the child-like qualities of Stratton's stage persona of Tom Thumb, but she also makes the following, rather more contentious remark: 'What is, in fact, lost in this idealized miniaturization of the body is sexuality, and hence the danger of power' (Stewart, 1993, p. 124). As my analysis below demonstrates, there is actually a considerable amount of evidence in the nineteenth-century construction of Stratton to suggest that sexuality is far from 'lost' in the depiction of his 'miniaturization'. Moreover, if the 'littleness' of dwarfism finds an association with the smallness of childhood, there is also a long-established historical tradition of representing dwarfism as connected with sexual knowledge and potency. For example, Betty M. Adelson's study of the cultural and social history of people with dwarfism offers evidence of this trope dating from Ancient Greek society in vase paintings which show dwarfs participating in Dionysian rituals of sexual excess and lasciviousness. However she also notes that such representation links to the figure of the satyrs who, whilst virile, 'are also often viewed as disappointed lovers – better known for desire that its fulfilment' (Adelson, 2005, p. 8). Adelson also points out that such sexualised images of dwarves are invariably male: 'There are very few women dwarfs among Greek artefacts, an apparent taboo that resulted from respect, modesty, or discomfort with female deformity' (Adelson, 2005, p. 8). This gendered division in the sexuality of people with dwarfism, and the motif of unconsummated desire will become apparent in both Victorian and neo-Victorian depictions of Charles and Lavinia.

Although this sexuality is coded as adult in the context of Ancient Greece – Adelson refers to 'bald men with exaggeratedly large penises' (Adelson, 2005, p. 8) – the association of dwarfism with transgression also finds resonance in relation to later tales of fantasy for children: 'A good part of the literature of dwarfs, elves, and fairies embodies aspects of the trickster myth. A trickster identity embodies duality: one may enjoy one's own virtue by disapproving of the immoral trickster or, conversely, delight in enjoying the forbidden behaviour' (Adelson, 2005, p. 105). The 'little person' is thus a stock figure of children's literature. Adelson does not elaborate upon what the 'immorality' of the trickster might involve, but, as we shall see in relation to the 'trickster' aspects of 'Tom Thumb's' nineteenth-century presentation, this certainly does shade in to sexual impropriety in his case. What I would also add to Adelson's comments here on the 'dual' enjoyment of trickster figures is the ambivalence as to *who* the joke is actually on with regards to representations of dwarfism. The audience might laugh with the trickster figure, but also laugh at him or her as well.

The concept of the person with dwarfism as a joke coalesces with another child-related issue in George M. Gould and Walter L. Pyle's book *Anomalies and Curiosities of Medicine* (1897). This volume is a compendium of accounts of various extraordinary medical conditions, liberally sprinkled with sensational anecdotes and decidedly lacking in 'scientific' rigour in places. Gould and Pyle offer the following account of dwarfism:

> There are two species of dwarfs, the first coming into the world under normal conditions, but who in their infancy became afflicted with a sudden arrest of development provoked by some malady; the second are born very small, develop little, and are really dwarfs from their birth; as a rule they are well conformed, robust and intelligent. These two species can be distinguished by an important characteristic. The rachitic dwarfs of the first class are incapable of perpetuating their species, while those of the second category have proved more than once their virility. A certain number of dwarfs have married with women of normal height and have had several children, though this is not, it is true, an indisputable proof of their generative faculties; but we have had instances in which dwarfs have married dwarfs and had a family sometimes quite numerous.
>
> (Gould and Pyle, 1898, p. 338)

This rather confusing classification of 'two species' of dwarfism does not actually map onto the situation of either Charles Stratton or Lavinia Warren; both were within the boundaries of 'average' weight and size at birth, but their growth slowed dramatically during infancy.[8] However, what is more significant here is the opinions on paternity which are being expressed. The stereotype of the sexually potent dwarf is reiterated, but alongside this is the figure of the dwarf as cuckold; their remark on the lack of 'indisputable proof' of paternity when men of short stature have children with women of 'normal' height insinuates adultery on the part of the mother. While this throwaway comment might simply be attributed to casual misogyny about female sexual promiscuity, it also might be taken as hinting that a 'normal' woman could not really be expected to be satisfied by a 'little' man and might have to take her pleasure elsewhere: the image of the dwarf man as impotent or, to use Adelson's terminology, as a 'disappointed lover' is invoked. Men with dwarfism might be tricksters, but they also might be tricked, and hence their family units might be based on deception. Ironically, no mention is made of Charles's ostensible paternity. Indeed, the circumstances involving the 'Tom Thumb Baby' was not exposed publically as fraudulent until the early twentieth century, as my later analysis of the newspaper story about Lavinia dating from 1901 indicates. But Gould and Pyle do make reference to Charles's famed sexual prowess in disparaging terms: 'It is said that in England alone he kissed a million females; he prided himself on his success in this function, though his features were anything but inviting' (Gould and Pyle, 1898, p. 342). Their palpable distaste for Charles's aesthetic appeal contradicts other contemporary accounts of Stratton's handsome, well-formed appearance and says much about their own prejudices,[9] but it also implicitly locates him in the 'species' of dwarf that might be virile, but also run the risk of being cuckolded as well, potentially due to physical unattractiveness.

However, when considering the specific circumstances of Charles Stratton with regards to nineteenth-century discourses of childhood, dwarfism, and sexuality, it is important to recognise that he was a young child when he began his career. Barnum's first autobiography gives an account of his first meeting with Charles. He remarks that 'He was exceedingly bashful, but after some coaxing he was induced to converse with me' (Barnum, 1855, p. 243). Considering Charles's youth, his 'bashfulness' is hardly surprising, but Barnum's perseverance is made apparent by his use of terms such as 'coaxing'; that Charles was 'induced' into conversation implies coercive strategies, and the overt power imbalance between the mature man and the little boy has ominous overtones. Barnum goes into some detail to explain his decision to bill 'Tom Thumb's' age as eleven:

> He was only five years old, and to exhibit a dwarf of that age might provoke the question, How do you know that he *is* a dwarf? Some

license might indeed be taken with the facts, but even with this advantage I really felt that the adventure was nothing more than an experiment [...] Mrs Stratton was greatly astonished to find her son heralded in my Museum bills as Gen. TOM THUMB, a dwarf of eleven years of age, just arrived from England! This announcement contained two deceptions. I shall not attempt to justify them, but may be allowed to plead the circumstances in extenuation. The boy was undoubtedly a dwarf, and I had the most reliable evidence that he had grown little, if any, since he was six months old; but had I announced him as only five years of age, it would have been impossible to excite the interest or awaken the curiosity of the public. The thing I aimed at was, to assure them that he was *really a dwarf* – and in *this*, they were not deceived. It was of no consequence, in reality, where he was born or where he came from, and if the announcement that he was a *foreigner* answered my purpose, the people had only themselves to blame if they did not get their money's worth when they visited the exhibition. I had observed [...] the American fancy for European exotics; and if the deception, practised for a season in my dwarf experiment, has done any thing towards checking our disgraceful preference for foreigners, I may readily be pardoned for the offence I here acknowledge.

(Barnum, 1855, pp. 243–44; original emphasis)

I have quoted Barnum's account of his initial shaping of Charles's stage persona at length for it reveals some important issues about the representation of dwarfism and childhood in the context of nineteenth-century freakery. What might be surprising for a twenty-first-century audience is the question that Barnum anticipates being 'provoked' by the age of 'Tom Thumb' is the authenticity of his 'dwarfism', rather than ethical concerns over the exhibition of such a young child. His attitude towards Charles is, at the outset, also rather calculating; the boy's entrance into the world of showmanship is an 'experiment', with Barnum thus figuring himself in the detached, disinterested stance of the scientist, hardly the compassionate and protective role which one might expect with regards to a five year old. In this vein, the 'astonishment' of Charles's mother as to the way in which her child has been billed is telling: while, as I shall detail below, the Strattons did have a significant role in the career of their son and a professional relationship with Barnum, Mrs Stratton was evidently not consulted about his billing. This perhaps suggests a failure of maternal care, yet also that Barnum has assumed control of the child.

Furthermore, Barnum's decision to change Charles's nationality forms an uncomfortable parallel between physical difference – in this case, dwarfism – and foreign 'otherness'. Barnum suggests that he is pandering to the tastes of his audiences and thus placing the blame for such 'deception' firmly with them, but as Chapter 1's discussion of Sarah Baartman demonstrated, there was already a long established tradition of ethnographic display in freak shows, one which Barnum himself would perpetuate and develop with other exhibits.[10] Of course, the purported 'exoticness' of Europe is hardly comparable to the denigrating spectacles of 'savagery' which framed some non-white, non-European performers in the nineteenth century, and Barnum's delineation of England as 'exotic' can easily be interpreted as a joke at the expense of Britain as the former colonial centre of North America. But the pseudo-'foreignness' of 'Tom Thumb' also serves to locate physical 'abnormality' beyond the borders of the American nation, and therefore at a safe remove for home audiences. If this passage is informed by Barnum's overt desire to justify his 'deceptions', then perhaps there is another, even more sinister reading of his remarks. Although the showman ostensibly does not articulate any qualms about Charles's youth with regards to the notion that childhood should be a time of protection from the outside world, this is not to suggest that such discourses were not brought to bear by 'Tom Thumb's' audiences in his own historical moment. A. H. Saxon's biography of Barnum reproduces an extract from Queen Victoria's diary, dated 23 March 1844, which records her first audience with 'General Tom Thumb' who she believes is twelve years old at the time (he was, in fact, just six). While she does appear amused by his routines and posturing, she also comments: 'One cannot help feeling very sorry for the poor little thing & wishing he could be properly cared for, for the people who show him off tease him a good deal' (Saxon, 1989, p. 132). She does not specify who the 'people who show [Charles] off' actually are, but it was Barnum who accompanied Charles on this visit.[11] Charles's 'littleness' in terms of height might be a reason for 'pity', but Victoria's concerns about the care – or lack thereof – that the boy might receive also alludes to his youth and thus need for protection. He clearly signifies as a child, despite Barnum's efforts to the contrary, and this has the potential to make at least one of 'Tom Thumb's' audience members feel uncomfortable.

Bearing this in mind, what other reason might there be for Barnum to fail to acknowledge the ethical quandaries of exhibiting a child? Put another way, which young members of nineteenth-century American society might not be considered to be privy to the discourse of childhood protection from the world of work – and attendant issues of consent and exploitation? My above summary of the conflicting attitudes towards nineteenth-century childhood indicated that race and class are the complicating factors here: enslaved children and working-class children were not protected in the same way by the white, middle-class ideal of innocence. Barnum's initial 'exotic' presentation of 'Tom Thumb' was rapidly supplanted by the young performer's framing as an all-American 'Yankee' character,[12] yet his prior suggestions of the 'foreignness' of Stratton, however incongruous, do hint at the boy being a racial 'other'. As we shall see below, the ways in which the persona of 'Tom Thumb' might be entwined with ambiguous racial identity is a facet of some of his performances. Moreover, Stratton's own class status should not be overlooked. His representation as 'General Tom Thumb' developed in to an example of the 'aggrandized' mode of freakery, suggesting refinement and cultural superiority (Bogdan, 1988, p. 108). Yet such social elevation belies Charles's more humble roots. Barnum's 'The Art of Money-Getting' recounts a story of the Duke of Wellington, on their first audience with Queen Victoria, enquiring after Charles's father's profession. On hearing that Stratton senior was a 'carpenter', the Duke exclaims: '"Oh! I heard he was a gentleman"' (Barnum, 1889, p. 183). In this context, Barnum refers to this incident as an example of English snobbery towards class and employment: those occupying certain professions can never be understood as 'gentlemen'. However, it is the case that Charles's career afforded his parents Sherwood and Cynthia Stratton access to money – and the attendant trappings of wealth – that their respective employments as carpenter and part-time cleaner could not have generated. As Eric D. Lehman's biography suggests, Charles's father and mother were considerably 'less affluent' than the other branches of the Stratton family (Lehman, 2013, p. 11). Both Sherwood and Cynthia accompanied their son and Barnum for much of Charles's early years of touring, and Saxon's biography of Barnum recounts how the Strattons were made full partners of the showman at the beginning of 1845. The amount of money that the family could make as a result of Charles's exhibition is an obvious – albeit cynical – answer to why his parents so readily agreed to their young son's entrance into the world of show business, and arguably this is not so far removed from the norm that working-class boys might need to undertake some form of paid work to contribute towards their family's income (Illick, 2002, p. 79). But, despite Barnum's generally gregarious – if comical – representation of the Strattons in his autobiographies, Saxon offers letters written during Barnum's association with Charles's parents which refer to them as 'brutes', and casts them in the role as 'vulgar, ignorant, common people' (Saxon, 1989, pp. 140–41). Put simply, I suggest that Barnum's recognition of the Stratton's 'lower' class status might have served as some degree of justification for his employment of their young child, smoothing the way for making the boy an adult before his time in a variety of ways.

Acting one's age?: *Hop O' My Thumb*

The motif of 'General Tom Thumb' as a particularly precocious child is very apparent in his characterisation in the play, *Hop O' My Thumb*. This play was written by Albert Smith, a good friend of Barnum's, in 1846, and was performed by Stratton for British audiences when he was seven years old (Chemers, 2008, p. 35–36). The published text's frontispiece states that it was written 'expressly for Tom Thumb', and so it can be understood as part of the discursive web which constructed Charles's persona as a performer. The play's subtitle – *A Romance of Nursery History* – indicates that the content would be suitable for a child audience, and the plot does feature nursery-tale-esque scenarios involving woodland fairies and ogres. However, the detail of 'Hop's' exploits in the play invoke the sexualised frame of reference for thinking about 'dwarf' sexuality which I detailed above. Margery and Solomon, a young married couple living next door to Hop's family, come calling to complain about Tom's disruptive behaviour:

> Sol.: He steals into my farm and drinks the milk,
> Marg.: Unrounds my reels, and tangles all my silk,
> And two nights since – confound his sleepy head –
> I actually found him in my bed!
> Sol.: Yes, think of that; it really is too much.
> I'm her young man; and will behave as such.
> Brid.: But, Margery, so proper and so steady
> Knows what to do
> Sol.: (angrily) She knows too much already.
> (Smith, 1846, p. 7)

The motif of creeping into other people's beds is a feature of the fairy tale – Goldilocks's housebreaking springs initially to mind – and Margery suggests that Hop's appearance in her bed is due to 'sleepiness' rather than any other activities. However, Solomon's jealous position as cuckold is transparent in his comment in two ways: he should be the one 'behaving' in this way as her lover, and also that his current anger is therefore justifiable 'behaviour'. Bridget, Hop's mother, might defend Margery's 'properness' (or, put another way, her faithfulness), but Solomon's concluding remark suggests her sexual knowingness, presumably at the hands of Tom. Hop's own retort to these accusations is to pop out of the 'salt box' and sing a version of 'Yankie Doodle':

> Yankie doodle is my name,
> America my nation,
> In ladies hearts I raise a flame
> Of general admiration [...]
> I love to kiss their pretty lips,
> As sweet as sugar candy.
> (Smith, 1846, p. 7)

To compare 'ladies' lips to 'sugar candy' suggests conspicuous – though childish – consumption. 'Hop' is a childish prankster and seductive trickster, embodying the transgressive pleasures of 'dwarf' identity.

Interestingly, 'Hop's' choice of song firmly locates 'General Tom Thumb' as a 'true' American, seemingly divested of his prior 'exoticism' at the hands of Barnum. Yet racial issues do make an appearance in the text of the play, albeit briefly: in one of the numerous song-and-dance interludes, Hop requests that the orchestra 'just play a nigger air' and the stage directions describe him as performing a 'nigger dance' (Smith, 1846, p. 10). Such casual racism bears an unpleasant relationship to one of Barnum's anecdotes published in the *New York Atlas* on 21 July 1844. Barnum explains that a 'negro' had attended one of Charles's performances in London:

> I made General Tom Thumb sing all the 'nigger songs' that he could think of [...] I then asked the General what the negroes called him when he travelled south. 'They called me little massa,' replied the General, 'and they always took their hats off, too.' The amalgamating darkey did not like this allusion [...] The General enjoyed the joke and frequently pointed his finger at the negro, much to the discomfiture of 'de colored gemman'.
>
> (Cited in Saxon, 1989, p. 84)

Barnum's egregious use of racist language does not sit comfortably with his well-publicised abolitionist values,[13] and Charles's collusion with this derision of a black audience member (including the story of how he was treated as a superior by black Americans living in the South) is perceived by Eric D. Lehman as a 'sad commentary on learned behaviour [...] disappointing and distasteful' (Lehman, 2013, p. 34). Lehman's response is pertinent and justifiable, but there is a further facet to this, for we should note Barnum's terminology: 'I *made*' (my emphasis). This frames Charles as a coerced worker, not necessarily acting under his own volition. While it is not appropriate to draw a direct parallel between the respective situation of Charles Stratton and enslaved people, especially considering the power inequalities which 'Tom Thumb' so gladly recounts in the above quotation, it does suggest some degree of connection. It is easy to interpret Stratton's performance of a 'nigger dance' in *Hop O' My Thumb* and the London show which Barnum describes as simply in the tradition of black-face minstrelsy, perpetuating derogatory stereotypes of race.[14] From another perspective, although highly controversial, blackface minstrelsy might also demonstrate the performativity of racial identity.[15] Stratton's ability to perform racially inscribed songs and dances might, albeit inadvertently, underscore his physical 'otherness' due to his unusual appearance, but it also adds a further context to the more sexually predatory aspects of his role in *Hop O' My Thumb*. Not only does he ensconce himself in Margery's bed, but he also kisses a 'washerwoman', leading to her fleeing the stage, a retreat which suggests that this is an unwelcome advance. Towards the end of the play, when the ogre has been vanquished and his family are imprisoned, Hop 'selects the smallest of the Ogre's children' to be his 'wife' (Smith, 1846, p. 24). There is no mention of the small 'wife's' consent, and she does not speak. Hop is thus constructed as a sexual adventurer with overtones of sexual aggression: a threat to all women he might encounter, which is disturbingly reminiscent of racist ideologies of the sexual threat of black men, alongside the aforementioned representation of dwarfism and lasciviousness.[16]

Despite some of the more sinister subtexts of the play, the overall effect is framed as comic. Hop's final speech is addressed to the audience:

> Although at night I may seem no great catch,
> I hope, kind friends, that you approve the match;
> Without your smiles and hands no luck can come
> To your devoted General, TOM THUMB.
>
> (Smith, 1846, p. 24)

This conclusion reveals the layers of performance involved in the play: Hop is played by Tom Thumb, who is played by Charles Stratton. And, in contrast to the rambunctious posturing of Hop, this version of Tom Thumb seems slightly more humble and self-conscious. His rampant sexuality is deflated: to be 'no great catch' in the context of the 'night' might allude to sexual impotency, a notable reference point with regards to Gould and Pyle's questioning of the ability of men with dwarfism to have children, and their scathing comments on Stratton's lack of physical appeal. 'Tom Thumb' is revealed as eager to please, desirous only of audience approval. Poignantly, this formulation foreshadows the neo-Victorian version of Stratton outlined in Carlson's novel, where Maud fears that the boy will look to audiences for 'all types of sustenance' (Carlson, 2011, p. 148). While presumably unintentional, Smith's conclusion gives us a brief glimpse into the potential vulnerability of Stratton's 'Tom Thumb' persona, the strange synthesis of power relationships and imbalances that has shaped Charles's life along the lines of disability, sexuality, and even race.

A *Sketch of the Life* of little men and women

As with the majority of other performers discussed in this book, a 'biography' of Charles and Lavinia was published in the genre of the 'true life story' pamphlet. Anonymously written, *Sketch Of The Life, Personal Appearance, Character And Manners Of Charles S. Stratton, The Man In Miniature, Known As General Tom Thumb, And His Wife, Lavinia Warren Stratton* was issued in 1863, giving an overview of the early careers of both performers with particular focus upon their celebrated wedding. Charles is represented as a darling of European nobility in his youth, but there is also an emphasis on his masculine maturity now that his career has been established: he 'attends his comfortable estate', is a successful landlord, and 'transacts all of his own businesses, like other men' (*Sketch*, 1863, para. 4). While his size makes him exceptional, his wealth and business acumen ensure his respectability and 'normality' in comparison to his male peers. He also engages in suitably masculine pursuits, such as yachting, horse-riding, and shooting (*Sketch*, 1863, para. 4). In the vein of the multi-voiced format of the genre, the pamphlet includes an extract from an article about 'The General' in the *Bridgeport Standard*, published in October 1862:

> Although General Tom Thumb has always lead a life of excitement, and twice, after retiring to public life, has felt compelled to exhibit himself again, to keep off the ennui, he remarked to the writer of this article last week, while quietly twirling his elegant little moustache, of which he seems quite proud, that he hoped one of these days to

> get married, 'in which event,' he added, with a roguish look, 'I guess that the cares of a family, added to my ordinary duties, will give me enough to occupy my attention, and prevent the necessity of again seeking the excitement of a traveling exhibition!'
>
> (*Sketch*, 1863, para. 5)

Importantly, Charles's career as a performer is constructed as being a pursuit for his own entertainment, not for financial gain: the emphasis is thus on his autonomy, agency, but also adventurous spirit. And this lust for 'excitement' hints at sexual interests as well. The 'excitement' of having a family is presumably not the 'cares' of domesticity, but the pleasures of a wife. The reference to his facial hair seems to allude to sexual maturity, but we should note that the 'littleness' of his moustache is also highlighted: the threat of 'dwarfish' impotency is still present, combined with the sense that this is, after all, perhaps just a 'little' boy pretending to be a man.

The pamphlet is also a useful reference point for exploring the nineteenth-century construction of Lavinia's public persona. She, like Charles, is depicted as a synthesis of childish dimensions, yet mature sensibilities: 'Although she has only the stature of a small child, she has the sense of a woman' (*Sketch*, 1863, para. 8). This 'womanly' sense manifests itself in feminine accomplishments: she can 'sew, knit, cook, and do all manner of housework', taught by her mother, is an excellent conversationalist, and is beautiful and refined (*Sketch*, 1863, para. 8) After giving Lavinia's measurements of height and weight, the reader is directly addressed by the pamphlet's narrative voice:

> The reader may choose from his lady acquaintances a sparkling woman, with dark hair and black eyes, symmetrical figure and soft voice, and, in his imagination, reduce her to the dimensions above named, leaving her mental and moral faculties fully expanded, and he will have an idea of this charming little woman; or, he may reverse the picture, and select a child of perfect mold, with a finely-arched brow, dimpled cheeks, large lustrous eyes, a nicely-chiseled mouth, a rich harvest of hair, and suddenly endow her with all the attributes and accomplishments of womanhood – a heart to love, a head to contrive, and a hand to execute.
>
> (*Sketch*, 1863, para. 8)

The reader is conspicuously gendered here: it is men who might be interested in imagining Lavinia. While the reader is assured of Lavinia's 'moral faculties', the description of 'selecting' a child to imbue with mature female qualities is disconcerting, to say the least, particularly as it is 'loving' that might be one of the benefits of such a 'charming little woman'. Interestingly, however, it is not Lavinia herself that might be an active sexual subject; there is no hint of her making bawdy, suggestive comments as in the characterisation of Charles, which is reminiscent of Adelson's earlier remark on the relative dearth of sexualised representations of women with dwarfism. Instead, it is left to the male reader's own agency to envisage the erotic potential of Lavinia, reiterating the traditional gendering of passivity with regards to women's sexuality.[17]

Much of the pamphlet is devoted to the wedding of Charles and Lavinia, which took place on 10 February 1863, in New York. As numerous commentators have explored, this was a glittering, enormously well-publicised event, which occupied the attention of the national press and reiterated Barnum's role as a master showman, and 'Tom Thumb's' celebrity status.[18] Lori Merish's excellent analysis of the wedding argues that the spectacle 'delighted its viewers because it *looked like children imitating adults*, thus assimilating the "freak" into a familial and familiar structure of domination and hierarchy [...] Domesticating the Otherness of little people entailed a curtailment of desire, especially sexual desire' (Merish, 1996, pp. 194–95). In terms of the 'curtailment' of sexual desire, she cites the pamphlet's reference to the newlyweds as '"smiling twins", as siblings rather than mates' (Merish, 1996, p. 195). While this conceptualisation of the couple does domesticate their relationship, which might hint towards asexuality, it also could be interpreted as alluding to incest, hinting at some underlying 'abnormality' or perversion in the otherwise heteronormative ritual. In many ways, the pamphlet's description of the wedding serves to consolidate the gendered – and sexual – roles that the couple have already been allotted: 'the world renowned General' enters the church with 'the fair one upon his arm, who was about to barter her maiden liberty' (*Sketch*, 1863, para. 35). This turn of phrase reminds the reader of Lavinia's virtue and respectability: she is a good, middle-class woman, who is a 'maiden' before her wedding day.[19] And lest we forget the sexual prowess of the General, at the conclusion of the ceremony he 'saluted his wife with an honest kiss, the last of nearly three million pressed in public upon the lips of his lady admirers' (*Sketch*, 1863, para. 37): evidently chastity is not a requisite for a man prior to his wedding day, regardless of his height. The couple are united, however, in their ability to perform their respective roles for the entertainment of an audience:

Stratton's multitude of kisses have seemingly only been in the 'public' domain, and Lavinia is 'bartering' her virginity – put another way, selling herself – for this spectacle. Again, there are more adult concerns underpinning this child-like spectacle. Finally, the pamphlet does make reference to the potential for consummation of the marriage. The General regales the crowd with a speech expressing his thanks for their support and enthusiasm, and concludes: 'But ladies and gentlemen, a little woman in the adjoining apartment is very anxious to see me, and I must, therefore, make this speech, like myself – short' (*Sketch*, 1863, para. 91). Stratton's remarks might be construed as self-aggrandising; he is so attractive to his wife that she cannot wait for him. Intriguingly, however, it also suggests that Lavinia is sexually demanding, and has the ability to exercise this control over her new spouse, moving him away from the public sphere which has been his sole domain to meet her desires. As Merish argues, the couple are repeatedly represented as both children and adults simultaneously: the 'Tom Thumb Wedding' was to become 'a ritual performance among children', with a volume about the wedding published in 1898 'as part of the series Baker's Entertainments for Children' (Merish, 1996, p. 191). At the same time, the pamphlet speculates on the ensuing parenthood of this ostensibly child-like couple, their potential to be 'the inventors of a small race of humanity' (*Sketch*, 1863, para. 113). The discourses of innocence and experience entwine in their representation.

Writing back to Barnum? Sylvester Bleeker, and Lavinia's Autobiography

Sylvester Bleeker, a friend and former colleague of Barnum's, oversaw the management of Charles and Lavinia in the latter stages of their career together, and, with the inclusion of Lavinia's sister, Minnie, and George Washington Morrison Nutt (billed as 'Commodore Nutt'), formed The Tom Thumb Company. On Barnum's suggestion, this group embarked upon a world tour between 1869–72, and Bleeker recorded his reminisces of this period in his book, *General Tom Thumb's Three Year Tour Around the World* (1872). Unlike the depiction of Charles as a man of action in the *Sketch* pamphlet, there is a tendency for Bleeker to depict both Stratton and Nutt as rather cowardly, particularly in comparison to the more robust and sensible Lavinia and Minnie. For instance, during the North American part of the tour the Company encounter some 'Indians'. Bleeker invites Stratton to visit them, yet he seems reluctant until chivvied by his wife: '"Why, General, *I* wouldn't be afraid to go, and I am a WOMAN. If I were a MAN, I would go in a moment"' (Bleeker, 1872, p. 12; original emphasis). Even the invocation of normative gender expectations is not enough to empower 'the General', for on the approach he exclaims '"Let's go back!" [...] giving my coat-shirt a pull that almost separated it from the waist, and hastily retreating behind me' (Bleeker, 1872, p. 12). Furthermore, during the scenario of a stagecoach containing the sisters and Bleeker's wife veering out of control, 'The General and Commodore covered their ears, ran into the inn, and closed the door to shut out the clattering sound' (Bleeker, 1872, p. 40). Upon rescue, neither Lavinia nor Minnie are phased: Lavinia only expresses concern for her parents if they were to hear of her death, and Minnie declaring '"I am not to be killed so easily"' (Bleeker, 1872, p. 41). Bleeker takes this opportunity to articulate his admiration for the 'ladies under my charge' in the various perilous situations they have encountered over the years: 'With them there has been no excitement, no screaming to increase the terror of those around them, and distract the efforts of those able to assist them, but always coolly looking forward to results and watching to take advantage of every favouring circumstance' (Bleeker, 1872, p. 41). Importantly, Bleeker represents the Warren sisters as defying the gendered expectations of their age; not only are they not given to hysterical reactions, they are positively calculating in their ability to turn situations to their advantage. This streak of canniness will become a significant theme in neo-Victorian versions of Lavinia and Minnie. In contrast, 'the General' is not so much a trickster, but consistently the butt of the joke, underscoring the bathos of his masculine styling.

Bleeker also relates the story of the Company's visit to Australia, and whilst in Sydney they attend a fancy dress ball given in honour of the Duke of Edinburgh. Minnie is costumed as Little Red Riding Hood, and attracts the attention of the Duke, who 'was particularly attentive'. In Bleeker's terms: 'It was the gossip for many days after, amongst the envious ones, that his Royal Highness had kissed that "mite of a thing". When I asked Minnie as to the truth of the report, her reply was "I never kiss and tell"' (Bleeker, 1872, p. 111). Considering the emphasis placed on Charles's propensity for kissing women in his heyday, we see a gendered role reversal take place. In fact, for Bleeker it is Minnie that is more inclined to fulfil the 'trickster' role, perhaps subverting gendered expectations, but not necessarily transcending the motif of people with dwarfism as transgressive, sexualised figures. Of course, the details of Minnie's liaison are kept coyly hidden, and it is neo-Victorian reimaginings of this incident that will 'tell' the details of her sexuality.

Bleeker's account of this tour bears an interesting relationship to the final text which has its origins in the final nineteenth-century text that I wish to discuss in this chapter: *The Autobiography of Mrs. Tom Thumb*, written by Lavinia under her later married name of Countess M. Lavinia Magri. Although this volume was only published in 1979, A. H. Saxon, who introduces and edits the text, suggests that it began to be written 'around the turn of the century' (Saxon, 1979, p. 12). Generally speaking, commentators who have paid attention to Lavinia's *Autobiography* have tended to bemoan its inadequacies: Melanie Benjamin's 'Author's Note' to her novel of the same name as the *Autobiography* complains that 'there is so much missing from all of these pages!', with the omission of the details of Minnie's death, the baby hoax, and 'her feelings [...] She never shares any disappointments, any frustrations about her size, her physical discomforts' (Benjamin, 2011, pp. 418–19). Saxon's introduction to the *Autobiography* raises comparable gripes, and both highlight Lavinia's substantial borrowings from other published sources: large sections of the text are almost exact reproductions of passages about Lavinia and Charles in Barnum's autobiography, and Bleeker's *Three Year Tour* (Saxon, 1979, pp. 13–14; Benjamin, 2011, p. 419). In summary, then, there is justification for considering the text as repetitive and self-censoring (and, of course, the latter trait provides fertile space for neo-Victorian re-memberings). However, I also want to make a claim for Lavinia's *Autobiography* as being more sophisticated with her sources than she has previously been given credit. For example, she quotes a paragraph from Barnum's autobiography about their first meeting, yet changes the first sentence from his 'In 1862 I heard of an extraordinary dwarf girl' (Saxon, 1979, p. 183) to 'In 1862 I heard of an extraordinary little woman' (Magri, 1979, p. 49). This alteration signifies in several ways: she does not wish to be solely defined by her physical difference, despite its importance for her career; furthermore, she does not wish to be infantilised – she is a 'woman', not a 'girl'. This latter point has compelling consequences in terms of distinguishing her career from that of her first husband, for she is making a mature, informed decision when embarking upon management by Barnum in contrast to Charles's potential coercion as a child. Cast in this light, Lavinia's 'borrowings' from prior sources can be understood as a subversive 'writing back' to the men who have scripted her life, a strategy of narrative manipulation which bears a striking resemblances to the neo-Victorian mode of transformation via repetition.[20]

Another aspect of Lavinia's narrative which might strike a chord with neo-Victorian readers is her assessment of Charles's treatment as a child performer. Offering an anecdote which emphasises Charles's enthusiasm for playing with children, she recounts her husband's explanation for this:

> 'Vinie,' he'd say, 'I like to watch them play. You know I never had any childhood, any boy-life.' And it somehow seemed pathetic to realize its truth. Mr. Barnum took him when only four years old, and from that time he was trained to speak and act like a man. He had, as he said, no childhood, and as he developed into manhood the sense of this loss made him particularly tender of children. Right here it may be said that for some the bad habits of which General Tom Thumb was blamed, the conditions of his daily life should be counted as extenuation. He was taught to take wine at dinner when only five, to smoke at seven and 'chew' at nine. This was a part of the education which supposably fitted him to fill the role he was expected to play.
> (Magri, 1979, pp. 115–16)

This passage offers an important echo of Queen Victoria's assessment of the vulnerability of Charles as a child performer. Lavinia's invocation of the concept of 'loss' in terms of Charles's interrupted childhood, which has in turn affected his development and personality as an adult suggests that he might be a somewhat damaged individual. It alludes to sadness, perhaps even trauma, particularly considering that she offers this detail as 'extenuation' for some of Charles's 'bad habits' as an adult. The notion of a young child being 'taught' to drink wine and smoke and chew tobacco is tantamount to abuse at the hands of Barnum. The compulsion for Charles to perform masculinity has been dictated by the conventions of how boys/men with dwarfism should appear for public consumption, and he has been corrupted by this. As my analysis of Charles's representation in *Hop O' My Thumb* and *Sketch* has demonstrated, the other aspect of appearing 'manly' before his time has been to be sexualised: although Lavinia does not make reference to this 'part of his education', it also chimes with her impression of his 'loss' of innocence.

If Charles might be understood as an abused child, his and Lavinia's participation in one of Barnum's 'humbugs' suggests that the couple were not wholly blameless in the use of children by the industry of the freak show. As part of Barnum's ongoing management of the public profile of their married lives, it was announced in 1864 that Lavinia had given birth to a child, and the 'Tom Thumb baby' was photographed with her parents by Matthew Brady (Lehman, 2013, p. 145). The details of this are not discussed in Lavinia's autobiography, but in a later interview published in 1901 after the deaths of Charles and Barnum, she reveals that the baby – actually a boy – came from a foundling hospital. However, the couple were concerned about the child's rapid growth:

> At the age of four years he was taller than his father [...] We appealed to Mr Barnum. He agreed with us. He thought our baby should not grow. Thus we exhibited English babies in England, French babies in France, and German babies in Germany. It was – they were – a great success.
>
> (Cited in Saxon, 1989, p. 210)

She does not express any further opinion on this ruse other than 'Mr Barnum was a great man' (cited in Saxon, 1989, p. 210). There are some troubling issues at work behind this glib account: for a child to be taken from a foundling hospital suggests their exploitation of abandoned and impoverished infants for their own financial gain. This is poignant, considering the reasonable presumption that it was the Stratton's own need for money that led to Charles's exhibition in the first place. That this pattern was replicated, at the couple's request, all over Europe compounds this use (abuse?) of vulnerable children. No record remains of what happened to this succession of 'Tom Thumb' babies, or of Charles's opinion – especially in the light of his own interrupted childhood – on this scheme. In summary, what this demonstrates is the ease with which the exploited child might become an exploiting adult, perpetuating a cycle which might be equated to abuse. Charles and Lavinia fulfil the role of 'tricksters', duping the gullible public, and this is couched in terms of physical size: ironically, the boundaries of 'normal' height become reconfigured, and an average child becomes too big in the context of their dwarfism, made freakish, as Lavinia states that 'our friends predicted that our son would be a giant'.[21] While such terminology might serve to justify and 'normalize' their own appearance, it does little to engage with other forms of social inequality – namely, the power relations of class, and between adults and children – that mark this event in their lives. In summary, the nineteenth-century textual representations of Charles and Lavinia discussed in this chapter have charted a series of shifting power relationships dealing with matters of gender, sexuality, class, and race. And it is the vexed boundary between childhood and adulthood in relation to discourses dwarfism which unites these concerns. I want to turn now to two neo-Victorian novels which centre on the lives of Charles and

Lavinia to explore the ways in which issues of disability, childhood and parenthood are re-membered in twenty-first-century texts.

Lost childhoods: Jane Sullivan's *Little People*

Jane Sullivan's novel *Little People* (2011) is set against the backdrop of the 'Tom Thumb Company's' tour, accompanied by the Bleekers, of Australia in 1870. It tells the story of Mary Ann, a governess who becomes pregnant by her employer. While contemplating suicide, she actually saves the life of Charles Stratton, who has fallen into the river. Mary Ann is taken in by the troupe, and employed as a dresser by Lavinia and her sister Minnie. Her description of Lavinia on their first meeting invites the reader to 'imagine' this 'society beauty' in a comparable way to the *Sketch* pamphlet discussed above. However, she continues: 'Now imagine she is just a fraction less perfect: cheeks a little too round and babylike. Now imagine she sips from the magic bottle labelled *Eat Me*, and she shrinks down, still in perfect proportion' (Sullivan, 2011, p. 12). Despite her beauty, Lavinia is still depicted as slightly aesthetically flawed, and it is notable that these imperfections become apparent with regards to the characteristic which might make her more 'babylike'. In contrast to the quasi-paedophilic framing of Lavinia in *Sketch*, to be child-like is not a marker of sexual attractiveness from the perspective of our narrator. Moreover, there is a hint of the dangers of sexualizing children in the reference to Lewis Carroll's *Alice in Wonderland* (1865) and the potion that the protagonist drinks to alter her size. For a neo-Victorian readership, the motif of Alice connotes the potential for inappropriate desire towards 'little people',[22] foreshadowing the theme of child abuse that will develop later in the novel.

Mary's first formal meeting with Charles judges him as a 'concentrat[ion] of masculinity' (Sullivan, 2011, p. 16), giving off a 'comfortable man scent of brandy and cigars' (Sullivan, 2011, p. 18). She thus encounters him as the polished specimen of manliness that he would become in his adult life, and is seemingly impressed by his bearing and composure. Nevertheless, she has encountered Stratton previously, in her rescue of him from the river: 'I had never seen any kind of little person, but I had touched one, as we struggled by the Yarra Yarra, and nausea rose when my fingers recalled the fishy wet skin. I thought of Mr Quilp the dwarf in Mr Dickens's book, with his hook nose and villain's smile' (Sullivan, 2011, pp. 11–12). To 'touch' a 'little person' might sound sexualised, yet rather than desire, Mary Ann feels a sense of repulsion; Charles is depicted as abject, not-quite-human on the one hand, or as villainous and ugly on the other. It is a textual representation of dwarfism – the cruel and grotesque Mr Quilp from Charles Dickens's *The Old Curiosity Shop* – which has shaped her prejudices, which makes an important point about the influence of fictional construction upon perceptions of physical difference or disability. Even though Mary Ann's initial feelings of disgust are challenged by Charles's masculinity, her discomfort resurfaces as she watches his reaction to a bad review of his latest performance in a local newspaper:

> He was enclosed in nothing but a tight garment like an acrobat's costume, the colour of cooked salmon flesh, that covered him from neck to wrists to ankles and glittered over the swell of his breast and paunch. I kept my eyes averted from his crotch. As we women stood transfixed, he stepped on to the mirror like a brave skater treading the ice. He glided slowly from one pose to another, pausing, staring constantly at the mirror beneath his feet. Muscles flexed, legs bent, arms swung, fat trembled. I wanted to laugh, then to vomit [...] All I could think of was a raw sausage dancing on a skillet.
>
> (Sullivan, 2011, p. 72)

Charles's clothing here reflects his actual garb when performing spectacles of masculinity as a young boy in his initial employment with Barnum,[23] but the description of his flabby, ageing body is a gross parody of the purported handsomeness and allure of the original 'Tom Thumb'. The colour of the suit alludes to the 'fishiness' of Charles in Mary Ann's rescue of him from the river, and furthermore, what we are forced to witness along with the assembled women (Mary Ann, Julia Bleeker, and Lavinia) is a vision of dwarf masculinity in crisis. For Mary Ann's perception of Charles is feminizing: his fatness has given him breasts, and she avoids acknowledging the signifier of his masculine sexuality by looking away from his 'crotch'. The image of 'a raw sausage dancing' might be considered phallic, but it is also an image of something to be consumed: put another way, perhaps Charles is being eaten away at by his audiences. He is comedic, but also nauseating, the realisation of Gould and Pyle's delineation of Stratton as 'anything but inviting' (Gould and Pyle, 1898, p. 342). We learn subsequently that this is 'how Mr Barnum used to teach him when he was a tiny boy' (Sullivan, 2011, p. 74), and Mary Ann concludes that 'he had looked like a bloated baby' (p. 75). He has regressed to infantile posturing, the training of his youth, to shore up his fading stardom.

Despite the negative chain of association which Mary Ann constructs in which dwarfism is equated with ugliness and childishness, the novel does offer a more sympathetic retelling of Charles's story in some ways. Mary Ann's observations are interspersed with first-person narratives from 'the little people', and in this we hear from 'Charlie Stratton':

> I am what the General used to be. The General is thirty-two years and three months old; he's pulling himself together, he's going onstage to astound the Antipodeans with his Napoleon. I'm four years old and I'm not going anywhere. I have been four for a long time. You can't see me, can you? [...] I'm good at hiding [...] What happened was the General came. He strutted in and he sat down, plonk, with his chest out and belly up and legs spread. He filled up all the space where I used to be [...] he was fully grown. He smoked cigars and drank wine and walked with a swagger and a stick with a lion's-head handle and a man-about-town way of wearing his hat any saying howdy-do to the ladies. His waistcoat held a manly chest and a thumping great heart and his breeches held I don't know what, but it something mighty important. He knew everything and was afraid of nothing. Did he know about me, then? I cannot tell.
>
> (Sullivan, 2011, pp. 38–39)

Charles is presented as having a split personality: due to his induction into the world of performing masculinity at such a young age, the child has become in some way stuck within the psyche of the adult Stratton. The process by which this has occurred is presented as traumatic: 'Charlie' explains how Barnum forced him to drink wine and smoke cigars even as it made the child sick, and despite the child's protestations that 'I'm not a man, Mr Barnum', Barnum laughs and responds with '"You want to grow up, don't you? All boys want to grow up"' (Sullivan, 2011, p. 40). Charles's narrative therefore depicts the impairment that the freak show construction of identity can enact upon a child. The mystery of what might be in the General's trousers presents a child-like confusion about sexual matters which draws a stark contrast with the eroticised and sexually potent construction of the General in nineteenth-century versions of Stratton, and Charlie's uncertainty about whether the General might know of his presence casts doubt on the maturity of the adult Charles and speaks of repression. Lavinia's sense that her husband has been damaged by his lack of childhood, as articulated in her autobiography, is thus realised by *Little People* in a twenty-first-century vocabulary of childhood abuse and trauma.

This has a generic significance for neo-Victorian representations of childhood beyond the specifics of Charles Stratton's situation. As Anne Morey and Claudia Nelson have pointed out, from the perspective of twenty-first-century understandings of childhood care: 'the Victorian period [...] is ostensibly a moment of abjection for children, who are controlled, worked, exploited, checked, trained, restrained' (Morey and Nelson, 2012, p. 4). In Marie-Luise Kohlke's terms, neo-Victorianism responds to this perception of the nineteenth century by representing childhoods that are traumatic, 'scarred by violence, exploitation, emotional and/or sexual abuse' (Kohlke, 2011, p. 135). In addition, she identifies that neo-Victorian childhoods both accentuate and capitalise upon 'the outrage of the depicted violations' (Kohlke, 2011, p. 135). Sullivan's depiction of Charles Stratton's experience of his early years as a performer as traumatic and highly damaging to his development as an adult does adhere to these expectations. Due to the absence of Stratton's personal opinion of his early career from the historical record, and the dubious circumstances of his management by Barnum, it is almost irresistible to fill these gaps with imagining various forms of abuse and oppression. Furthermore, the novel also perpetuates Kohlke's observation on neo-Victorianism's 'emphasis on the long-term after-effects of childhood trauma [which] effects an inadvertent re-marginalisation of its fictional children to a state of passive latency and non-agency, and a re-silencing of the child's voice purportedly being recuperated' (Kohlke, 2011, p. 145). While the novel does accord 'Charlie' a narrative voice, the latent child in Stratton has no opportunity to influence the events of the novel, only record his suppression in the General's psyche.

His childhood experiences have left Charles apparently confused and immature about sexual matters, indicated by his naïve assumptions about how the child that Mary Ann is carrying might be his own. As Mary Ann's pregnancy begins to show, Stratton becomes convinced that through some pseudo-scientific process of conception he impregnated Mary Ann as she became entangled with him in the water (Sullivan, 2011, pp. 54–55). As I shall explain in further detail below, Lavinia and Charles are unable to have children and so come to believe that this baby will be truly tiny enough to become their child permanently, unlike the prop infants who must be disposed of when they begin to grow. A pianist with the group, Franz Richardson, is seemingly in love with Mary Ann, and warns her of the couple's tendency to discard 'Tom Thumb babies' who grow too big: 'So many orphanages, foundling homes, baby farms [...] They disappeared. No one has ever mentioned them again. It was because they grew too big' (Sullivan,

2011, p. 174). Slightly more information is given in Franz's revelation than in Lavinia's 1901 interview, and the mention of typical signifiers of Victorian child exploitation – orphanages, baby farms – further casts Charles and Lavinia in the role of abusive villains. Their 'disappearing' is ominous, alluding to abandonment or even worse. On learning this information, Mary Ann reflects on why she does not ask more questions on her arrangement with the couple: 'But I was so grateful to be housed and fed and given purpose and future. Above all, to the spared disgrace and destitution. And I had so little power – or so I thought' (Sullivan, 2011, pp. 49–50). Although not made explicit in the novel, Mary Ann's commentary forms a pertinent parallel with the situation of many of the freak show performers discussed in this book: they do not feel that there is any other option, and so are not always able to achieve the 'best possible arrangement' for themselves. Considering Charles's own experiences, the exploited child has becomes the exploiting adult of both infants and their working-class mothers in turn.

Mary Ann and Richardson elope to rescue her unborn child from future exploitation and ultimate disposal. However, Richardson is actually a paedophile, and also working for Dr Musgrave, a collector of human oddities who wants to keep the 'miniature' child preserved in his private collection. She discovers a letter from the doctor to Franz: '*About four years old, I think, would be the perfect age. Secure it for me and I will build it a glass Iranistan, a beautiful grotto*' (Sullivan, 2011, p. 281; original emphasis). 'Iranistan' was the name of P. T. Barnum's elaborate home, and the novel thus features a crazed doctor figure who is aligned with the freak show, but, in the vein of Cuvier in Chapter 1 is more interested in the ultimate objectification of post-mortem exhibition. Furthermore, the age at which the child will become Musgrave's possession links it to Charles and it is telling that Mary Ann begins to call her 'bump' Thomas, despite knowing full well that it is not Stratton's child. When the female child is born – and they are rescued from the clutches of Richardson and Musgrave – she decides to call her Alice after 'the adventurous little girl in the book' (Sullivan, 2011, p. 314). In the context of the baby's rescue from the care of a paedophile and fate of being a freakish medical specimen, this allusion to Alice in Wonderland is hugely significant. She circumvents the fate of 'General Tom Thumb', the abused, disturbed male child, and reappropriates the name Alice as an expression of female agency rather than the potential victim of an older man with inappropriate desires. And we are reminded, of course, of Mary Ann's initial comparison of Lavinia to a shrinking Alice. In comparison to the perversions of Richardson and Musgrave, Lavinia's treatment of children seems rather less monstrous and her persona might even be a source of inspiration.

It is in this spirit that the novel tells the story of an alternative version of Lavinia and Charles's relationship, which borrows from nineteenth-century stereotypes of dwarfism, sexuality, and parenthood even as they are redressed and complicated. Lavinia's narrative tells us that she has made a conscious decision not to have children due to warnings from her mother that childbirth for a woman of her size would be fatal. Lavinia's immediate response is to scoff at her mother's warnings:

> But I began to dream of formless, heaving things. Mother's words had planted a cold blue embryo in my womb. On the eve of my marriage, I had a little talk with Charlie, and we came to our arrangement [...] I try not to think about babies, even when they sit in my lap. I imagine they are clockwork creatures you might wind up in Mr Barnum's museum. It's easier that way.
>
> (Sullivan, 2011, p. 28)

This passage furnishes the reader with an explanation as to why the 'baby hoax' is not discussed in the historical Lavinia's autobiography: thoughts of maternity are something to be repressed for 'little' women. The image of children being like 'creatures' to be manipulated provides a poignant echo of Charles's own childhood manipulation at the hands of Barnum. Lavinia might be somewhat cold in her dealings with children, but this is for her own emotional and physical protection: she cannot run the risk of maternal feelings or experiences.

The details of Lavinia's 'arrangement' with her husband become clearer in a conversation between Lavinia and Mary Ann:

> 'I had a talk with my husband before our wedding day [...] He is an admirable man, has always respected my wishes. As for his wishes.... [...] Forgive my indelicacy, but you are – were – a married woman, so I can speak to you [...] He taught me how to give him oral satisfaction. It is not hard, and he never seems to tire of it.' I stopped my gasp just in time. Charlie was indeed admirable: I could not imagine how such a virile soul would ever be content with kissing.
>
> (Sullivan, 2011, p. 209)

Although the reader has previously assumed that Charles is sexually naïve, we discover here that the couple do manage a sex life, engaging in fellatio rather than procreative sex. Comically, however, Mary Ann is exposed as the truly naïve character: she misses the allusion and, deluded by the tales of 'General Tom Thumb's' predilection for 'kissing' his female admirers, she believes that this is all Lavinia can imagine as well. Put another way, it reveals Mary Ann's own problematic assumptions about Lavinia's immature, child-like sexuality.

A further dimension to the representation of sexuality in *Little People* is the characterisation of Minnie Warren. Elucidating the hints at her interest in men in Bleeker's text, she is depicted as a sexual agent from a young age. In her part of the narrative, she describes how she 'squeezed my thighs together. I had done this ever since I was a child. First, it was comforting, and then, it was invigorating. So invigorating, I wanted to do it all the time, and could not understand why Mother slapped me' (Sullivan, 2011, p. 143). This depiction of the suppression of childhood sexual experimentation – a fictionalised version of Michel Foucault's masturbating Victorian child – is thought-provoking in the context of the more sensationalist portrayal of children as vulnerable to abuse elsewhere in the novel. Children – 'little people' – are not so innocent as adult society would like to suppose, and the self-exploration of sexuality is not problematic here: it is adult desires to conceal masturbation that leads to abuse (in this case physical, the 'slap' from Minnie's prudish mother). But the blurred boundary which dwarfism treads between childhood innocence and adult sexuality becomes more apparent in Minnie's adult exploits. Even Commodore Nutt, himself of restricted growth, finds Minnie's choice of costume for the fancy dress ball with the Duke of Edinburgh challenging. As in Bleeker's memoir, she is dressed as Little Red Riding Hood: 'A red dress, knee-length, like a little girl's smock. But little girls don't wear satin, nipped in at the waist and cut scandalously low. She pushed past me, eyes fixed on the Duke' (Sullivan, 2011, p. 199). However, as Jack Zipes has argued, the fairy tale version of Red Riding Hood can be understood as a parable about burgeoning sexual maturity and the dangers it might pose,[24] and so to present Minnie as simultaneously sexualised and childlike is not necessarily specific to her short stature.

Subsequently, Minnie's narrative makes her sexual agency explicit. Detailing how she flirts with men that she finds attractive, she explains: 'the usual rules for a young lady did not apply to me [...] I didn't have time to wait for a gentleman to declare himself. I had to come forward, to make discreet but firm declarations of my own' (Sullivan, 2011, p. 214). She justifies her own sexuality and refuses to fulfil the passive, feminised expectations of her era, but she perceives this boldness as necessitated by her physical size: 'I don't deceive myself that all will be well with me. I will grow old with no man, no babies. All I want is a few memories of beauty that I can hold in my heart' (Sullivan, 2011, pp. 215–16). She believes that she cannot sustain the attention of a man, as her size is more likely to attract men with sexual fetishes for 'little' women (due to either a prurient fascination with 'freakish' sexuality, or sublimated paedophilic inclinations). Her sexual conquests thus become a matter of taking her pleasures where she can but having to subject herself to perverse imaginings at the hands of her lovers, which somewhat undermines the liberatory potential of this neo-Victorian reimagining of Minnie Warren. Sullivan's novel stops short of detailing Minnie's fate, but this theme will take a central role in Melanie Benjamin's fictionalisation of the sisters' lives.

The dangers of belittlement: Melanie Benjamin's *The Autobiography of Mrs Tom Thumb*

As I suggested in my discussion of the historical Lavinia's autobiography above, Benjamin overtly positions her novel as a development of the hints and omissions which are apparent in the original *Autobiography of Mrs Tom Thumb*. However, in many ways, the text's characterisation of Lavinia, Charles, and Minnie is also indebted to Bleeker's *General Tom Thumb's Three Year Tour*. For Benjamin's Lavinia is an intelligent, courageous and determined woman. She demonstrates heightened feminist consciousness about how she is perceived as a woman of short stature, railing against the patriarchal bias of her employer's derision at her enquiries about her wages when she begins working as a school teacher (Benjamin, 2011, pp. 19–20), refusing to be confined to the domestic sphere by pursuing travel and wealth in her career as a freak show performer (Benjamin, 2011, p. 21; p. 273), and working alongside Barnum to develop her persona and orchestrate her marriage to Charles Stratton (Benjamin, 2011, pp. 197–98). In fact, in a comparable vein to Bleeker's nineteenth-century narrative, Charles is repeatedly depicted as being rather inadequate and foolish, particularly in comparison to his clever wife. He is represented as an apt pupil to Barnum's schooling in performing the ultra-manly role of General Tom Thumb, but also as a slightly pathetic, damaged character:

> I peered at him, attempting to see beyond the obviously calculated appearance – he tried too hard to resemble a gentleman of the world, with his careful grooming [...] Yet despite his earnestly grown-up manner, his brown eyes were appealingly boyish, almost bashful;

> I found myself wondering what it had been like to live in the public spotlight since the age of five. It must not have been easy for him; it was little wonder he had learned to cloak himself in practiced attitudes and rehearsed speeches!
>
> (Benjamin, 2011, pp. 183–84)

This is a neo-Victorian re-membering of Charles which is already familiar to us from Sullivan's novel: he is a child trapped within the performance of masculinity, hiding his vulnerability behind a script orchestrated by Barnum and somewhat restricted in emotional development because of this. Although Lavinia expresses some level of sympathy for him, she also explains that she never perceived Charles 'to be my intellectual equal' and experiences 'feelings of frustration' over Charles's 'immature ways' (Benjamin, 2011, p. 250). As I shall detail below, Lavinia's romantic affections are directed elsewhere, but despite occasional feelings of companionship and pride, she rarely articulates anything other than contempt and irritation towards Stratton during their lives together.

This culminates in their final interaction before Charles's death: according to Eric D. Lehman, Lavinia was visiting Sylvester Bleeker in Brooklyn, 'discussing business' at the time of her husband's demise (Lehman, 2013, p. 206), but Benjamin re-members this absence as a result of an argument between the couple. Some months earlier, they had narrowly escaped from a fire at the Newhall House in Milwaukee, Wisconsin. In Benjamin's novel, Charles has been manhandled by the fireman and 'tossed, unceremoniously, to the street', after 'the entire lower half of his body was sticking out, uncovered, for all the world to see' (Benjamin, 2011, p. 384). This rescue scene is a notable departure from the historical record of their escape from the burning building; in Lehman's biography, Charles 'descended the ladder', with his wife being carried to safety (Lehman, 2013, p. 201). In Benjamin's version, Charles's reaction is hysterical: he lies 'sobbing' in the street, and explains to his wife that the humiliation of exposure in this way was 'mortifying' (Benjamin, 2011, p. 386). In their final confrontation, he reminds her of this incident and the way in which this has damaged his sense of agency and confidence. Lavinia tells us that she realises that he is a 'coward'. She looks at him with 'his arms full of clippings, a morose figure in his dressing gown and worn slippers':

> The shades were drawn, but I could still see the stumps of cigars in every ashtray, the papers and photographs and citations and ribbons

> and, above all, memories; remnants of memories, threadbare, worn almost to shreds from a lifetime of use, lying in tatters at his feet. The room smelled like sadness, like stale breath and cheap cigars and musty papers that hadn't seen light in decades. It reminded me of a deserted, desolate circus tent long after the crowd had gone.
>
> (Benjamin, 2011, p. 396)

These shabby accoutrements, of a faded celebrity clutching onto past glories, are highly poignant; the culmination of his abuse at the hands of Barnum represented by the cigars to which he has become addicted.[25] In this framing, the former child star has never fully made the transition to an adult life, and he is preserved in the trappings of freakery: stuck in a room like a 'desolate circus tent' when there is no audience left to shore up his fragile sense of self. Charles is engaged in his own process of 're-membering' here; searching through the textual remnants of his career to make sense of the man child that he has become. But we see that this is futile and offers no comfort or respite, an interesting reflection on neo-Victorianism's attempts to reconstruct freak show performers – and the past more broadly – via textual fragments. This is the fruition of Maud's concerns expressed in Carlson's *Among the Wonderful* which I discussed at the beginning of this chapter: he still 'looks to sustenance' from his audiences, but they are gone, and so is his wife. Impatient to keep her appointment with Bleeker, she responds harshly to his pleading, responding '"I'm quite mad at you, if you want to know the truth"' before she leaves (Benjamin, 2011, p. 396). Lavinia is figured as the chastising mother to Charles as imploring child, and she abandons him to his lonely death. Benjamin's version of Stratton can never move on from his childhood experiences, and is fixed in an image of a desperate desire to revisit his past which alludes to trauma.

Stratton-as-perpetual-child is not the novel's only engagement with the nineteenth-century discourses surrounding dwarfism and children, however. As in Sullivan's *Little People*, Benjamin's Lavinia has a horror of maternity stemming from overhearing a conversation between her mother and her sister Delia discuss the impossibility of Lavinia surviving childbirth due to her size (Benjamin, 2011, p. 25). As a consequence, Lavinia avoids any sort of sexual encounters, despite being subject to lascivious advances from men during her work in the freak show on the Mississippi show boat (Benjamin, 2011, p. 96–97; pp. 113–15). The sexual allure of the child-size woman – and freakery more broadly – is certainly apparent in the ways in which men interact with Lavinia, but she refuses to be exploited or objectified. Furthermore, her marriage to Charles remains chaste: there is no attempt at the 'oral satisfaction' alluded to in Sullivan's novel. Her reaction to the succession of 'Tom Thumb' babies the couple procure with the assistance of Barnum is, nevertheless, comparable to Sullivan's Lavinia: she avoids bonding with the children by perceiving them as non-human; on one occasion she holds an infant and is reminded 'of the time I had dressed up a baby pig in dolls clothes, back when I was a girl' (Benjamin, 2011, p. 252). More significantly, however, it is the baby hoax which is reimagined as inaugurating Minnie's maternal instincts – she becomes 'alarmingly attached' to the children (Benjamin, 2011, p. 243). For Lavinia consistently perceives Minnie as a child-like innocent – 'My dear, simple little sister!' – and due to her own experiences of prurient interest from men as a freak show performer, is committed to her staying this way, 'remaining unspoiled for the both of us' (Benjamin, 2011, pp. 124–25). Due to Lavinia's first person narration, we are limited by this perception of Minnie; pointedly, there is no question of her being the sexualised 'trickster' figure of Bleeker's hints and Sullivan's realisation. Thus it is a surprise for us when Lavinia suddenly informs us that her sister is married and expecting a child. Lavinia's reaction to his announcement is important:

> I let go of her hands, as if she were contagious, as if having a baby was a disease that I could catch from her touch [...] 'But how? But, Minnie, you – and Edward?' I was shocked, sickened. Yes, my sister was married. But so was I. I knew she and Edward shared a bed, but – didn't she know the dangers of allowing a man to touch her, she who was so delicate, so vulnerable – even more vulnerable than me?
> (Benjamin, 2011, p. 299)

In Lavinia's view, maternity is couched as disability, and her shock and disgust at Minnie as sexually active belies her sense of Minnie as a child and therefore supposedly being sexually innocent. For Minnie to be pregnant is tantamount to sexual abuse of a minor, yet, of course, Lavinia's error is clear: Minnie is not a child. The most powerful message of the novel concerns the risks and dangers of infantilising adults of short stature, but the irony is that this comes from Lavinia herself. However, Lavinia comes to believe that refusal to recognise Minnie's adult status leads to her younger sister being unaware of the dangers of pregnancy, and that this results in Minnie's death in childbirth. Although this is not the case – Minnie is aware of the dangers, but still proceeds with the pregnancy – Lavinia recognises that the limits of her own maturity are not due to her small size, but her own prejudices and assumptions about 'little people'.

In this vein, the novel offers an alternative reading of the historical Lavinia's subtle distancing of herself from the label of 'dwarf' in her autobiography. Initially, when Colonel Wood, her manager on the showboat, refers to her in this way, Lavinia's outrage is explained in the following terms: '*I will not let my size define me*' (Benjamin, 2011, p. 67; original emphasis). In this sense, her repudiation of the term 'dwarf' is couched in terms of her feminist sensibilities, a refusal to be 'belittled' in a man's world. However, much later in her career, she is employed in Barnum's travelling circus, and is introduced to some other 'small people':

> I had seen them hanging about wherever we went, trailing Charles and me like shadows, whispering and pointing. But they weren't like us. They had large heads on small, barrel-chested bodies, oddly proportioned arms and legs [...] They made me uneasy; they made me ashamed, for how the audience howled with laughter whenever they jumped up and down, flapping their grotesque arms, rolling their bulging eyes! I did not wish to make their acquaintance [...] [The hand] was odd, ugly, disfigured, with short stumps for fingers and a very fleshy palm. I placed my own delicate, perfectly formed hand – my nails buffed a pretty pink – in hers.
>
> (Benjamin, 2011, pp. 360-61)

There are complex and troubling politics at work in this quotation. Lavinia is invoking a point of distinction between herself and other performers of short stature which was familiar in the nineteenth-century freak show: as Robert Bogdan explains, people with 'hypopituitary' dwarfism, 'who tended to be well proportioned and physically attractive' were cast in the aggrandised mode of presentation, whereas performers with 'achondroplastic' dwarfism, 'whose head and limbs tend to be out of proportion to their trunk, were cast in the exotic mode' (Bogdan, 1988, p. 112).[26] But Lavinia also, perhaps inadvertently, reveals herself to have internalised these freak show discourses in several ways. Firstly, she has come to believe in her own 'aggrandized', elevated status as a performer and is horrified when an old friend, Carlotta, suggests to Lavinia that she thought '"you all might get along"' (Benjamin, 2011, p. 362). What she therefore must confront is that her own self-perception of her persona as dignified, feminine and refined is not necessarily interpreted in this way by others: for Carlotta, all little people are the same. Secondly, the imagery which Lavinia employs – the image of these 'other' performers as like 'shadows' to herself and Charles – invokes the spectacle of freakery as defining the boundaries between self and other for the freak show audience. Ironically, the points of contrast that she draws between her own body and theirs offers a microcosm of the metaphor of freak show performers as 'mirrors' which I discussed in the Introduction to *Neo-Victorian Freakery*. They are the part of the self which she repudiates, which she defines herself against, yet which are what she fears that she really might be. After her initial horror, she becomes more reflective: 'I didn't know what to call them. Because I didn't know what to call myself. Dwarf? Tiny? Perfect woman in miniature? None of them, all of them; had I ever been simply Lavinia Warren Stratton? To anyone – even myself?' (Benjamin, 2011, p. 363). The fact that these questions are never entirely satisfactorily answered in Benjamin's 'autobiography' of Lavinia articulates her own conflicts and confusions over her identity. Perhaps this ambivalence does offer an important lesson about the problems of political labelling. Betty M. Adelson, for instance, points out that 'group identity is still a work in progress' for people with dwarfism due to anxieties about reiterating stigma, but also because of differing experiences of living with restricted growth (Adelson, 2006, p. xvii). Lavinia's struggles with identification versus repudiation thus chime with contemporary disability politics, and the difficulties apparent in assuming collective identity and terminology.[27]

In my earlier analysis of the historical Charles Stratton's performances as Tom Thumb, I highlighted the, somewhat uncomfortable, connections between the 'blackface' elements of some of his routines as a child and enslaved labour. It is notable, therefore, that racial inequalities do have a place in Benjamin's novel. As one of the appendices to the historical Lavinia's *Autobiography* details, on a trip to New Orleans before the Civil War during her time under the management of Colonel Wood, she received an 'embarrassing' gift from a 'wealthy plantation owner'. Apparently due to the 'particular attention' she paid to 'a beautiful mulatto girl' in his company, Lavinia was offered the enslaved woman as her own: 'Of course, I couldn't think of becoming a slaveholder; but the poor girl used to visit me at the hotel in the firm conviction that she was my chattel' (Magri, 1979, p. 176). Benjamin's version of Lavinia re-members this incident in similar terms: 'A beautiful girl, so graceful and delicate [...] I was unable to take my eyes off her' (Benjamin, 2011, p. 85). She also refuses the 'gift' but struggles to persuade the 'girl' to return to her master. Lavinia explains that she is on the side of the abolitionists: 'no human being should ever be given as chattel!', and expresses regret that she did not keep the 'girl' and take her back to the North to freedom: 'Even as I realized this, however, I remembered that I was almost as indentured as she; Colonel Wood would not have allowed it [...] I dreamed about the girl many nights after; she appeared, silent and reproachful, staring at me before vanishing into a soupy southern mist' (Benjamin, 2011, pp. 85–86). Lavinia's ostensibly egalitarian reaction surely appeals to neo-Victorian revisionary sensibilities; although the historical Lavinia expresses her rejection of the role of slave-holder, Benjamin's Lavinia offers a – seemingly – politically-correct denunciation of the whole institution of slavery. The connection she forms between the enslaved woman and her own 'indentured' role as a vulnerable performer is, to an extent, pertinent: I made a comparable association earlier in this chapter in terms of thinking about Charles's (potentially compelled or coerced) performances of 'blackness'. However, we should remember the oppressive implications of the identification which Slouka's version of Chang Bunker made between himself and Lewis, an enslaved man, which I discussed in Chapter 2. Lavinia's sense of recognition does in fact expose power imbalances between her situation and that of the enslaved woman's. In either the historical or fictionalised version of Lavinia's narratives, the enslaved woman is consistently referred to as a 'girl'. As Wilma King has identified, the convention of slave-holding discourse in the nineteenth century was that 'social customs rather than chronological age determined if one called a bondservant "boy" or "girl"' (King, 2011, location 189). More broadly, enslaved people were generally infantilised and considered as in need of protection and/or correction (King, 2011, location 145). Benjamin's Lavinia's replication of this convention is telling; it is an invocation of her sense of superiority based on race, but also potentially the mistreatment of a child as well. Both issues also coalesce in the neo-Victorian Lavinia's palpable interest in the enslaved person's physical attractiveness. She is 'unable to take her eyes off her', a turn of phrase which constructs the enslaved 'girl' as an object of the colonial and sexualised gaze. The latter might be a moment of queerness, but this appropriation of the gendered gaze does nothing to reappropriate power inequalities. And that the object of the gaze's age is uncertain again raises the spectre of the inappropriate sexualisation of children. That Lavinia is haunted by memories of the 'girl', who is 'silent', 'reproachful', and 'staring', speaks of her guilt to secure her emancipation, but also perhaps her self-consciousness about her own relatively privileged status. Unlike this fictionalised version of Lavinia, the 'girl' has no voice,[28] and is 'staring' rather than gazing; a demand for mutual recognition and engagement rather than the reiteration of racial inequalities (Garland-Thomson, 2009).

Although Lavinia is imbued with a self-reflectiveness which is lacking in Benjamin's representation of Stratton – he is offered no self-consciousness about race, or any other social power inequalities in this novel – there is an over-riding theme of this version of Lavinia which remains troubling. In Lavinia's introduction to her story, she remarks that 'I suppose it would be fashionable to admit some reservations as I undertake to write the History of My Life', and explains that this prescription for reserve is gendered: 'We women are timid creatures [...] we must retire behind a veil of secrecy and allow others to tell our story' (Benjamin, 2011, p. 3). She is thus overtly aware of the patriarchal inflection of the 'official' record of history, but positions her narrative in defiance to such oppression: 'I have let others – one other, in particular – tell my story for far too long' (Benjamin, 2011, p. 3). Is the 'other' she refers to Charles Stratton? This is a reasonable assumption, considering the title of the novel: Lavinia has always been, after all, defined in relation to her husband. Yet what emerges from Benjamin's novel is Lavinia's love for Barnum. Although their relationship is at times fraught – for instance, she partially blames him for persuading her to allow an introduction to Minnie, which inaugurates the latter's career and a chain of events leading to her death – Lavinia's adoration for Barnum is transparent (Benjamin, 2011, p. 173; p. 307; p. 330). Benjamin's 'Author's Note' makes no apology for this romance: 'it became clear to me that this is a love story [...] P. T. Barnum was always the light she was seeking [...] the companion, the true partner, she could never find in Charles Stratton' (Benjamin, 2011, p. 420). Although there is no sexual relationship represented between Lavinia and Barnum, Benjamin claims, for both her fictional heroine, and the historical Lavinia, that Barnum 'was the great love of her life [...] everything she did began and ended with him' (Benjamin, 2011, p. 420–21). So, although Benjamin's afterword to the main body of the novel explains how her writing of the book was motivated by Lavinia being routinely represented as an extension of her husband rather than a woman in her own right (Benjamin, 2011, p. 419), her decision to limit her fictionalisation of Warren's life to her years working with Barnum is surely questionable. In effect, she replaces Stratton with Barnum in Lavinia's life, which inadvertently reiterates the child-like dependency which the historical Lavinia was sometimes depicted as having upon men.

Conclusion

This chapter's discussion of the conflicted construction of Victorian childhood demonstrated that the tension between innocence and experience – especially in relation to sexuality – finds resonance with the representation of Charles Stratton and Lavinia Warren in both nineteenth-century and neo-Victorian narratives. 'General Tom Thumb' was fashioned as a hyper-sexualised, trickster figure in his life time, but also as having the potential to be something of a joke himself: immature and impotent. More seriously, there are suggestions of his use and abuse as a young performer at the hands of Barnum which intersect with broader power inequalities of race and class. Lavinia is similarly positioned at a dubious boundary between childish innocence and adult sexuality, particularly in the 'true life story' pamphlet about her and Stratton's relationship. However, other nineteenth-century narratives such as Sylvester Bleeker's book and Lavinia's own autobiography are more inclined to highlight her assertive and intelligent qualities, despite simultaneously invoking tropes of cowardice and vulnerability in relation to Charles.

In his biography of P. T. Barnum, A. H. Saxon opines that 'it is virtually impossible to distinguish between the real Charles Stratton from the General Tom Thumb of Barnum's creation' and speculates that Stratton's youth when coming under the management of Barnum might have 'prevented the real Charles Stratton from developing an individuality of his own' (Saxon, 1989, p. 130). Neo-Victorian versions of Charles do attempt to look beneath the persona of 'General Tom Thumb' and what they re-member is a damaged individual who is perpetually trapped in a state of arrested development. *Little People* represents the loss of childhood innocence as being traumatic for Charles, and the Warren sisters – Lavinia and Minnie – as having to negotiate the difficulties of adult sexual experience. Charles and Lavinia might be exposed as manipulating and exploiting their 'Tom Thumb' babies – thus the abused become abusers in turn – but their dealings with children pale in comparison to the sexualised and murderous machinations of Richardson and Musgrave. When the Strattons realise that Mary Ann has absconded with the baby that Charles desperately imagined might be his own, which would remain permanently in scale, the couple are genuinely bereft. But this experience does inaugurate a new intimacy between the couple; Lavinia decides that the time is right to consummate her marriage with her husband, regardless of the consequences, and looking at their embrace in the mirror in the room, she ponders: 'there is nothing in the frame to show how large or how small they are, only that they fit each other to perfection. I think I will stop looking in the mirror now' (Sullivan, 2011, p. 330). Hence, their story in Sullivan's version of their lives seeks to look beyond distorted reflections of the sexuality of people with dwarfism, and imagine Charles and Lavinia's lives regardless of size. However, the characterisation of Charles is still informed by themes of impotency, a troubling reiteration of nineteenth-century denigrations of dwarf masculinity.

Benjamin's novel re-members Lavinia's feminism at the expense of her husband, who again is a figure of immaturity and tragedy. Yet Lavinia is not idealised: she is exposed as subject to her own confusions about the boundaries between innocence and experience in relation to Minnie. Lavinia's inability to understand her sister as an adult woman due to her short stature offers a thought-provoking commentary on the dangers of infantilizing 'little people'. Lavinia's repudiation of other performers with dwarfism – and her problematic sense of identification with the slave 'girl' she meets – bring the power relationships of disability and race into sharp focus. Despite her own vulnerability as a woman of short stature in a patriarchal world, she is still inclined to invoke ambivalent currencies of repudiation and identification in relation to 'others', which ironically deploys the more oppressive impulses of the nineteenth-century freak show. Both neo-Victorian novels are attuned to the dangers of 'belittlement' and exploitation for adults and children alike. Yet Lavinia and Charles are still belittled in their own way: Benjamin's novel can only define Lavinia's identity in relation to the men in her life, and in both texts Charles is defined by his childhood experiences. Both novels have their revisionary aspects, but ultimately struggle to think beyond nineteenth-century discourses of dwarfism in their attempts to render the Strattons as adult agents.

5

The Strange Case of Joseph and Jack: Joseph Merrick and Spectacles of Deviance

Joseph Merrick suffered with extensive facial and bodily disfigurement, and was exhibited as 'The Elephant Man' in late nineteenth-century England and continental Europe. Born in Leicester in 1862, Merrick was of 'normal' physical appearance for the first few years of his life, but began to develop thickened skin on his body and large growths over his face and flesh during childhood. After attempting to make a living by rolling cigars in a factory, and subsequently hawking goods, he left home and entered a work house aged 17. In 1884, he contacted a showman, Sam Torr, with the proposal that he might find work as a freak show exhibit. Merrick soon came under the management of a successful freak show proprietor named Tom Norman, and was exhibited in a shop in Whitechapel, London under the name 'The Elephant Man'. A surgeon named Fredrick Treves attended one of Merrick's performances, and persuaded Norman to allow him to take Merrick to the London Hospital to be photographed and examined for the purposes of medical research. Merrick spent some time travelling Europe, but had his savings stolen and was forced to make his own way back to England. Discovered by the police with Treves's card, Merrick returned to the London Hospital and was permitted to live in lodgings there. He became something of a cause de célèbre during his final years at the hospital, receiving visits from prominent society figures under the supervision of Treves. Merrick died in 1890; he was unable to sleep lying down due to his deformities, and yet Treves's theory was that Merrick suffocated whilst attempting to sleep in a 'normal' posture.[1]

Kenneth Sherman's *Words for Elephant Man*, first published in 1983, offers a series of poems about key incidents in Joseph Merrick's life, written from Merrick's perspective. Early in the sequence, 'Freaks' imagines Merrick's musings on an exhibition of wax models of the victims of Jack the Ripper which is taking place in Whitechapel over the street from his own display under the management of Tom Norman. The very title seems to associate the eviscerated sex workers with freakery; however, this connection becomes more complicated as the poem develops. The crowd who come to view the figures – and who, presumably, might be enticed in to see 'The Elephant Man' as well – are described in the following terms:

> black silk hats
> white scarves
> women's parasols.
> (Sherman, 2012, p. 20)

The audience's apparel codes them as sophisticated and respectable, but also speaks of a middle-class prurient interest in disfigured bodies, whether due to a medical condition as in the case of Merrick, or due to brutal murder as in the case of the Ripper's victims. The conclusion of the poem underscores the commercial aspect of this exchange: women are murdered in the evening, but 'In the light of day/they are sold' (Sherman, 2012, p. 20). Women's flesh as a commodity signifies in several ways here: it reminds us that, despite the dangers, women are still working the streets, but also that this 'selling' does not stop with death – victimisation might continue with posthumous objectification and exhibition. Furthermore, such exploitation is evidently not confined to women, for it underscores a connection with Merrick: he too must sell his body for consumer entertainment and gratification. To return to the poem's title, then: who are the 'freaks' – who is made monstrous by this exhibition? The sex workers, the showman who 'bags pennies' from displaying these 'terrors' (Sherman, 2012, p. 20), the audience who pay to see both freak show performers and spectacles of gruesome murder, or Jack, the man who has murdered these women in the first place? This question, it seems, is not easily answered.

In cultural mythology of fin-de-siécle Whitechapel, the respective myths of Joseph Merrick and Jack the Ripper are entwined in various ways. Peter W. Graham and Fritz H. Oehlschlaeger's study of 'interpretations' of the 'Elephant Man' detail some key points of connection: Merrick was a resident of the London Hospital in the same year – 1888 – as the series of brutal murders of Whitechapel sex workers by an unknown killer who became known as 'Jack the Ripper'.[2] Perhaps more significant than mere geographic and temporal proximity, the suspicion that the Ripper might be a medical man due to the anatomical knowledge involved in the killing of the victims meant that some of the doctors attending Merrick also could fall under scrutiny: 'if the doctor could be seen, on the one hand, as a benefactor to the poor [...] he could also be seen as a potential malefactor, a being capable of preying on the poor in the foulest of ways' (Graham and Oehlschlaeger, 1992, p. 29). However, they also highlight the sheer range of suspects in the Ripper case: not only doctors, but royals, Jews, dockland workers, and butchers fell under suspicion, amongst many others.[3] In this sense, Jack the Ripper crossed social boundaries of class, as did the audiences for Joseph Merrick both in his time as a freak show performer and during his stay at the London Hospital. Finally, Graham and Oehlschlaeger note the connection with which this chapter opened: the exhibition of garish models of the Ripper victims took place in the same area as Merrick's 'freak show' career in London, and both shows would be shut down by the local police on the grounds of offending public decency (Graham and Oehlschlaeger, 1992, p. 29).[4]

However, there is an even more pernicious connection between Joseph and 'Jack': the internet, unsurprisingly, is awash with websites dedicated to debating potential suspects behind the Ripper murders, and even a cursory search will reveal that Merrick's name often is mentioned in the more fanciful speculations about 'Jack's' real identity.[5] Mike Holgate's book focusing on the 'celebrity suspects' in the Ripper case names both Joseph and Fredrick Treves as potential Rippers: Treves due to his possession of the requisite anatomical knowledge, Merrick due to his access to medical implements. Moreover, Holgate notes that both might have motive in terms of the misogyny evidenced by the murders: Treves apparently took a dim view of women employed in sex work, and Merrick might have been spurred on by rejection by women: 'His experience with [...] women who found him repulsive supposedly developed into a bitter hatred' (Holgate, 2008, p. 18). While Holgate quickly dismisses both accusations as absurd, the notion that Joseph might have been 'Jack' rests on the assumption that inner self is reflected by outward appearance. Put simply, Joseph Merrick looked 'monstrous' and so his personality and behaviour must also be deviant. According to Lennard J. Davis, the cultural link between criminality, deviance, and disability becomes heightened in the nineteenth century with the construction of the concept of 'normality' (Davis, 2010, p. 7), and in the terminology of David Mitchell and Susan Snyder, the conflation of Merrick's physical difference with moral delinquency in the Joseph as Jack story is a narrative prosthesis: the 'crutch' upon which to lean to account for the extremity of Merrick's deformity and the disfiguring horror of the Ripper's crimes (Mitchell and Snyder, 2010, p. 276).

Of all the performers studied in *Neo-Victorian Freakery*, Merrick is undoubtedly the most famous, and he has been the subject of considerable attention from popular culture, biographers and critics. The perspective on Merrick which I take in this chapter is to trace the ways in which a set of anxieties about sex workers, disfigurement, monstrosity and gender apparent in Frederick Treves's *The Elephant Man and other Reminiscences* (1923) are re-membered in neo-Victorian versions of Merrick, with particular focus on the connections between Merrick and Jack the Ripper. I begin with a brief discussion of the ways in which sex workers were constructed as disfigured in nineteenth-century discourses on prostitution, which feeds into the spectacle of grotesque female bodies as a result of the Ripper murders. In the light of such associations, Frederick Treves's memoir will be discussed for the insights it offers about Treves's perspective on femininity, sexuality, monstrosity, exhibition and propriety. In contrast to the other chapters in this book, I have made the decision to explore just one key nineteenth-century depiction of Merrick as, due to its formative influence upon neo-Victorianism's engagements with Joseph Merrick, it merits analysis at length. I seek to highlight the ways in which Treves fashions Merrick's 'deformity' around conflicted images of nineteenth-century femininity: the 'fallen woman', the 'angel in the house', and, rather queerly, the dandy. Treves's construction of Merrick's feminised 'deviance' is, to an extent, challenged in Bernard Pomerance's play *The Elephant Man* (1979) and David Lynch's 1980 film of the same name. Pomerance represents the hypocrisy of the nineteenth-century medical profession and 'Victorian values' in the form of Treves's prudishness. Lynch, whilst more generous towards Treves, positions Merrick as a victim of sexual violence at the hands of working-class 'monstrous' masculinity. The quandary of whether Merrick should be perceived as a victim or villain becomes heightened in a series of neo-Victorian sources which explicitly engage with the Merrick-Ripper connection. The neo-Victorian fascination with Jack the Ripper and his victims, and prostitution more broadly, is oft-remarked in scholarship on the genre,[6] but the politics at work in the way in which Merrick has also been associated with the Ripper (villain) and/or sex worker ('victim') – sometimes simultaneously – deserves further scrutiny. In Iain Sinclair's novel *White Chappell, Scarlet Tracings* (1987), Alan Moore and Eddie Campbell's graphic novel *From Hell* (1999) and the Hughes Brother's film adaptation of the same name (2001), it is the figure of the Victorian doctor which bears the burden of moral monstrosity in the shape of William Gull as the chief culprit of the Ripper crimes. In this sense, these examples crystallise the theme of 'medical sensationalism' which has run throughout *Neo-Victorian Freakery*. However, we shall see that the Ripper's depravity is contagious, and Merrick himself becomes implicated in these brutal murders in various ways. Yet Treves's feminisation and orientalisation of Merrick is also a key theme, which aligns him with the selling of flesh in prostitution/freakery, and as an artefact of Empire. As a counterpoint to these problematic currencies of prurience and pity, I explore the ways in which the BBC's television series *Ripper Street* (2012–) works to represent Merrick as a figure of integrity and agency, albeit still a victim of a corrupt establishment.

Sexual spectacles: Prostitution and disfigurement in the Victorian era

As numerous critical studies of nineteenth-century attitudes towards gender have indicated, there is no figure which embodied conflicted social anxieties about women's sexuality so much as the Victorian prostitute. Characterised variously as poverty-stricken victims, aberrations of womanly propriety, dangers to home and nation, and threatening femme fatales, nineteenth-century sex workers were a locus point for debate in medical, religious, legal, political, and popular media discourse, as well as being subject to copious cultural representation in the spheres of art and literature.[7] For the purposes of this chapter, however, it is the construction of the sex worker as disfigured, and potentially disfiguring which is of particular interest. In the nineteenth century concerns about prostitution became heightened around the issue of contagion: the spread of venereal disease, particularly syphilis. This lead to the passing of a series of Contagious Diseases Acts of 1864, 1866, and 1869. These Acts, initially aimed at naval and garrison towns, were focused upon at halting the spread of sexually transmitted infections, as Lynda Nead explains: 'The Acts provided for the registration of prostitutes and their supervision by a special police force. Prostitutes were subjected to compulsory examination and, if found to be diseased, could be detained in special hospitals until cured' (Nead, 1988, p. 22). Various campaigns were galvanised for the repeal of the Acts,[8] yet the ideological implications were clear: sex workers were a corrupting threat to the physical and moral health of men. While, as I shall detail below, there was a strand of discourse on prostitution which focused on the disfiguring effects of sex work upon women, it is worth noting here that a primary concern about the physical influence of syphilis was about the ravages which it might enact on male bodies. Elaine

Showalter writes of the disease's 'dramatic inscriptions on the male body', with particular emphasis on the havoc wrought on the skin via 'macules, papules, tubercules, pustules, blebs, tumors, lesions, scales, crusts, ulcers, chancres, gummas, fissures, and scars' (Showalter, 1992, pp. 192–93).[9] Of course, in offering this detail I am making no claims for Joseph Merrick's physical appearance as being associated with syphilis,[10] but the motif of disfigurement being conflated with 'deviant' sexuality will become important for understanding the connection between Merrick and fears and fantasies about physical and moral 'monstrosity'.

In terms of representing the disfigured body of the sex worker in nineteenth-century discourse, images of corruption were not just related to the symptoms of venereal disease, but became conflated with a broader sense of physical monstrosity resulting from vice. For example, Fraser Harrison relates the sermon of the Reverend William Arnot, spoken to his congregation in Glasgow in 1860: '"Look at the fruit of your doings [...] in that imbruted soul and bloated body, with hardly any features left, a mass of incurable corruption now. That lump of living flesh was once a woman"' (quoted in Harrison, 1979, p. 245). While this indictment ostensibly lays the blame of the physical degeneration of the sex worker with the men who visit her, the disgust towards the monstrous corporeal appearance of the prostitute is palpable. The distorted body of the sex worker is no longer recognisably gendered; it becomes subhuman, abject, positively freakish. Harrison himself notes that such rhetoric was actually hyperbolic, as other commentators at the time were at pains to demonstrate. For instance, Dr William Acton's tome, *Prostitution, considered by its Moral, Social, and Sanitary Aspects*, first published in 1857 and running to an expanded second edition in 1870, initially works hard to dispel the assumption that women working as prostitutes were disproportionately affected by venereal disease, or that they suffered physical damage from their trade. He remarks: 'The Gorgon of the present day against whom we should arm our children should be a woman who, whether sound or diseased, is generally pretty and elegant' (Acton, 1870, p. 28). His use of the term 'Gorgon' might invoke the vocabulary of monstrosity, but this is quickly undermined by the emphasis on the 'prettiness' of most women employed in sex work. In fact, the force of Acton's argument rests on the incongruity between the alluring aesthetic appearance of such women, and their monstrous lack of morality. He develops this thesis by comparing the physical state of a prostitute of thirty five with that of her 'sister', who might be 'the married mother of a family': 'we shall seldom find that the constitutional ravages often thought to be a necessary consequence of prostitution exceed those attributable to the cares of a family and the heart-wearing struggles of virtuous labour' (Acton, 1870, p. 39). Acton seems rather disgruntled by this lack of justice in the meting out of the aging process, but his observations do sound a cautionary note in assuming that all nineteenth-century discourse on the appearance of sex workers emphasised grotesquery. However, his prose later fall prey to this very stereotype in his account of the numbers of women employed in sex work in London, and the potential this has for spreading 'loathsome poison' which not only effects the men who pay for sex, but 'are too often transmitted to his issue and bear their fruits in tottering limbs and tainted blood' (Acton, 1870, p. 74). In this formulation, sex workers become a contaminating and disabling force on the population at large. He continues: 'Broken constitutions, sickly bodies, and feeble minds are times out of number the work of the prostitute [...] It exercises an evil influence on the nation at large, depraving the mind and lowering the moral tone. It is the case of disease, premature decay, untimely death' (Acton, 1870, p. 74). Belying his previous arguments, this emphasis on physical and moral decay reunites the discourses of disability and deviancy, as outer appearance again comes to reflect inner self.

Another notable perspective on the disabling and disfiguring effects of prostitution upon the women involved comes from Henry Mayhew in his compendious *London Labour and the London Poor* (1862). Although he frequently comments on the physical attractiveness of sex workers as he details the various 'types' or 'classes' of prostitutes, he has recourse to dwell on the horrific appearance of the most 'degraded' of sex workers, the 'Park women' who frequent public parks and gardens after dark:

> [They] consent to any species of humiliation for the sake of acquiring a few shillings [...] These women are well known to give themselves up to disgusting practices, that are alone gratifying for men of morbid and diseased imaginations. They are [...] by their appearance utterly incapacitated from practicing their profession where the gas-lamps would expose the defects of their personal appearance.
>
> (Mayhew, 1862, n.p.)[11]

Again, the register for articulating the horrors of prostitution is of the gothic, and the 'degradation' of these women is evidently contagious: the men who visit them are morally 'sick' ('morbid and diseased') and the appearance of the Park women is such that they are effectively disabled ('incapacitated') from working in any other location or with any other pool of customers. Mayhew offers a case study of a woman he has interviewed who was originally a 'very pretty' young woman, but, after many years of unsuitable sexual partners, was 'infected with a disease [...] it attacked my face and ruined my features to such an extent that I am hideous to look upon' (Mayhew, 1862, n.p.) Furthermore, she is so grotesque that she must wear a 'long thick veil, that concealed her features, and made her interesting to the unsuspicious and unwise' (Mayhew, 1862, n.p.) This detail about the erotic allure of veiling, which might disguise a horrific appearance, becomes a notable trope in several neo-Victorian versions of Joseph Merrick. In summary, however, it seems that despite the diversity of appearance of nineteenth-century sex workers, for certain Victorian commentators to emphasise the disfigurement and generalised monstrosity of prostitutes had a compelling rhetorical import which offered the opportunity to offer warnings to both men and women about the potential for physical and moral corruption.

Such fevered imaginings found a specific focus in the media coverage of the Whitechapel murders of 1888. Considering the occupation of the murder victims, and the gynaecological nature of the mutilation of some of the bodies, the newspaper reports on the crimes were inclined to construct the murder as a 'Gothic sex beast', to use Judith Walkowitz's expression. She cites several key descriptions:

> Declared the *Daily Telegraph*, 'we are left... to form unpleasant visons of roving lunatics distraught by homicidal mania or bloodythirsty lust... or finally we may dream of monstres, or ogres.' In the East End, monstrous metaphors assumed a literal status: 'People allowed their imagination to run riot. There was talk of black magic and vampires'.
>
> (Walkowitz, 1992, p. 197)

The absence of a tangible perpetrator to describe physically left a vacuum for public imagination to fill, and this was gratified by images of monstrosity: vampires, ogres, lunatics. The flipside of these visions was to imagine an outwardly socially acceptable and respectable looking individual – the doctor – who was capable of morally monstrous acts.[12] Interestingly, therefore, the speculations over the Ripper's identity – and physical appearance – inadvertently echoed the conflicted accounts of the physiognomy of prostitutes: would moral ugliness find resonance in physical horrors, or, perhaps more threatening, would a socially conventional or even an attractive appearance mask debilitating deviance?

It was Archibald Forbes, a journalist from the *Daily News*, who proposed that the killer might be a vengeful '"victim" of a "specific contagion"', crazed by syphilis and seeking reprisal by murdering the purported harbourers and perpetuators of the disease (Walkowitz, 1992, p. 210) As the commentaries on prostitution and disease leading to disfigurement above suggest, such a condition might mean that the murderer was physically marked, but also casts some degree of blame on the victims as potentially diseased and disfigured themselves. More significantly, though, it was the brutality of the murders which exposed the susceptibility of prostitutes to being maimed and defaced. According to Judith Walkowitz, the reporting of the crimes which dwelled on the mutilations enacted upon the victims invoked 'cultural fantasies about the grotesque female body' (Walkowitz, 1992, p. 191). She explains:

> To middle-class readers of the *Times* and the *Morning Post*, the murders constituted a morality tale of stark proportions. These were economically desperate women, who violated their 'womanhood' for the price of a night's lodging, and for whom the wages of sin were death. Outside of Whitechapel, the victims were viewed as unsympathetic objects of pity – by radicals and conservatives alike. Whatever guilt middle-class readers may have experienced over the 'mangled ruins' of Annie Chapman, their compunctions were soon overwhelmed by feelings of fear and loathing towards the spectacle of the victims themselves.
>
> (Walkowitz, 1992, p. 201)

While the women were certainly constructed as victims in some respects – obviously in their status as prey to the Ripper, but also of poverty – they were also denigrated as objects of horror, disgust and abjection. The misogynistic implication is that such sex workers not only deserved their fate, but that in death their moral aberrations were compounded by the grotesque state of their bodies. In a sense, the 'spectacle' of their corpses became conflated with the polymorphous monstrosity of the Ripper himself, hence the roles of victim and villain combine via the discourse of physical and moral disfigurement which becomes associated with gendered and sexualised transgression.

Saving 'fallen' monsters: Frederick Treves's *The Elephant Man and Other Reminiscences*

The specific deployment of the themes of grotesque sex workers and the Ripper murders become apparent in later neo-Victorian representations of Merrick, but the broader tropes of monstrous spectacles, and gendered and sexualised deviancy are still at play in Treves's writings on Merrick in his memoirs. His chapter on his relationship with Joseph – or 'John', as he insists on renaming his subject[13] – opens with a description of Merrick's exhibition under the management of Tom Norman. On first viewing him, Treves explains that, while his medical career has routinely brought him into contact with deformity, 'mutilations and contortions', 'at no time had I met with such a degraded or perverted version of a human being as this lone figure displayed. He was naked to the waist, his feet were bare' (Treves, 1923, p. 3). His use of vocabulary is suggestive, as it intimates sexual as well as physical aberration. Treves's conceptualisation of Merrick's body as 'degraded' might remind us of Mayhew's description of the 'Park' prostitutes as well, who are similarly marked by extreme disfigurement. Merrick's nakedness is presumably to display his deformity more clearly to the audiences, yet in Treves's account it becomes associated with the notion of a 'perverted' body: a spectacle which is debauched and deviant. This connection becomes more pronounced when Treves reports approvingly on the closure of Merrick's exhibition:

> In England the showman and Merrick had been moved on from place to place by the police, who considered the exhibition degrading and among the things that could not be allowed [...] The official mind [...] very properly decreed that the public exposure of Merrick and his deformities transgressed the limits of decency. The show must close.
>
> (Treves, 1923, p. 9)

Nadja Durbach's gloss on these remarks is pertinent: 'forms of bodily commodification, such as prostitution – or, in this case, the exhibition of a freakish body – challenged norms of respectable behaviour' (Durbach, 2010, p. 49). Merrick's career as a freak show performer is thus placed on a continuum with prostitution in Treves's formulation; continuing the theme of the sexualised elements of the display of unusual bodies which has been repeatedly identified in *Neo-Victorian Freakery*, the ways in which freak shows become conflated with sexual prurience is palpable, and the reaction of Treves and the late Victorian authorities to Merrick's exhibition invokes this. Furthermore, the very notion that his display 'could not be allowed' and might trouble 'the limits of decency' implicitly suggests that Merrick's exhibition might deprave others; his bodily deformities represent a corruption of the flesh, but could also inspire moral corruption in his audience. Thus another connection between Merrick and the fears and fantasies surrounding the body of the Victorian prostitute emerges: both might contaminate, literally in the case of sex workers, and metaphorically in the case of Merrick.

Treves offers a fulsome description of the intricacies of Merrick's deformities, variously comparing his tumours to 'cauliflowers', his skin as hanging like that of a 'lizard', his face to a 'block of gnarled wood', his hand to 'a fin or paddle', his thumb to a 'radish', and his fingers to 'thick, tuberous roots' (Treves, 1923, pp. 4–5). In the midst of his struggles to articulate whether Merrick might be most closely aligned to mineral, animal, or vegetable, he comments on the 'remarkable' contrast which his subject's left arm provides: 'It was not only normal but was, moreover, a delicately shaped limb covered with fine skin and provided with a beautiful hand which any woman might have envied' (Treves, 1923, p. 5). Merrick is overtly feminised, a theme which will be developed as Treves describes his securing of his ward's new residence at the London Hospital. While the description of Merrick's time in the freak show aligns him with the deviant, abject body of the prostitute, the mention of his limb's delicate shape, the fineness of his skin and the beauty of his hand suggests that he has the potential to be (re)constructed as approaching a more refined, respectable version of femininity. Several commentators have highlighted the ways in which Treves's narrative constructs Merrick within gendered discourses, coding his behaviour as feminine in terms of his 'gentle' and 'affectionate' nature, 'as amiable as a happy woman' (Treves, 1923, p. 17) and his propensity for emotional outpourings as he 'sobs' when first being kindly met by a 'pretty widow' (Treves, 1923, p. 22).[14] To develop this trope further, I argue that Treves stages his relationship with Merrick – his 'rescue' of him from the degradation of freak show exhibition and establishment as a member of respectable middle-class society – by engaging with the motif of the 'fallen' woman, reiterating the ambivalent depiction of Merrick as a prostitute-esque figure. As Amanda Anderson's study of the 'rhetoric of fallenness' in Victorian culture has suggested, the concept of 'fallenness' is applied to a wide range of women:

> Prostitutes, unmarried women who engage in sexual relations with men, victims of seduction, adulteresses, as well as variously delinquent lower-class women. A wide umbrella term, the designation cuts across class lines and signifies a complex of tabooed behaviours and degraded conditions.
>
> (Anderson, 1993, p. 2)

However, she argues that these various identities are united by 'attenuated autonomy and fractured identity'; put another way, fallen women become figures of cultural anxiety because they represent of a loss of control over the self and the failure to sustain an acceptable performance of the nineteenth-century gendered expectations (Anderson, 1993, p. 2). In this sense, Merrick's representation by Treves offers some significant parallels to the figure of the fallen woman: firstly, as discussed above, in his 'degradation' as a freak show performer, and secondly, as I shall explore below, in his 'saviour' at the hands of Treves. However, this reformation is an ambivalent process.

A further facet of Merrick's feminisation in Treves's narrative is the emphasis placed on his domestication. Now residing permanently at the London Hospital, 'Merrick had now something he had never dreamed of, never supposed to be possible – a home of his own for life' (Treves, 1923, p. 13). If Merrick was initially equated with the role of prostitute – a 'fallen' woman – he has seemingly now been saved, placed in the private, domestic sphere. He becomes, as Nadja Durbach points out, 'the Victorian feminine ideal, the angel in the house' (Durbach, 2010, p. 50). However, Treves's text also inadvertently exposes the problematic elements of this gender role for Merrick, and perhaps for Victorian women more broadly. Treves explains: 'He had no possessions. His sole belongings, besides his clothes and some books, were the monstrous cap and the cloak' (Treves, 1923, p. 18). Yet the home, and the possessions he acquires under the protection of Treves, are always gifts. He is no longer afforded the agency to make his own money, as he now has no means of making an income. Durbach's analysis of Tom Norman's memoir highlights the ways in which the showman believed that Merrick's employment as a freak show performer offered him autonomy and working-class masculine respectability, in the sense that he was able to earn his living (Durbach, 2010, pp. 46–52). Ironically, therefore, at the hands of Treves, Merrick now becomes the equivalent of a 'kept' woman.

The fluctuations in Merrick's ambiguous gendering – and attendant respectability – in Treves's memoir are also apparent via his relationship to the gaze in the public and private spheres:

> Another trouble was his dread of his fellow men, his fear of people's eyes, the dread of being always stared at, the lash of the cruel mutterings of the crowd. In his home in Bedstead Square he was secluded; but now and then a thoughtless porter or a wardmaid would open

> his door to let curious friends have a peep at the Elephant Man. It therefore seemed to him as if the gaze of the world followed him still.
> (Treves, 1923, p. 19)

As Amanda Anderson identifies, 'fallen' Victorian women in the form of the prostitute might also be known as 'public' women as well (Anderson, 1993, p. 2). The conflation of female sexual immorality with the dangers of the 'public' sphere of the streets where women become a 'spectacle' (Walkowitz, 1992, p. 21) coheres with Treves's description of Merrick's situation: he is vulnerable to the gaze whilst in public. However, the domestic sphere is revealed as not the secluded haven that one might expect, for Merrick is still subject to prurient 'peeping' here as well. Nevertheless, Treves explains his strategy for making Merrick feel more secure: he opines that Merrick needs to be treated 'as a normal and intelligent young man and not as a monster of deformity' (Treves, 1923, p. 20). Normality is 'manliness', and it is the company of women that will ensure 'his transformation' (Treves, 1923, p. 20). This formulation is interesting in itself, for it suggests that Merrick needs to be 'made' a man – revealing the ways in which gender is a process of becoming rather than a 'natural' given – but also that Merrick's prior role as degraded freak/prostitute, and his current position as a delicate kept woman, both align him with being 'a monster of deformity'. It is after Merrick is introduced to Treves's 'young and pretty widow' friend that he 'began to change, little by little, from a hunted thing to a man' (Treves, 1923, p. 22), and can thus presumably transcend his monstrous femininity. The evidence that Treves offers for his 'transformation' is in relation to Merrick's altered attitude to social engagement: 'He liked to see his door pushed open and people look in' (Treves, 1923, p. 23). This suggests that Merrick can now look back at his 'audience', and enjoy this 'seeing' now he is on the road to becoming properly manly. Yet Treves's phrasing is still ambiguous: people 'looking in' might mean social enquiries as to his well-being, but also still bears the insinuation of him being the feminised object of the gaze. His degraded, victimised identity is not fully rehabilitated.

Treves is at pains to emphasise Merrick's interest in women, which does seem to accord him some status in terms of the norms of heterosexual masculinity, but even this is couched in feminised terms:

> Merrick had an admiration of women of such a kind that it attained almost to adoration. This was not the outcome of his personal

> experience. They were not real women but the products of his imagination. Among them was the beautiful mother surrounded, at a respectful distance, by the heroines from the many romances he had read.
>
> (Treves, 1923, pp. 20–21)

This is one of several references to the ways in which literary representation shapes Merrick's perception of the world. This also has gendered implications, for certain nineteenth-century discourses suggested that women were more inclined to be emotionally influenced by the reading of books. Significantly, this propensity also had moral implications as well: for example, an anonymous article entitled 'Moral and Political Tendency of Modern Novels', published in *Church of England Quarterly Review* in 1842, warned that women being 'more sensitive, more impressable' which meant that the influence of fiction might be 'peculiarly mischievous' (Anon., 1842, pp. 287–88). It is 'love stories' that are Merrick's favourite reading matter, and they fuel his romantic passion: 'His bodily deformity had left unmarred the instincts and feelings of his years. He was amorous. He would like to have a lover' (Treves, 1923, p. 29). This desire to be the 'hero of many a passionate incident' seems relatively innocuous, but this strange combination of feminine susceptibility towards literature and manly passion makes for a queer construction of Merrick's persona. This strand of queerness becomes most clearly manifest in Treves's description of his gift to Merrick one Christmas: he requests a 'dressing bag with silver fittings', and Treves spends some time detailing the incongruity of this desire to aspire to a certain version of masculinity: 'Merrick could not wear the silk hat of the dandy nor, indeed, any kind of hat. He could not adapt his body to the trimly cut coat' (Treves, 1923, p. 27). Nevertheless, he acquires the bag, and tells how Merrick takes pride in arranging his impractical accoutrements. Merrick might learn to perform masculinity in this sense, but his construction as 'dandy' has dubious connotations: as Andrew Smith also notes, the 'dandified fop' signifies the 'highly ambiguous domain of gendering' that would become the focus of sexological debates on homosexuality (Smith, 2000, p. 299).[15] Merrick's gendered persona thus still has connotations of performance; he is not really so far away from the spectacle that he embodied when Treves discovered him. Furthermore, he is still associated with sexual transgression, not only a fallen woman, but a sexual deviant as well.

In her analysis of Treves's writing on Merrick, Christine Ferguson suggests that 'as a tale of metamorphosis, "The Elephant Man" remains incomplete', as Merrick's identity is always presented as a process of becoming: 'while no longer "elephant", he is not quite fully developed "man" either' (Ferguson, 2008, p. 128). In my terms, he is constructed in a variety of gendered and sexualised roles: a monstrous, depraved and corrupting prostitute; a fallen woman rehabilitated into the angel of the house; a queer dandy. His identity, as Ferguson highlights, is never stable. Ironically, these disparate characterisations ultimately do accord with Amanda Anderson's conceptualisation of the Victorian fallen woman as having a 'fractured' identity (Anderson, 1992, p. 2). Moreover, for William Rathbone Greg, writing for the *Westminster Review* in 1850, the fallen woman can never be wholly 'saved': 'the prostitute may not pause, may not recover' (cited in Fisher, 1997, p. 62). Treves's memoir similarly indicates that Merrick's inclination towards deviant, sexualised spectacle cannot be transcended. I turn now to neo-Victorian reimaginings of Joseph Merrick to consider the ways in which the themes of prostitution, gender, and monstrous sexuality are revisited.

Freaking out the Victorian Doctor: Bernard Pomerance's *The Elephant Man*

Bernard Pomerance's *The Elephant Man*, first staged in 1979, makes an interesting departure from the other neo-Victorian versions of Joseph Merrick discussed in this chapter, as the 'Introductory Note' to the text dictates that the actor playing Merrick should not be required to reproduce his 'appearance and his speech naturalistically'; instead, slide projections are offered of the historical Merrick to accompany the action on stage (Pomerance, 1980, pp. v–vi). In Scene Three, however, the actor playing Merrick is required to 'contort himself to approximate projected slides of the real Merrick' (Pomerance, 1980, p. 5). Presumably in response to this direction, the 'Introductory Note' also states: '*No one with any history of back trouble should attempt the part of MERRICK as contorted. Anyone playing the part of MERRICK should be advised to consult a physician about the problems of sustaining any unnatural or twisted position*' (Pomerance, 1980, p. vi; original emphasis). On the one hand, such a warning seems to pathologise the 'real' Merrick. By trying to emulate him, the actor himself could become disabled hence Merrick's deformity is couched as potentially contagious, a disconcerting echo of the impression of contagion and corruption which surrounds Treves's account of the ways in which Merrick's exhibition might morally contaminate its audiences, and the broader discourse of contagious disease which shapes nineteenth-century debates about prostitution. On the other hand, Graham and Oehlschlaeger argue that there is a 'subversive message' at work here, for the note implies that it might be, in fact, the ostensibly 'normal' (and norm-defining) physicians who are inclined towards being 'twisted' or 'unnatural'; this suggestion of the 'deformity of normality' is a trope throughout the play (Graham and Oehlschlaeger, 1992, pp. 85–86) and offers an important counterpoint to the deviance of Merrick which is insinuated at various points in Treves's memoir. Furthermore, considering the undermining of the authority of medicine which also occurs in the course of the play's narrative – particularly the character of Treves himself – the notion that a doctor might be a reliable or respectable figure of authority is in fact exposed as questionable. Put another way, the Introductory Note also introduces the trope of the corruption of the medical profession, a theme which will reach fruition in the Jack the Ripper/surgeon connection which is alluded to in Pomerance's play, Iain Sinclair's novel, and the graphic novel and film versions of *From Hell*.

We witness Merrick in a freak show environment. His manager, Ross, is acting as the barker for the performances, exclaiming: 'See Mother Nature uncorseted and in malignant rage! Tuppence' (Pomerance, 1980, p. 3). Such presentation suggests that the freak show is a space of sexualised disarray, which is overtly gendered as feminine. Yet the swift reference to the admission cost – and its cheapness – undermines this hyperbole: the grandiose claims of sex, violence and horror is bathetically deflated by the mundane reality of economic exchange. Even so, the historical Treves's outrage at the moral dubiousness of the freak show finds resonance in the police intervention depicted in Scene IV, 'This Indecency May Not Continue': 'This is a brutal, indecent, and immoral display. It is a public indecency, and it is forbidden here'. He then 'smacks' Merrick, calling him an 'indecent bastard' (Pomerance, 1980, p. 10). The repetition of the word 'indecent' articulates spluttering moral outrage, but also an obsessive, almost masturbatory focus upon the purported sexual deviance on display. The hypocrisy of this attitude is made clear by the group of 'pinhead' characters[16] who take up the chorus: 'Indecent, indecent, indecent, indecent!' (Pomerance, 1980, p. 11). Their point of reference is not the degradation of the freak show, however, but the witnessing of Merrick being beaten by a man of the law. Police brutality is the shocking exhibition, the 'freakish' and corrupt behaviour on display.

Subsequently, when Merrick is ensconced in the London Hospital he is visited by Ross, who draws a pointed comparison between his previous career as a freak show performer and his 'audiences' with the upper-class visitors who come to visit him in his rooms: 'So I figure you're selling the same service as always. To better clientele. Difference now is you ain't charging for it' (Pomerance, 1980, p. 51). Merrick's response is pertinent:

> Merrick: You make me sound like a whore.
> Ross: You are. I am. They are. Most are. No disgrace, John. Disgrace is to be a stupid whore. Give it for free. Not capitalize on the interest in you.
>
> (Pomerance, 1980, pp. 51–52)

Prostitution – the making of bodies into commodities – is universalised in this formulation; Merrick is normalised, as is 'whoring', which challenges the scandalised horror directed at both sex work and freak show performers in the Victorian discourses discussed above. To be a 'whore' is to be neither a villain nor a victim, but the human condition. In these terms, Merrick is actually more exploited in the context of the medical profession by which he is 'kept' rather than making his own money, which coheres with Nadja Durbach's analysis of Merrick's career as depicted by Tom Norman. Nevertheless, what the play also demonstrates is that some characters are more likely to be compared to 'whores' than others. In a conversation between Treves and Mrs. Kendal, a contemporary actress who was enlisted by the historical Treves to raise the profile of Merrick's case for having a permanent residence at the London Hospital,[17] the surgeon expounds upon this theory that the company of women would be beneficial to the normalisation of Merrick. Although other women have expressed horror at Merrick's appearance, Treves remarks: 'an actress could help. I mean, unlike most women, you won't give in, you are trained to hide your true feelings and assume others' (Pomerance, 1980, p. 29). This version of Treves thus invokes the Victorian anxiety about actresses violating their proper gender role: as Kerry Powell suggests, this was related to the public spectacle of the actress in contrast to the expected private, domestic role of 'respectable' women, but also the established stereotype that associated actresses with prostitution, for the actress might make a 'commodity' of her 'thoughts and feelings, as well as bod[y]' (Powell, 1997, p. 31). Moreover, a further connection is made between Kendal and Merrick, as he remarks on their first meeting: 'You must display yourself for your living then. Like I did' (Pomerance, 1980, p. 32). Although this continuum between actresses, Merrick, and sex workers seems to reiterate the association between Merrick and deviant, 'fallen' femininity which is apparent in Treves's memoir, we must remember Ross's words: everyone in this world is some sort of 'whore', and Merrick's capacity for self-awareness in this scene imbues him with an ownership of his identity which is lacking in Treves's rendering of his pathetic naivety.

Pomerance's version of Merrick is indeed a knowing, sexually desiring subject, but is not adverse to invoking some of the more troubling associations between prostitution and deformity which becomes manifest in Victorian writings on sex work. He discusses with Kendal his desire to see 'a naked woman', and he explains: 'A woman not worn out early. Not deformed by awful life. A lady. Someone kept up. Respectful of herself. You don't know what fairgrounds are like' (Pomerance, 1980, p. 47). Ironically, Merrick has internalised certain aesthetic – and patriarchal – conventions of the requisite for feminine attractiveness, which is intrinsically associated with class and moral values as well. An 'awful' life (or, put another way, moral degradation) leads to physical deformity and the space of the 'fairground', the freak show, is where this is likely to happen. Pomerance therefore leaves unquestioned the conflation of prostitution and physical and moral monstrosity. The play has previously reminded us of one of the oft-quoted details of the historical Treves's medical paper on Merrick published in *The Transactions of the Pathological Society of London* (1885); after detailing Merrick's physical condition, Treves comments: 'It is remarkable that the skin of the penis and scrotum were perfectly normal in every respect' (quoted in Fielder, 1981, p. 176). Pomerance's Treves, when questioned by Kendal about this detail, splutters 'No, no, no, it is quite normal' (Pomerance, 1980, p. 30). For Leslie Fielder, as for Treves, this information turns Merrick's genitalia into a metaphor for his sexual frustration (Fielder, 1981, pp. 176–77). Yet another interpretation of Merrick's 'normal' genitalia in the context of Pomerance's play would be that, beneath his obvious physical differences and his susceptibility to being pathologised and feminised, Merrick has the same conventional patriarchal prejudices as his male contemporaries, dictated by the possession of a 'normal' penis and the gendered entitlements which this connotes.

Kendal obliges Merrick's curiosity by showing him her naked body, but the scene is interrupted by Treves, who is outraged: 'But – have you no sense of decency? Woman, dress yourself quickly [....] Are you not ashamed? Do you know what you are? Don't you know what is forbidden?' (Pomerance, 1980, p. 50). This evidently exposes Treves as a paragon of Victorian sexual repression, yet it is ambiguous as to who the latter lines are actually addressed. The sexually uninhibited actress and the sexually-desiring 'freak' are conflated in a phrase – 'do you know what you are?' – which questions their humanity. Merrick is monstrous, but so is female sexuality, and Treves's remark on 'what should be forbidden' has resonance with the historical Treves's approving commentary on the closure of Merrick's public exhibition as 'among the things that could not be allowed' (Treves, 1923, p. 9). Later in the play, Treves is depicted having a dream in which a role reversal takes place: he is placed in Merrick's role as 'freak' and his ward is the authoritative doctor, expounding upon the 'terrifying' normality of Treves's body: 'The left arm was slighter and fairer, and may be seen in typical position, hand covering the genitals which were treated as a sullen colony in constant need of restriction, governance, punishment' (Pomerance, 1980, p. 62). Merrick appropriates Treves's vocabulary but ultimately we see that it is repressive, anxious attitudes towards sexuality that are constructed as freakish. In the audience of this alternative lecture, one of the 'pinheads' responds: 'It is a pity and disgrace. It is an indecency in fact' (Pomerance, 1980, p. 62). The politics at work are transparent; Victorian prudishness is monstrous and indecent, and the historical Treves is rendered 'freakish' in turn.

After the debacle of Kendal's nakedness, Merrick challenges Treves about his reaction by highlighting his hypocrisy:

> Merrick: Is it okay to see them naked if you cut them up afterwards?
> Treves: Good Lord. I'm a surgeon. That is science.
>
> (Pomerance, 1980, p. 56)

When Merrick further questions Treves's value judgements, the surgeon retaliates: 'And it is not okay. If they undress if you cut them up. As you put it. Make me sound like Jack the, Jack the Ripper' (Pomerance, 1980, p. 57). Treves's reaction is defensive, and this is hardly surprising considering the weight of suspicion upon men with medical knowledge in the wake of the Ripper crimes. Yet, as Graham and Oehlschlaeger identify, the surgeon actually finds it difficult to articulate what it is that distinguishes him from the Ripper (1992, p. 110). The medical profession becomes associated with a monstrous, misogynistic masculinity. It is tempting to conclude that this, along with the play's commentary on the ubiquity of 'whoring', poses a satisfying redress to nineteenth-century associations of femininity and monstrosity, and exposes the precarity of the medical profession's construction of the boundaries between the 'normal' and 'abnormal', the 'respectable' and the 'deviant'. However, it is important to note that Treves's and Merrick's identities have already been placed on a continuum by the play, explicitly by Treves's dream of their role reversal, and implicitly by Merrick's internalisation of the patriarchal privileging of women's beauty and 'respectability'. From this perspective, could it be that Merrick also becomes associated with the moral monstrosity of the Ripper? Pomerance's play does not pursue this connection, but it does problematize understanding this version of *The Elephant Man* as a straightforward reappropriation of Merrick's 'monstrosity'. And, as we shall see, the potential for connecting Joseph Merrick with Jack the Ripper will surface again in his neo-Victorian afterlife.

Sexual victimhood in David Lynch's *The Elephant Man*

The film of *The Elephant Man* (1980), directed by David Lynch, is perhaps the most famous depiction of Merrick's life and it also relies very heavily on Treves's memoir of Merrick. The reading that I offer here of the film suggests that, while it deals with comparable themes as Pomerance's play in terms of monstrosity and sexual danger in relation to Merrick, it is concerned with constructing Merrick as sexually vulnerable, a victim that needs to be protected from exploitative villains and predators. As with Treves's memoir, but in distinction from the other neo-Victorian examples I discuss in this chapter, the film does not make explicit reference to the Ripper story. However, sexualised violence – and how this might be negotiated by the medical profession – is a central theme of Lynch's *The Elephant Man*. Peter W. Graham and Fritz H. Oehlschlaeger have argued that the central motif of Lynch's version of Merrick's story is his love for his mother (Graham and Oehlschlaeger, 1992, p. 135). In Treves's memoir we hear that she deserted him in childhood, and she is denigrated as 'worthless and inhuman' (Treves, 1923, p. 16). Subsequent research has indicated that this was not in fact the case,[18] and she is certainly idealised by Lynch's Merrick. After the film's opening shot of her face, we witness a scene of her being trampled by an elephant. According to Merrick's 'autobiographical' pamphlet, which is reproduced in Michael Howell and Peter Ford's biography,[19] his deformity was caused by his mother being 'frightened by an Elephant' while pregnant: 'she was pushed under the Elephant's feet, which frightened her very much' (Howell and Ford, 2001, p. 173). It is thus maternal impression which is offered as the reason for his condition and, as Chapter Three explained, such theories have the ideological consequence of placing responsibility for 'abnormality' with the mother. In Lynch's film, this scene is recast as a sexual assault on the woman: she is spread out on the ground, turning her head from side to side and screaming as the phallic trunk lunges towards her.[20] In one sense, perhaps this quasi-rape can be understood as alleviating Merrick's mother from blame – this is violence beyond her control – yet it also inaugurates the strand of sexual violence that will run throughout the film. While Lynch's Merrick is never represented as an aggressive, sexualised man – quite the opposite – it suggests that the 'freakish' part of him, his physical deformity, is associated with this monstrous, animal sexuality. The 'Elephant Man' is forged in sexual violence, and will be framed by this threat for his entire life.

However, the primary sexually predatory characters in this film are working-class men associated with the exhibition of Merrick as a freak. When Treves first meets Bytes, Merrick's manager who is a version of Tom Norman, he requests to be allowed to examine Merrick at the Hospital. As the arrangements are finalised, Bytes extends his hand to Treves, but then pulls him closer, almost into an embrace, speaking deliberately: 'We... understand each other [...] More than money has changed hands'. Treves stumbles slightly as he is pulled closer, and Bytes continues: 'We understand each other completely my friend'. Bytes maintains an intense gaze upon Treves throughout this exchange, and his raised eyebrow adds a lascivious air to this menacing interaction. Treves is palpably uncomfortable; he crosses his arm across his own body to push Bytes away. The scene is thus evocative of a coercive sexual advance. After Merrick returns from his sojourn to Bytes's tawdry residence, his manager is intoxicated. Bytes questions him aggressively: 'Where have you been? What did you do?' and beats Merrick with a stick, slightly snivelling and shaking with emotion. Bytes thus appears jealous, as if he is a cuckolded lover abusing his partner for a sexual transgression.[21] Merrick is taken ill after this assault, and Treves is summoned to care for him. As Bytes is thanking Treves he grabs his collar and again pulls him close, saying 'There are a lot of things I could do for you', referring to moving in the right circles for 'this sort of thing [...] in fact, anything at all, if you take my meaning'. The men lock eyes again, until Treves peels Byte's hand off him and pulls away. In summary, then, the characterisation of Bytes elaborates upon Treves's construction of Norman as 'the vampiric showman' (Treves, 1923, p. 19) by developing Bytes into a queer figure.[22] His violent, sexualised advances feminise both Treves and Merrick by highlighting their vulnerability to mauling at his hands. William E. Holladay and Stephen Watt's analysis of the film suggests that Bytes's comments to Treves about what he could 'do for him' demonstrates a merging of the 'businesses of pornography and the exhibition of freaks' (Holloday and Watt, 1989, p. 876). Bytes presumably refers literally to the procurement of more freakish bodies for study, but also underscores that both trade in bodies. Bytes is tantamount to a pimp, and Treves is the punter brokering a deal for access to Merrick's flesh.

For Treves to overcome Bytes's hold over Merrick and rescue him from the degradation of his freak show manager reiterates the theme I identified in the historical Treves's memoir: Merrick is depicted as a 'fallen' woman saved by the doctor from an abusive professional and personal relationship. But, as is hinted by Treves's memoir, Merrick is not safe from prurient intrusion at the hospital either. The hospital porter, Jim, takes over Bytes's mantle as Merrick's pimp. Firstly, he enters Merrick's attic room with a woman. The couple are kissing, but he suddenly grabs her head and forces her to look at Merrick. She screams, and Merrick screams in response. Bruce Kawin argues that such scenes underscore the aphrodisiac function of freakishness, a tradition 'which is a well-recognised function of horror-film dates' (Kawin, 1981, p. 24). Yet the shared scream of horror offers a conceptual connection between Merrick and the woman; both are victims of a forced meeting, and both react in a feminised, hysterical manner. Spurred on by the prospect of making money from bringing paying guests to visit Merrick, he later rounds up a throng of men and women from the pub, and they progress to Merrick's rooms. The scene is cut with shots of Merrick laying out the items in the dressing case that Treves has given him, combing his sparse hair in an elaborate, stylised fashion, and posing with his cigar. As Jim forces his way into the room, he mockingly comments: 'You look beautiful, darlin'. I wouldn't change a thing. You look like the bleedin' Prince of Wales'.[23] At the window, there is a close-up of the face of a dirty and dishevelled older man, who leers in at Merrick while ogling two women he is embracing. As the characters look upon Merrick with disgust, he begins to kiss one's neck, and then turns to kiss the other on the mouth. When Jim lets the group inside, the blonde woman is held up towards Merrick, and he is held in the same way. They are made to kiss, and she is then pinned down on the bed on top of him. To return to Kawin's analysis of the erotic potential in spectacles of horror, we too as the audience of this film are implicated in this voyeuristic frisson. Merrick is then passed between the men, who pour drink over his face and clothes while the soundtrack swells into raucous carnival music. Jim's parting shot is to throw a coin on Merrick's bed. Merrick is again associated with women, this time in their shared status as victims of a sexual assault. The shared mauling of Merrick, accompanied by the fluid pouring over his face and body, connotes a gang rape. Merrick's performance of sophisticated masculinity – 'the bleedin' Prince of Wales' – is punished by him being made into a passive sexual object, and the giving of money emphasises that his body is still a commodity; he is brutally reminded of his role as prostitute freak, worth only a pittance. Lest we miss the over-wrought symbolism of this scene, the aftermath of the visit is represented in a shot scanning across Merrick's bedroom in which his model of a church is shattered[24] and a bunch of broken blooms are strewn across the floor. Faith (or morality) has been crushed, and Merrick has been deflowered. Interestingly, however, the fate of the women who were pushed into participating in this spectacle remains unknown. Granted, their characterisation is not relevant to the plot as Merrick's experience is the focus, yet their simultaneous abuse is down-played. They are coarse and disposable, unlike the graceful and dignified society women who are figured as important in Merrick's recovery. In a sense, therefore, the film colludes with the use and abuse of working-class women's bodies, a movement which comes perilously close to reiterating the economy of nineteenth-century prostitution.[25]

It is impossible to ignore that this has happened in the context of Treves's purported 'rescue' of Merrick, and at times the film does engage with the problematic aspects of Treves's role as a doctor and the justification for his interest in Merrick. Bruce Kawin has commented on the significance of the delayed revelation of Merrick's body in the film (Kawin, 1981, p. 23). This sense of suspense accords with the genre of horror film, the anticipation created by freak show advertising, but also with the titillation of the strip tease. It is here that the trope of the veil in relation to nineteenth-century and neo-Victorian representations of Merrick becomes pertinent. Leslie Fielder has analysed the historical Treves's suspense-filled detailing of Merrick's body in his memoir and medical reports as a form of 'strip-tease' (Fielder, 1981, p. 177). We should remember that the trope of the veil to cover disfigurement but also as a device of erotic allure is a feature of Henry Mayhew's account of 'Park' women. More broadly, however, the veil has been historically associated with femininity. Elaine Showalter explains:

> Veiling was associated with female sexuality and with the veil of the hymen. The veil thus represented feminine chastity and modesty; in rituals of the nunnery, marriage, or mourning, it concealed sexuality. Furthermore, science and medicine had traditionally made use of sexual metaphors which represented "Nature" as a woman to be unveiled by the man.
>
> (Showalter, 1992, p. 145)

There are a succession of veils/unveilings in Lynch's *The Elephant Man* which the viewer experiences before we are actually permitted to see Merrick's appearance in full, and these have gendered and sexualised implications, and also take place in the context of a medical man. Firstly, when Treves secures a private viewing of Merrick with Norman, the showman pulls back a curtain: we see Merrick's body briefly, but the main shot is a close-up of Treves's shocked face, as tears of pity fall from his eyes. The second teasing shot of Merrick is when Treves examines him privately in his office at the hospital, and Merrick is enrobed in his travelling clothes.[26] In this, Treves briefly assumes the role of predator in relation to Merrick's body as his ultimate prize. Treves slowly paces around the room after Merrick, and requests: 'Will you take your hat off? [...] Don't be frightened, I simply want to look at you [...] Take your hat off'. He edges up behind Merrick, repeating 'Don't be frightened', but begins to take his garment before Merrick consents. Before the revelation, the shot fades to black. The doctor's attempts at persuasion become a compelled removal of clothing, hence the scene is cast as an abuse of power as well as a seduction. The third near-revelation of Merrick's body is in the context of medical exhibition. Treves addresses his peers, and a screen is pulled back to reveal the shadow of Merrick's body: we see the shape, but not the flesh. Treves runs clinically through his description of Merrick's anatomy, commenting on the 'normality' of his subject's genitals, at which point the assistants remove Merrick's loincloth. Yet the screen is redrawn as the camera shot returns to the front. The veiling/unveiling of Merrick in these terms becomes associated with the dynamics of the strip-tease; the object of the doctors' (and the film's viewers') prurient desire – Merrick's deformed body, particularly his penis – is suggested and yet withheld, in a dynamic which feminises and sexualises him at the hands of the medical community.[27]

However, unlike the persona that the historical Treves presents in his memoir, Lynch's Treves is gifted with insight into his ambivalent role as the new exhibitor of Merrick. As his friendship with Merrick develops, he confesses to his wife: 'I'm beginning to believe that Mr Bytes and I are very much alike [...] It seems that I've made Mr Merrick into a curiosity all over again'. The continuum between the freak show and medicine, and points of departure, have been repeatedly highlighted throughout this book, but in the case of this version of *The Elephant Man*, it is a medical man that vanquishes the exploitative elements of freakery. When Treves discovers that Merrick has left the hospital after Jim's intrusion into his room, he has a violent confrontation with the porter: 'You're the monster, you're the freak'. Put another way, the film presents working-class masculinity as monstrous, and the more involved that Merrick becomes in the respectable circles of medicine and polite society, the more 'normal' he becomes as well. Doctors are saviours rather than murderers or exploiters; it will be for neo-Victorian versions of Merrick and Treves which engage with the Ripper myth to develop the theme of the monstrous medic.

Jack or Joseph? The Ripper and Merrick narratives of Iain Sinclair and *From Hell*

I want to turn now to a cluster of depictions of Merrick which crystallise a series of themes: the synthesis between physical and moral monstrosity; prostitution; and Jack the Ripper. A key reference point for the connections between Iain Sinclair's *White Chappell, Scarlet Tracings* (1987), Alan Moore and Eddie Campbell's *From Hell* (1999) and the subsequent film adaptation by the Hughes Brothers (2001) is the source text of Stephen Knight's *Jack the Ripper: The Final Solution* (1976). This sensational study argued that the women were murdered to cover up a secret marriage between Prince Albert Victor (who was second in line to the throne at the time of the killings) and a working class woman named Annie Elizabeth Crook, who was friends with the murder victims. According to Knight, these women knew of Annie's secret marriage, and were thus a threat to the lineage and integrity of the British crown. In a complex masonic conspiracy between the Royal family and the painter Walter Sickert, involving various other eminent Victorians, it was decided that William Gull, a respected doctor and physician to Queen Victoria, would be tasked with the elimination of these women. Although Knight's theories have now been widely discredited, it is not difficult to imagine why this heady mix of aristocratic corruption, clandestine sexual relationships and insane doctors would have appealed to the popular imagination. Interestingly, however, Knight does not mention Merrick in his book with regards to the Ripper plot; this is an addition of Sinclair's which is subsequently reiterated by Moore and Campbell. Both texts ostensibly locate Gull as the Ripper, yet they also engage overtly with the impossibility of ever knowing the 'truth' of the murderer's identity and so are inclined to spread the blame further to the medical community and, in some ways, to Joseph Merrick himself.

Sinclair's *White Chappell, Scarlet Tracings* is an esoteric, at times hallucinogenic, and often surreal engagement with the mythologies surrounding the Ripper murders. It offers a dual time frame between the late twentieth century and 1880s (indeed, these periods also become entwined at points), and broadly features three main strands of narrative: a group of book sellers in the late 1970s, 'Sinclair'[28] and Joblard's fascination with the Ripper case and their psychogeographic musings about London, and the arcane thoughts and activities of Gull as the main Ripper figure. However, there are various 'Rippers' in this novel, not least the Ripper enthusiasts who become obsessed with solving the mystery of the crimes, as Joblard identifies: 'There's something inherently seedy and salacious in continually picking the scabs off these crimes, peering at mutilated bodies' (Sinclair, 2004, p. 47). The act of attempting to make sense of the past in this sense becomes a queasy combination of disfigurement and spectatorship. This is reminiscent of Sherman's poem discussed at the beginning of this chapter, for this salacious 'peering' at the Ripper victims aligns them with freaks, and those who wish to look at them as the morally monstrous audience. This blurring of identities between freak and spectator becomes more explicit when 'Sinclair' and Joblard gain access to the skeleton of Joseph Merrick in the London Hospital Medical College Museum:

> As we approach the skeleton cabinet, we approach our darker selves. Joblard's meat outline is imposed on the twisted bone armature. My face stares out from the skull cast [...] The glass is a mirror [...] the eyes of the audience are brought to this place to look into themselves, to look out, from the painted shadow of what a man was, to the three dark shapes crossing the floor to join with him, in one unbroken moment.
>
> (Sinclair, 2004, p. 100)

The metaphor of the freak as a mirror, as detailed in this book's Introduction, is here made literal: Joblard, 'Sinclair', and the doctor who guides them to the cabinet (he is the other of the 'three dark shapes crossing the floor') are visually imposed upon Merrick. This incident is couched as if they actually become him, but, of course, reflections can be deceptive. The confrontation with Merrick aligns him with 'darkness', the sense of inner corruption which leads the men to 'pick the scabs' of the Ripper case. It is the audience who make Merrick monstrous, who seek to find their own self within his body, but he only become a point of identification for horror, brutality, and prurience and, as we shall see, the novel does little to redress this obliteration of the historical Merrick's identity.

Yet *White Chappell, Scarlet Tracings* is also flagrantly aware of the dissolved boundary between 'history' and 'fiction' as the tangled rewriting of the Ripper murders and the cast of fictional, mythological, and actual historical characters demonstrates. Indeed, Treves's memoir is described in comparable terms:

> Treves' simple act of charity had to be explained. Fiction was its truth. There were errors in the account he gave: the names of streets faltered, time flowing always in the direction of decay, improving upon a clumsy excess of detail. The truth can only be remade out of lies. What horror! A life struck out of pure invention.
>
> (Sinclair, 2004, p. 97)

In these terms, Treves's rewriting of Merrick has much in common with some aspects of neo-Victorianism: the sense that fiction offers another, paradoxically more 'truthful', account of history, or is driven by the impulse to impose a coherent narrative structure on the messy unknowability of the past. But, in the case of Treves's version of Merrick, the fictionalised aspects of his remembering make his subject more monstrous. At one point in the novel, 'Sinclair' opines that certain authors – Conan Doyle, Robert Louis Stevenson – create a 'presence', fictional characters which exceed their control: 'figures [...] like Rabbi Loew's Golem, [who] became too much and too fast to be contained within the conventional limits of that fiction. They got out into the stream of time, the ether: they escaped into the labyrinth. They achieved an independent existence' (Sinclair, 2004, p. 117). Put another way, certain fictional creations are so compelling that they take on a cultural afterlife of their own. The pantheon of late-Victorian characters who can be categorised in this way are familiar to neo-Victorian audiences: Sherlock Holmes; Dr Jekyll and Mr Hyde; Dracula. Indeed, Jack the Ripper, with the reimaginings and fictionalisations which swirl around his obscure historical personage can be perceived in a comparable vein. And, in *White Chappell, Scarlet Tracing*'s world, Joseph Merrick – first fictionalised by Treves – takes on a similar role.

The novel imagines Treves ritually summoning up his 'creature', a Golem,[29] which the surgeon addresses: '"Thou shall be called Joseph and thou shalt lodge within my house. Thou, Joseph, must obey my commands, when and whither I may send thee [...]." [...] And then it began' (Sinclair, 2004, p. 98). What 'begins' is a process of obsessive care and control of Merrick, 'But, equally, Merrick controlled him; appearing in the seductive guise of pure deformity. Making Treves vampire; returning compulsively' (Sinclair, 2004, p. 98). The reference to the vampire is important, for it damns Treves with the very terminology he used to describe Tom Norman's exploitation of Merrick, but also associates him with the images of the Ripper as a monster or vampire in the nineteenth-century press. Merrick is cast as culpable in the symbiotic relationship which develops between them. On leaving his role as public performer with Norman:

> He willingly abandoned himself [...] to the sensationalism of his history. The victim drew the hand of the author over the paper [...] Treves worked with surgical precision; cut away all extraneous dialogue, local colour, architecture, weather. Merrick was the nerve of all of this: and it was at the cost of his own existence [...] Uninstructed, the Golem, like one mad, began running about in the Jewish quarter of the city, threatening to destroy everything [...] The sideshow freak becomes Presence.
>
> (Sinclair, 2004, p. 99)

While Merrick is named 'the victim', he also becomes like a muse to Treves. In the process of his inspiring Treves's fictionalisation, however, his own 'existence' becomes lost. He becomes a 'presence' or fictional 'figure' and this is what makes him monstrous, the 'Golem' who lurks in Whitechapel, which forms the bond between Merrick and the Ripper.

Elsewhere, the novel refers to Treves's story of Merrick as constructing him as 'Ganesa of the Last Days, Elephant Head' (Sinclair, 2004, p. 97). This alludes to Treves's description of Merrick as 'hideous as an Indian idol' (Treves, 1923, p. 21). The orientalism of this association goes unremarked upon in Sinclair's text, but instead becomes a way to connect Merrick with the role of sex worker. A subsequent chapter splices scenes of Treves and Merrick's activities in the nineteenth century with 'Sinclair' and Joblard's exploits with a stripper. She is described as wearing 'a lizardskin coat around her shoulders, naked otherwise' (Sinclair, 2004, p. 138) which forms an interesting point of comparison with Treves's detailing of the 'bag of [...] repulsive flesh' which resembled 'a dewlap suspended from the neck of a lizard' (Treves, 1923, p. 5). Sex worker and freak show performer are conflated in an image of degeneration, but more significant is the way in which the text's description of Merrick's as Treves's 'Hyde' blurs into the following passage: 'When she is naked [...] they bring out the mask, the great Elephant's Head of Ganesa. So she sways, she lifts her arms [...] She threatens the moon with her tusk [...] Now it spears Joblard's side' (Sinclair, 2004, p. 141). The association of Treves/Merrick with Jekyll/Hyde is not the only strategy of doubling in this scene, for the sex worker becomes Merrick's double as well, taking on a mask which makes her a grotesque yet sexualised spectacle. But clearly this is not an entirely passive role, for it allows her to penetrate the body of one of her male spectators, the tusk as a 'spear' in Joblard's side. She is thus also a potential Ripper, conflated with Merrick, a queer figure of freakishness and monstrous muse presiding over the sexual misrule.

For the nineteenth-century narrative's part, we learn that 'Treves was beginning to take a positive relish in introducing Joseph to new experiences: subtle pleasures could be derived from watching' (Sinclair, 2004, p. 137). What these experiences are, and precisely what is being watched is never made entirely clear due to the text's obscurity, but a scene is described of two women visiting Treves's rooms:

> The old woman on the bed appears to be eating her way into the other, a witch – Merrick shrinking back – black mouth towards the head of the unborn child. The apprehension and creation of his own deformity; he pushes back into the chair. Treves has shed his coat, sleeves rolled, no water, pulls the old woman by the shoulder and will lift his creature up into her place. The coachman leading her out into the courtyard [...] The coachman lifting and banging the woman against the wall, repeatedly driving against her; her head almost broken from her beck, shaken loose, a dried-up orange in a torn stocking. Tongue lolling and dribbling. The waters. Dead eyes. Finishing with her, she falls into the doorway of the house [...] Holding Merrick above the body of the girl, so that he stares directly into her face. And sees whatever Treves cannot see [...] And they are all, just then, entirely one being.
>
> (Sinclair, 2004, p. 142)

The references to Treves's rolled sleeves, the location of these events in his consultation rooms, and the reference to the 'head of the unborn child' seem to suggest that the younger woman has come to have her baby delivered by the surgeon. However, the image of the older woman appearing to be 'eating her way into the other' might suggest a sex act, cunnilingus, performed for the benefit of the spectators. Similarly, images of sex and death are at work in the violence of the coachman towards the older woman: she might be being physically assaulted, even murdered, yet at the same time raped. That this takes place in collusion with Treves, and the gynaecological theme of the younger woman's exhibition, associates the surgeon and his coachman with the Ripper. Merrick is not merely a spectator, but a participant, and the lifting of his body on top of the girl suggests, as Brian Baker identifies, a sexual encounter (Baker, 2007, p. 75). Yet Merrick is described in passive terms, 'lifted' into this position; we are reminded of Lynch's Merrick's enforced intimacy with the woman who visits his room in *The Elephant Man*. At the same time, Merrick is gifted with some sort of visionary abilities here, the extra-sensory perception to see something – unspoken – into the girl's experiences. In the final line, the novel returns to the image of Merrick as a mirror: he is the conduit for the birth, sex, and death that has taken place, the inspiration for abuse and exploitation even as he is subjected to these experiences himself. He unites the identities of abused working-class women, young and old, the brutal working-class man, the perverted doctor. In short, Sinclair's Merrick comes to represent the monstrosity and degradation of the age, but also coexists as a reference point for sex workers in the late twentieth century. While the novel acknowledges that cultural afterlives of fictional characters can run away from authorial intentions and become monstrous, it ultimately compounds this monstrosity by figuring Merrick as gothic villain and feminised victim in turn.

As Brian Baker has identified, Alan Moore and Eddie Campbell's graphic novel *From Hell* is indebted to Sinclair's text in a variety of ways (Baker, 2007, p. 60) and the inclusion of the Merrick-as-Ganesa theme is explicitly acknowledged in Moore's annotations as inspired by Sinclair (Moore, 2001, Appendix I, p. 8). In Chapter 2, William Gull is invited by Treves to meet Merrick. Gull suggests Merrick's physical resemblance to 'Ganesa [...] the Indian God of Wisdom [...] Just think – in India you would be worshipped' (Moore and Campbell, 2001, Chapter 2, p. 24). Merrick questions 'Worfipped?' in response. As Gull leaves, the illustration shows Merrick sitting on his bed in the dark. He repeats 'Worfipped', as an affirmation rather than a question (Moore and Campbell, 2001, Chapter 2, p. 24). The rendering of Merrick's speech is important; Christine Ferguson has identified that in Treves's memoir, the development of Merrick's speech is related to the process of his becoming 'human' in the doctor's eyes (Ferguson, 2008, pp. 114–33). In *From Hell,* Merrick is already marked by his physical appearance in the illustrations, and so perhaps this infantilised manner of speaking further alienates him from the reader – at times, it is extremely difficult to understand the phonetic spelling of his utterances. However, a strange consequence of this difficulty in reading the words is that they begin to make more sense when read aloud. Put another way, we are encouraged to speak as Merrick to comprehend his utterances, and this might offer a sense of identification which is not just us imposing our fears and fantasies onto Merrick (as the Merrick-as-mirror motif often is in the examples discussed above). Nevertheless, this empathy is subsequently complicated. In Chapter 5's detailing of the night of Polly Nicholl's murder, Gull's carriage stops outside the London Hospital. The illustrations depict Merrick wearing his cloak and cap, and picking a rose in the garden (Moore and Campbell, 2001, Chapter 5, p. 28). Holding her face against the window, Gull requests she repeats after him '"Salutation to Ganesa". Can you say that?' She responds: '"Ha... I... I think I can, sir. Sa...sal'tation to Ga-nee-sha"' (Moore and Campbell, 2001, Chapter 5, p. 28). Gull's hands close around her neck, and two consecutive pictures show Polly's choking, bloated face next to Merrick slightly crumpling a rose by smelling it, the petals falling away (Moore and Campbell, 2001, Chapter 5, p. 29). This victim of the Ripper thus becomes a sacrifice to Merrick. Again, his physical appearance is the inspiration for brutal deviance. Merrick plays a role in the crimes of the Ripper, and his pride in Gull's compliment to him in Chapter 2 of the graphic novel serves to make him, albeit unwittingly, collusive in this. The close-up of her bloated face underscores the theme identified above of his disfigurement being contagious. The positioning of Merrick with the flower is interesting. Although on one hand this might feminise him by representing his refinement and delicacy, on the other the image of the broken flower offers an echo of the 'deflowerment' of Merrick in Lynch's film. The crucial difference, of course, is that it is he who is responsible for the damaged bloom, restating that he is connected with masculine villainy rather than feminine victimhood.

However, the orientalism of Merrick-as-Ganesa might be another way of signalling his femininity. In the scene described above, Merrick is represented as wearing his face covering in the hospital garden, in effect a 'veil' and, as Doy discusses, the veiled woman is a key trope of orientalism (Doy, 2001, p. 130). On Gull's second visit to Merrick, he tells him a story of a man living in India who is believed to be an incarnation of Ganesa. When this man is sleeping, 'each movement's studied; taken as an omen for the nation as a whole [...] If he starts violently from sleep, it augurs war'. As Gull departs, he warns Merrick to 'do nothing sudden in YOUR slumber [...] lest our British Empire come to dust' (Moore and Campbell, 2001, Chapter 5, p. 13; original emphasis). In the context of the plot of *From Hell*, Merrick's death in his sleep does not occur, but Moore's Appendix notes the 'irony' of this detail, 'given that John Merrick and the British Empire died in their sleep at roughly the same time' (Moore and Campbell, Appendix I, p. 18). Merrick is, albeit in jest, depicted as a threat to the British establishment and nation, which subtly aligns him to the sex workers of the graphic novel who must be murdered to keep their knowledge of Annie Crook's illegitimate child – and her potential claim to the throne of the Empire – a secret. Again, this neo-Victorian version of Merrick fluctuates queasily between masculine 'monster' and feminised victim.

The way in which Moore and Campbell's version of Merrick is translated into the film version of *From Hell* is even more disturbing. He makes two brief appearances, firstly in one of Detective Abberline's opium inspired visions. A shakily angled camera – presumably simulating someone lurching down the streets of Whitechapel – comes across various images of rot and decay: filthy slums teeming with rats. We witness prostitutes having sex with clients against walls, and amidst these scenes of squalor features a brief shot of Merrick's face. His face and head are uncovered and we get a full look at his deformed face. The scene then cuts to a man opening a bag containing surgeon's knives and rapid flashes of the knife working across a woman's exposed body. Merrick's depiction is incongruous in terms of the historical figure, for Treves makes no mention of him being able to wander the streets alone, and even if he did, he would be unlikely to go out without the protection of his headdress. The symbolism of his positioning in this shot is transparent: he, along with the other scenes, is cast as a signifier of the city's corruption and dissipation, its grotesquery, its moral monstrosity. Furthermore, this generalised degradation – crucially, including Merrick – is pictured as feeding in to, and perhaps feeding off, the Ripper's crimes. This is Whitechapel as Hell, of which Merrick is a denizen condemned as a sinner due to his physical appearance. By implication, the backstreets of the East End of London become a freak show for our consumption, degrading the women who work there, and reducing Merrick to a mere horrific spectacle. That he is conjured in an opium-induced vision reiterates his role as 'oriental' other. His only other appearance is within the 'conscious' world of the film, but is no less troubling. Merrick is shown being exhibited to the medical students and professionals at the London hospital; he is fulsomely introduced by the doctor, and dramatically unveiled to the gasps and horrified expressions of the medical men in attendance. He turns slowly, as if on a podium, allowing the audience present and us spectators of the film, to take in the full horror of his appearance. The unveiling of him invokes again the dynamics of the striptease. His flesh is there to be consumed and defined by his audience, deemed hideous, abnormal and deviant; not so far removed, of course, from the 'deviant' bodies of the sex workers that are also being exposed and dissected by medical men throughout the film.[30] Gull is in the audience, and stares with a slightly opened mouth, not appalled but fascinated. In the documentary *Born Freak* (2002), Mat Fraser explores the potential continuum between Victorian freak show performers and contemporary actors with physical impairments. He discusses Merrick, and his conclusions on the 'problems' of reclaiming Merrick as a positive role-model for twenty-first-century performers are summarised by David Mitchell and Susan Snyder:

> Whereas most freak performers sought to establish a rapport with their audiences, Merrick turned himself into a pure object. The Elephant Man act cultivated no verbal interaction and allowed himself to be gazed upon without interruption. Thus, Merrick 'realized' the full promise of the freak show: permission to stare without recrimination in the encounter with another's humanity.
>
> (Mitchell and Snyder, 2005, n.p.)

If we accept Fraser's analysis, what the exhibition of Merrick in *From Hell* signifies is a conflation of the freak show with medical exhibition, for this is precisely what happens to him in this film. He is afforded no verbal interaction, for he utters no audible words, and is the object of interrupted gazing. Gull's presence at Merrick's 'unveiling' might be interpreted as reiterating the trope of Merrick-as-inspiration for the Ripper's crimes, but the film does not develop this link and, without prior knowledge of the graphic novel, Merrick's role in the adaptation of *From Hell* with regards to the plot remains obscure. He is, in Fraser's terms, 'a pure object'.

Peeping Joseph: Rethinking Merrick as an agent in *Ripper Street*

The BBC's *Ripper Street* is set in the aftermath of the Whitechapel murders. The local branch of the police force, 'H Division', are responsible for this area of the East End of London but obviously have failed to arrest the killer. The Ripper murders cast a shadow over the dramas which unfold but Jack himself is always already absent: a spectre which haunts Whitechapel's inhabitants, but never fully materialises. Yet the series is set in a world which produced and has been further shaped by the Ripper, with crime, bloody violence, poverty, and prostitution being rife. The first two series also feature the trope of disfigurement in a variety of ways: Inspector Reid, the central protagonist, is revealed to have burns covering his body as a result of a boat accident in which he lost his daughter;[31] Fred Best, a scurrilous journalist, loses his ear and wears a prosthetic; Detective Sergeant Bennet Drake bears the scars of his brutal boxing matches; a gang of women suffering from 'phossy jaw' take their revenge by kidnapping the men they hold responsible for their ravaged faces and health.[32] Most significantly, the first two episodes of Series 2 feature Joseph Merrick who is in residence at the London Hospital.

In Series 2, Episode 1 (entitled 'Pure as the Driven'), Reid, Drake, and Homer Jackson (a former US Army Surgeon and Pinkerton's detective who now works for H Division), visit the London hospital to question a police officer who has been impaled upon an iron railing and is under the care of Treves. The men walk across the courtyard over which Merrick's window looks. In the audience's first glimpse of Merrick he sits at the window draped in lacy curtains, framed by its pane which has flowers at its base. He is positioned as resting in the feminised, domestic sphere set apart from the masculine world of action which the detectives inhabit. Yet as Reid pauses to speak with him, a conversation out of earshot of the viewer, and Jackson comments in surprise: 'Reid knows the Elephant Man?', Drake responds sharply: 'That's Mr. Merrick to you. On rare occasions he may travel and leave the city for a while. When he does, the men of H Division provide escort'. The nature of these travels remain unspecified, as do the 'new experiences' which Merrick has under the tutelage of Treves in Sinclair's novel, or the reason why Merrick is wandering the streets of Whitechapel in the film of *From Hell*. Yet unlike these other examples, in *Ripper Street* Merrick's outings are not a sign of unspecified deviance. The police escort that he receives is presumably for his own protection but, in Drake's eyes, it is also a mark of status and respect, hence his instruction that Jackson should dignify Merrick with a formal name rather than his freak show appellation. The presence of Treves on these visits is not mentioned, which imagines Merrick a life beyond the sequestered domestic sphere of the Hospital and as an agent independent of the medical world.

This sense of agency becomes further developed in his participation in the plotline which runs over the two episodes. Inspector Jedediah Shine kills his injured sergeant at the Hospital to cover up his own involvement in the heroin trading taking place in Whitechapel and the only witness is Merrick, who observes the murder through a window whilst on one of his night-time wanders around the hospital grounds. Merrick is now positioned as bearing witness, possessing the power of the gaze rather than being a spectacle. Furthermore, he becomes a key source of information about the circumstances of a fellow freak show performer. In Series 2, Episode 2 (entitled 'Am I Not Monstrous?'), Stella

Brooks, a young woman with a tail at the base of her spine has been murdered and her child abducted. Seeking information about her life from the freak show performers with which she worked, Reid is directed to Merrick as her one friend. He explains to Reid about the relationship between Stella and John, her child's father. Merrick also directs Reid towards the perpetrator of Stella's murder and the baby's kidnapper: John's father, Dr. William Corcoran, who is obsessed with ridding his family of an inherited degenerative disease. Hence, Merrick is also a source of knowledge and intelligence, and his friendship with Stella belies the historical Treves's construction of Merrick as unmanned due to his lack of association with women.

Despite struggling under the threats of Shine, he makes the decision to seek out Reid to offer the crucial testimony of his witness of the murder and is compelled to travel across the city alone to find the police at the museum where Corcoran works.[33] Merrick arrives at the venue to find John about to kill himself and his child to spare the infant the trials of living with a disability, but Joseph is able to talk him down with reference to the 'joy' he experiences in his life despite being 'monstrous':

> I hear the bells ring from my room... the chatter of nurses. Once, beyond my window... I... I... watched one of their number make love to the Night Porter. I have never known the secret intimacy of a woman that might have told me that I was desired, beautiful in another's eyes. You've known that [...] Would you deny him that joy, that hope?

It is this invocation of John's ability to attract women and produce a son – and the prospect of this son in turn becoming a lover of women when an adult – that convinces him to climb to pass the child to safety in Merrick's arms. Merrick is a desiring subject in this scenario rather than the romantic child in Treves's memoir, and he demonstrates compassion, sensitivity, and bravery: a combination of traditional masculine and feminine qualities. Yet there are some troubling aspects to this characterisation: Merrick's role as voyeur to sex, while couched in tender and heteronormative terms, is a rather more dubious form of bearing witness in comparison to his nobler role as the possessor of righteous knowledge of Shine's crime. He must also function as a metaphorical mirror for John's superior sexual appeal; John possesses what he never could, and the spectacle of Merrick's deformed face and body makes him grateful for his own relative aesthetic qualities. It thus seems that the dynamics of the freak show are never far from neo-Victorian versions of Joseph. Nevertheless, Merrick is celebrated as the hero of the hour. Reid praises him in glowing terms: 'Forever and always, Mr Merrick, I shall remember you for this' and to consolidate his position on the side of the good, Merrick also imparts to Reid his knowledge of Shine's crime.

This neo-Victorian version of Merrick therefore delivers him from the role of villain and (almost) manages to restrain itself from presenting him as a sexual deviant. But even if the world of *Ripper Street* can rewrite history to re-member Merrick as an active hero, it cannot quite bring itself to free him from the position of victim. Shine learns of Merrick's witness to his crime, and visits his bedroom. As he enters, Merrick falls back on his bed gasping, his legs slightly open. He threatens Merrick to not tell what he has seen, and compares his need to sleep upright to being 'a marionette on a puppeteer's string'. We return to a familiar image: Merrick being violated in his bedroom, and his comparison to a puppet returns him to the position as a passive object to be manipulated as others see fit. The concluding scene of Merrick's cameo in the series is his death. Shine knows that he has told Reid of what he saw and returns to his room. The connotations of rape are reiterated, as Merrick struggles on the bed, Shine gently takes away his supportive pillow as Merrick begs 'Please, please'. What is the significance of this reimagining of Merrick's death as murder? It surely consolidates his role as victim, but it represents institutional deviance in the form of a corrupt officer of the law. In these terms, Merrick is a victim of Shine's ruthlessness just as many other characters are in the series. He is not exceptional, but a victim of the system like numerous socially disenfranchised characters in *Ripper Street*. Also, he does not, as Treves's memoir sentimentally supposed, die from lying down so he can sleep 'like other people' (Treves, 1923, p. 36). Aside from his desire to find love, Merrick does not appear to feel the need to assimilate, to conform to 'normality' in this version of his life; he thus seems to accept his physical difference, rather than it being a source of sadness, tragedy, or anger. It is also notable that the theme of feminised orientalism in relation to Merrick is redressed. As Shine murders Merrick, he remarks 'What will men say? The Elephant Man hoped to lay down and rest like any other Englishman'. Why should Shine invoke national identity at this moment? In contrast to Moore and Campbell's *From Hell*, Merrick is apparently not a threat to the Empire, but is imagined as desiring to be assimilated within it. Indeed, it is Shine who is marked as an 'orientalist' subject in this series: he has worked in Hong Kong under the auspices of the Empire yet has ostensibly turned 'native' in his relationship with a Chinese lover, Blush Pang. When his torso is revealed in the boxing ring in Series 2, Episode 7, he is marked with a tattoo of an oriental ideogram. Ironically, his orientalism is written on his body, mirroring the positioning of Merrick as orientalised due to his deformities. Yet Shine uses and abuses the Empire for his own gains, engaging in the trading of opium and heroin and discarding Pang to save his own career (Series 2, Episode 1). His representation is an indictment of the power relations of Empire which lead to Merrick's depiction as a 'hideous [...] Oriental idol' in Treves's memoir and which has fed into other neo-Victorian depictions of Merrick as Ganesa.

At the conclusion of 'Am I Not Monstrous?', Treves is grief-stricken by Merrick's death, and, although previously he was holding the balance of both Reid's and Shine's respective fates as both were suspects in the murder of Shine's sergeant, he does not appear to have the heart to assist in any further investigations. He simply tells Chief Inspector Frederick Abberline that the sergeant died from natural causes. It is Treves's affection for Merrick which leads to this miscarriage of justice and allows Shine to continue in his criminal activities. Perhaps this does taint both Treves and Merrick as, albeit inadvertently, the closeness of their relationship allows villainy to continue. In fact, although Treves is clearly respected by Reid and designated as a 'good man' by Shine, he is not beyond threatening violence: when Shine bursts into his operating theatre in the course of Treves's treatment of his sergeant in Episode 1 of Series 2, the surgeon remarks: 'You will move yourself from my operating theatre or I shall remove your nose from your face'. The motif of the surgeon as having the potential to disfigure offers a brief, though pointed, nod to the Ripper-as-doctor theory. Yet a small detail which redeems this version of Treves is his ability to remember his patient's proper name: Joseph. *Ripper Street*'s Merrick is neither John, nor Jack.

Conclusion

There is a dualism at the heart of the representations of Joseph Merrick that I have considered in this chapter: is he a victim or villain? Ironically, perhaps it is this uncertain multiplicity of identity which leads us back to the fears and fantasies surrounding the Victorian prostitute. My initial discussion of discourses surrounding the figure of the 'fallen woman' emphasised the ways in which she was constructed as potentially disfiguring to her male clients, but also disfigured, an allegory of moral monstrosity which reaches a horrific zenith in the grotesque spectacle of the Ripper victims. Fredrick Treves's memoir dwells on the depravity and corruption of the freak show and positions himself – and medicine more broadly – as the saviour to the 'fallen', feminised state of Merrick. Yet Treves's narrative still struggles to fix his subject in a securely gendered role. These oscillations of Merrick's identity – and the sexual politics at play in these fluctuations – shape the depiction of Merrick's body and subjectivity in neo-Victorianism. In Pomerance's play, everyone might be a 'whore', but the site of 'real' monstrosity resides in Victorian sexual prudery which restricts the lives of women and freak show performers alike. Ironically, though, this stereotype of Victorianism – the play's unquestioning deployment of the 'repressive hypothesis', in Michel Foucault's terms – is perhaps guilty of the same hyperbole and misrepresentation as freak show discourse. Freakery – or physical and/or moral monstrosity – does become something of a free floating signifier in neo-Victorian versions of Joseph Merrick. Although Lynch seems content to fix Merrick as a feminised victim of sexual violence, it is the film's working-class men who are depraved and corrupt in mind, if not flesh. Monstrosity is associated with the medical profession in the Ripper-as-doctor narratives of Sinclair, Moore and Campbell, and the Hughes Brothers. Yet Merrick is consistently tainted by association to the medical profession, a figure of identification, repudiation, and horror at various points. Furthermore, racial power relationships coalesce with the politics of sexual villains/victims: Merrick is sometimes Ganesa, sometimes an exotic veiled feminine spectacle, sometimes an ironic threat to the British Empire. Whilst murderous medics and pitiful prostitutes might also become figures of freakery, this does little to rehabilitate Merrick from monstrous, generalised otherness. However, I suggest that *Ripper Street* offers the most complex and thought-provoking re-membering of Merrick. He is not completely idealised, nor victimised, but emerges as subject to comparable experiences, oppressions, and triumphs as the rest of the milieu of Whitechapel. Refusing to be fixed in a finite role, there are multiple possibilities of identity for – and identification with – this version of Joseph Merrick, whilst still recognising the specific, material circumstances of his life.

Afterword: The Neo-Victorian Enfreakment of P. T. Barnum

The inclusion of Phineas Taylor Barnum in this study might initially seem incongruous in several ways; he is not strictly a Victorian (being born and living in America, when not on tour) and was of 'average' physical appearance. Indeed, Barnum is famous for his role as a showman, and moreover being repeatedly involved in celebrated 'hoaxes' involving his performers. Born in Connecticut in 1810, he owned a business and founded a newspaper before moving into the exhibition business in the 1830s. His first foray into exhibiting 'curiosities' came with his purchase of Joice Heth, a formerly enslaved women who was billed as being the nurse of George Washington and as being over 160 years old. Upon her death, an autopsy revealed Heth to be no more than 80. Undeterred by the negative press he received for this hoax, he purchased Scudder's American Museum in New York in 1841, renaming the establishment 'Barnum's American Museum' and populating the building with a range of performers with extraordinary bodies. He also made considerable amounts of money through his management and promotion of Jenny Lind, a singer, and Charles Stratton as 'General Tom Thumb'. He branched out into theatre and circuses in the later years of his life, produced several autobiographies and self-help books, and dabbled in politics. He died in 1891, hailed as an American hero of self-fashioning and showmanship.[1] However, it is important to recognise that Barnum had a role in the careers of five out of the seven performers discussed in this book: he promoted the Bunker twins, Stratton and Warren, and Anna Swan. Furthermore, he was acquainted with and a certain source of inspiration for Tom Norman, the manager of Joseph Merrick,[2] and his exhibition of Heth and a later succession of ethnographic 'freaks' surely has some uncomfortable resonances with the career of Sarah Baartman. As a way of reflecting on *Neo-Victorian*

Freakery's analyses of these performers' narratives lives and cultural afterlives, then, this Afterword offers brief readings of three neo-Victorian novels which fictionalise Barnum: Stacy Carlson's *Among the Wonderful*, Melanie Benjamin's *The Autobiography of Mrs Tom Thumb*, and Angela Carter's *Nights at the Circus*. I argue that these versions of Barnum self-consciously subject him to the hyperbolising and often exploitative discourses within which he himself framed his exhibits; put another way, in neo-Victorian accounts of Barnum, it is he that becomes a curiosity, the 'other', the 'freak'. But, as my discussion of the Victorian and neo-Victorian freak show in this book has emphasised repeatedly, the construction of freakery is an ambivalent process. So, what might the enfreakment of Barnum tell us about the politics of neo-Victorian freakery more broadly?

Carlson's version of Barnum has a very limited narrative voice, and is often an elusive figure; the performers and other employees of the American Museum are often seeking him to ask for information, or waiting in vain for him to visit. The reader is largely left to construct an image of him based on the speculations and perceptions of his employees. On the brief occasions he does meet either Ana or Guillaudeu, he is couched in quasi-mythological terms: 'Not quite leonine, was he, but what? What does a griffin look like?' (Carlson, 2011, p. 122). The concept of Barnum as almost animalistic seems to imply an 'exotic', bestial mode of presentation. Put another way, the freak show performers project their own fears and fantasies upon him; an ironic reversal of the one aspect of the dynamics of freakery discussed throughout this book, in which the 'freak' becomes a mirror against which the audience reflect upon their own relative 'normality'. For Guillaudeu, Barnum becomes tantamount to an apocalyptic portent. Considering the havoc that Barnum has wreaked upon the scientific, scholarly environment of the old Scudder's Museum, the taxidermist is reminded of a work by his 'hero', Baron Georges Cuvier, who writes of 'long periods of equilibrium on earth' being terminated by 'fire or flood', after which a new age would dawn. Guillaudeu 'had the uncomfortable sensation that Cuvier's theory explained more than just an ancient scenario: A dark whirlwind, he realized, had struck the museum in the form of Phineas T. Barnum' (Carlson, 2011, pp. 9–10). The invocation of Cuvier's name is significant; as Chapter 1's discussion of Sarah Baartman demonstrated, Cuvier's 'scientific' view of Sarah's body – informed by patriarchal and colonial power relationships – was the cause of her posthumous exhibition as an objectified 'specimen' and, in turn, spawned the neo-Victorian attempts to reclaim her life as a subject with agency and dignity.

Barnum's introduction of live human performers into his American Museum, and his disregard for taxonomising principles of display, is depicted as an overthrowing of the old order of scientists such as Cuvier.

Such an undermining of scientific authority is also apparent in his employment of three 'Professors', who ostensibly should '"add Scientific Authority to selected exhibits and performances"' (Carlson, 2011, p. 119). Guillaudeu is initially delighted that scientific rigour is being restored to the Museum, yet on quizzing the men, he is told: '"we are actors by trade [...] We are here to give the *illusion* [...] of science"' (Carlson, 2011, p. 121). In a development of Alice Domurat Dreger's commentary on the way in which medical discourse might be appropriated by the nineteenth-century freak show to frame the extraordinary bodies on display (Dreger, 2004, pp. 123–24), Carlson's Barnum does not only appropriate 'science' to the purposes of constructing freakery, he aligns 'scientific authority' with a mode of performance. 'Science' – or 'medicine' – is an 'illusion', as is freakery, and hence scientific discourse itself becomes akin to a freak show performer. The challenge to scientific and medical authority has been a compelling theme throughout the neo-Victorian sources discussed in this book and, furthermore, medical exhibition is repeatedly depicted as more oppressive and exploitative than the freak show ever could be. In Chapter 1, both Parks and Chase-Riboud depict Cuvier as predatory and perverse; in Chase-Riboud's formulation, he is murderous and sub-human. In Chapter 3, Susan Swan's version of Anna Swan figures her unwitting exhibition during a medical examination as a form of rape. Jane Sullivan's rendering of Charles Stratton and Lavinia Warren, as discussed in Chapter 4, might highlight their own collusion with the procurement of children for exhibition, but this is hardly comparable to the horrors of Dr Musgrave's plans for the murder of the 'Tom Thumb baby'. This trope reaches its culmination in the depictions of doctors as pimps or even Rippers in Chapter 5's exploration of Joseph Merrick. In summary, then, neo-Victorianism tends to position scientific attitudes towards extraordinary bodies as 'monstrous'.

This is not to suggest that the freak show is idealised in neo-Victorianism. It is still sometimes a site of degradation and dehumanisation for the performers involved. But the sense remains that some exhibitions are conceptualised as more exploitative than others. This too becomes an issue in Carlson's novel. Guillaudeu and Mr Archer, one of Barnum's publicity men, discuss Barnum's previous exhibition of Joice Heth: '"I'm surprised Barnum doesn't have Joice Heth in here," Mr. Archer said. "That would seem an appropriate finale to his first enterprise in the show business, wouldn't you agree? Displaying her mummified remains to the paying public?" Guillaudeu cringed' (Carlson, 2011, p. 31). The exhibition of Joice Heth has been a source of considerable critical controversy and debate, with some commentators considering Barnum's procurement and manipulation of Heth as a form of enslavement, while others arguing that Heth can be understood as exercising a sense of agency in her performance of race which duped Barnum along with her paying public.[3] Here, the source of horror in Archer's imaginings as to how low Barnum might sink to generate wealth from his exhibits – the thought which makes Guillaudeu 'cringe' – is the exhibition of a performer after death. However, despite Guillaudeu's squeamishness, he ironically becomes such an exhibitor; as Chapter 3's analysis demonstrated, he is ultimately the possessor of Ana's posthumous textual body, which he promotes for his own gains. It is the metatextual implications of the cultural afterlives of performers, and to what uses they are put, which offers a compelling point of connection for all of the neo-Victorian examples of freakery examined in this book, for sites of exhibition are staged in each. For Suzan-Lori Parks, this comes in the metatheatrical device of blurring the boundaries between the audience and the action onstage, for we are rarely allowed to lose sight of our collusion with 'Venus's' (dis)rememberment as a spectacle in life and death. For Barbara Chase-Riboud, this comes in our bearing witness to Sarah's dissection. In both Darin Strauss's and Mark Slouka's versions of Chang and Eng, we are voyeurs to the entanglements of conjoined sexuality. For Susan Swan, Anna is self-conscious of her role as commodity, just as the reader is reminded of their own consumption of her body in their perusal of the novel. Both Jane Sullivan and Melanie Benjamin draw our attention to the dangers of 'belittlement' and reflect upon assumptions about 'childhood' innocence and experience. Metatextual and metafilmic elements are at work in neo-Victorian representations of Joseph Merrick; the emphasis on the shock of his physical appearance – and the meanings that might be attached to this – signify ambivalently in every re-visioning of his face and body. We might be encouraged to vilify Merrick, pity or even identify with him, but the neo-Victorian consumer is always watching these various reanimations of his flesh. As I have indicated, some re-memberings of performers are more self-conscious of the politics of constructing freakery than others. But Guillaudeu's 'cringe' is symbolic of some neo-Victorian freak shows' own anxiety about the ethics of revivification. The point of distinction between medical and freak show exhibition in neo-Victorianism appears to come in the latter's transparent sense of 'illusion' (or, in other words, fiction), rather than the claim to objectivity and 'truth' from which science has traditionally benefitted. Freak show representation certainly does become the carrier of dubious ideologies of gender, sexuality, race, class, and disability. Yet identity is not static in this context, but endlessly made and re-made in a process of self-conscious fabrication. Unlike the fixed spectacle of a body in a medical cabinet with a taxonomic description which represents the imparting of superior knowledge to a passive observer, the self-reflective constructions of neo-Victorian freakery often invite imaginative audience/reader participation and interaction with, and even contestation of, the subjects on display.

Neo-Victorianism's fictions of freakery find resonance with the genre of the 'true life story' pamphlet, a key component of the construction of nineteenth-century freak show performers. The neo-Victorian investment in bio-fiction as a way of rewriting the lives of nineteenth-century individuals might re-centre historically marginalised subjects, or complicate our received knowledge of eminent Victorians. And the perceived problems in the fictionalising tendencies of nineteenth-century 'true life story' pamphlets thus become sites of creative engagement in neo-Victorian re-tellings of the lives of freak show performers. Even though not all of the texts discussed in this book perform their indebtedness to this genre of freak show writing as overtly as Carlson's novel, they can still each be understood as neo-Victorian versions of 'true life story' pamphlets, in which 'truth' and 'stories' are irrevocably entwined. At times, these still might offer oppressive or exploitative constructions of freakery, yet our role as audience to and reader of these textual performances means that the 'story' does not end, but can continue to be reanimated via our interpretations. *Among the Wonderful* depicts a conversation between Ana and Barnum where he examines her own beginnings of a 'true life story', and she questions him as to his definition of the Museum he is creating. He responds:

> 'Walking through these halls, people encounter nothing but mystery. They interpret what they see according to the patterns of their own lives and relate it to the larger pattern of our city, of the world. So to answer the question, How do I define this place? I give you this: I never will. It is true that I will hire people to do it. That is the way of our time. But just as in this book, there are many authors: interpretation is infinite. And so mystery lives'. (Carlson, 2011, pp. 124–25)

Barnum's emphasis on the 'mystery' of the exhibitions he oversees might remind us of his role as the orchestrator of 'exotic' modes of freak-show presentation. He could be condemned for reiterating the boundaries between 'self' and 'other' which is perhaps one of the most oppressive functions of the freak show. Yet he is also encouraging his audiences to be not only readers ('interpreters'), but 'authors' as well. His definitions – and the way he might participate in the commercial transactions of exhibition – are but one version of the 'truth', but there are many competing stories which resist narrative closure. The 'mystery' is what the audience want to make of it; the burden of making meaning of freakery is placed with us and the uses to which we put it to make sense of the performers' and our own place in society. In this sense, Barnum, his audiences, and also us as readers are all neo-Victorian freak show proprietors. But he accords equal significance to Ana's own perception of events as well. Nevertheless, the acceptance and incorporation of performers' perspectives on their exhibition is a neo-Victorian dream; as I have indicated in the previous chapters, the 'voices' of nineteenth-century performers have largely been lost to history. Yet perhaps the polemical power of the neo-Victorian 'true life story' is that it can imagine the potential for these perspectives, even as they might be undermined and problematised by the very ambiguity of this genre of freak-show writing.

Melanie Benjamin's rendering of Barnum in *The Autobiography of Mrs Tom Thumb* can be understood as an 'aggrandized' pattern of presentation. Lavinia is initially suspicious of Barnum's motives for promoting her, yet he is continually positioned as sensitive, intuitive, and inspiring. His only flaw – standing in for the 'anomaly' of the freak show performer – is his love of money, and yet even this trait is overcome in his devotion to Warren and his other exhibits. Although the relationship is never consummated, Barnum is constructed as Warren's 'true love', the noble hero of a great romance, and the guiding light of her career. In another context, such aggrandisation of this showman might function as a signifier of the deluded exploitation of a freak show performer, yet the novel consistently encourages the reader to trust Warren's judgement and recognise her intelligence and perception. The description of her first meeting with him offers the opportunity to think about the politics of looking and identification which are a significant theme in neo-Victorian representations of freakery:

> His eyes [...] were piercing gray and alert, the most watchful eyes I'd ever seen. They were kindly, however; observant, wary, yet kindly [...] He took my hand solemnly, shook it, then suddenly bent down to peer directly into my face. His eyes were level with mine, so close that I could see myself reflected in them, and I had the startling,

> dizzy impression of a carnival, of colors and sounds and mirrors of every shape and size; of music, joyous, merry music tooted from horns and plucked by fiddles. How one man's gaze could engage so many senses, I had no idea; I only knew he did. It nearly knocked the breath out of me; my heart did a riotous somersault as the back of my neck tickled with excitement, and I fought an undignified urge to giggle.
>
> (Benjamin, 2011, pp. 143–44)

That Barnum's eyes are 'piercing' might invoke the penetrative, sexualised gaze which attends various examples of looking at freak show performers in neo-Victorianism: the violating gaze of Chase-Riboud's Cuvier; the spectacle of Chang and Eng's sex life; the prurient voyeurism of Swan's version of Martin Bates; the medical scrutiny upon Merrick in the film version of *From Hell*. Yet Barnum's meeting of Lavinia's stare is about 'levelling', which speaks of mutual recognition. This leads her to visualise a quasi-freak-show environment, but a scene associated with the joy of permutations of identity and sensory (sensuous?) engagement. Idealised as this version of the freak show might be, to see such images as a shared vision between Barnum and his performer suggests possibilities of understanding, community, and even identification. However, is not the reference to Lavinia being 'reflected' in Barnum's eyes, which inaugurates this impression, somewhat troubling? Is she seduced by his vision of what she might be, which occludes the 'reality' of her experiences? The previous chapters have explored the politics of imagined identification which the neo-Victorian freak show offers. While this can, at times, be an avenue of empathy, understanding and insight into the lives of people who performed in nineteenth-century freak shows, it has also emerged as a precarious strategy. Lest we forget the deceptions of neo-Victorian mirrors, which reflect back only what we project on to the Victorian era in the first instance. Furthermore, as Bogdan suggests, an aspect of aggrandised freak show presentation is in the potential for identification of the audience with the performer (Bogdan, 1988, p. 109) and, in Rachel Adams's terms, the projection of the self into the other which might be facilitated by the freak show encounter also risks obliterating the personhood of the performer (Adams, 2001, p. 31) Importantly, the ethical violations which this can produce have been dramatized in various examples of neo-Victorian freakery explored in this book, particularly in relation to the power inequalities of race: the colonisation of Sarah's exhibition under the auspices of feminist feeling in Chase-Riboud's fictionalisation of Jane

Austen; Slouka's Chang's desire to 'connect' conjoinment with enslavement; Benjamin's Lavinia and her uncomfortable identification with the slave 'girl'. What is notable in relation to several of these examples is that it is the performer themselves who claims the sense of inappropriate recognition. Should such misplaced expressions of empathy be explained away as symptomatic of the historical era in which the texts are set, or even as a subtle condemnation of the individual performers themselves? I think not; instead, it is more productive to consider these projections of self as pertinent allegories with metatextual implications. Neo-Victorian freakery's distorted reflections can also hold a mirror up to the limitations of our own desire to project twenty-first-century concerns back on to the nineteenth century, and dramatize the multiple sites of power which shape historical and contemporary identities.

The final neo-Victorian version of Barnum I want to consider is distinct from the others discussed above: Angela Carter's Colonel Kearney, the circus owner in *Nights at the Circus* hails from Kentucky (in contrast to the Connecticut origins of P. T.) and is not a direct bio-fictional representation of Barnum: the Colonel is instead self-consciously inspired by the earlier showman, as at one stage he strives to 'recall how his great predecessor, Barnum' marketed one of his acts (Carter, 1985, p. 162). Yet the Colonel's love of humbug and endless pursuit of dollars position him as a Barnum-esque character, and one particular facet of his characterisation offers an interesting point of comparison with all of the neo-Victorian freak show performers explored in this book. Colonel Kearney has amorous designs upon his star turn, Fevvers, and finally manages to engineer an evening alone with his famous *aerialiste*. However, he turns to drink to calm his nerves, which has a deflating effect upon his plans for romance:

> [Fevvers] enjoyed well-chilled champagne while the impresario lapsed into slumber on the couch beside her. Removing the bourbon bottle from his fist, she poked curiously into the aperture of his fly, which he'd just fumbled open before he passed out, and withdrew a string of little silk American flags.
>
> (Carter, 1985, p. 171)

Aside from being a satirical reflection on the impotency of the Colonel's colonising impulses – his lust for importing Yankee-style showmanship across the globe is literally derailed by an explosion in Siberia – what we witness here is a bathetic re-membering of a freak show manager, rather than a freak show performer. A consistent theme in both nineteenth-century and neo-Victorian constructions of freakery is the sexual prurience attached to the exhibition of unusual bodies, whether as a source of moral outrage, disgust, or a frisson of desire. Rather predictably, considering the broader neo-Victorian fascination with sexuality, the sexual exploits (and exploitations) of freak show performers have featured prominently in each of the texts discussed, which I have understood as part of the concept of 're-membering'. More specifically, the genitals of freak show performers (the 'members' which are reimagined) are a uniting theme across the chapters. As I have outlined, this aspect of making textual flesh of the past generally reiterates oppressive power relations for the performers discussed. So for a Barnum-esque character to be re-membered as lacking and impotent – essentially unmembered – should give us pause for thought. It contributes towards undermining the construction of neo-Victorian freak shows as places of sexual abuse; in this instance, predatory sexuality is emasculated, and performers themselves can be re-membered instead as sexually knowing subjects rather than as passive victims. This is not to suggest that Carter's novel – or, indeed, the others discussed in *Neo-Victorian Freakery* – are in any way trying to trivialise the ways in which performers might have been highly vulnerable to sexual exploitation. It is quite the opposite, for the texts considered in this book are often all too eager to furnish the reader with the salacious details of the uses and abuses of unusual bodies. But this comic re-membering of Barnum does suggest that the promise of forbidden pleasures and transgression of taboos that the neo-Victorian freak show appears to offer might in fact be a façade for something more mundane; an intoxication with the imagined sexual thrills of freakery which actually prohibits any consummation of our desire to possess the past. Put another way, could we as readers who might seek to peep at the extraordinary re-memberings of neo-Victorian performers as sexual subjects be aligned to the rapacious yet ridiculous Colonel Kearney, lost in prurient fantasy, unable to see the performers for what they actually were? This is surely an uncomfortable sense of identification, but I maintain that neo-Victorian readers and critics should be prepared to reflect on their own desires for sexual re-membering of the freak show.

For perhaps the most important message of the neo-Victorian freak show is that textual constructions of bodies, extraordinary or otherwise, really do matter. Consider the way in which the version of *The Hottentot Venus, or Hatred of Frenchwomen* in Parks's play influences the Baron's treatment of 'Venus' in their subsequent relationship. Or how Slouka's Chang's ability to enjoy his relationship with Sophia is undermined by Dumat's reading of Victor Hugo's novel. Stacy Carlson's image of Barnum as a 'griffin' reappropriates the ostensibly 'normal' showman as a monstrous creature assembled from different animal parts. Thus I return to the gloss of Kate Mitchell's understanding of neo-Victorianism as 're-membering' which I offered in the Introduction, where fragments of texts become like 'dismembered' bodies to be pieced together by authors and readers. Who will be re-membered in monstrous form in this process? Judging from the examples I have explored in *Neo-Victorian Freakery*, it is the ostensibly 'normal' Victorians who seek to denigrate, exploit and abuse those delineated as 'freakish' who are often exposed as the 'true' monsters of the neo-Victorian freak show; it is the doctors, managers, sensation-seeking audience members who are ultimately subjected to a process of 'enfreakment'. Hence, the boundaries between audience and performers, the 'normal' and 'abnormal', the 'self' and 'other' are in a constant process of negotiation and reconstruction. To suggest that neo-Victorianism as a genre of distorted reflections and re-membered bodies of all sorts is always already something of a freak show is clearly a hyperbolic move, and ironically in keeping with the fantastical exaggerations and embellishments which typify freak show discourse. But, at its most self-reflective, the neo-Victorian freak show can exceed the confines of being just an oddity or curiosity, and might even return an interrogative stare upon the audiences of the genre more broadly.

Notes

Introduction: Distorted Images and Re-membered Bodies: Constructing Neo-Victorian Freakery

1. See Jacques Lacan, 1977, pp. 502–09.
2. For a comparable discussion of Lacan's 'mirror stage' from a disability studies perspective, see Margrit Shildrick (2002, pp. 79–81).
3. For example, see Lennard J. Davis on the construction of the 'normal' body in the nineteenth century (2010, pp. 3–19).
4. Other appellations have been suggested for contemporary fiction set in the nineteenth century (for instance, Sally Shuttleworth's concept of the 'retro-Victorian', 1998, p. 253; John Kucich and Dianne F. Sadoff's use of the term 'post-Victorian', 2000, p. xiii; Cora Kaplan's 'Victoriana', 2007). And, despite the influence of Ann Heilmann and Mark Llewellyn's definition of neo-Victorianism, as detailed in the Introduction, it is worth noting here that current criticism in the field is still preoccupied with tailoring this classification. See, for example, Marie-Luise Kohlke, 'Mining the Neo-Victorian Vein: Prospecting for Gold, Buried Treasure and Uncertain Metal' (2014, pp. 21–37).
5. See Helen Davies, 2012, pp. 2.
6. It is this level of self-conscious critical engagement with the aesthetics and ideologies of nineteenth-century culture which is perhaps still the most contentious issue in defining what 'neo-Victorianism' actually designates. For example, Kohlke's recent re-definition of neo-Victorianism advocates 'employing "neo-Victorian" (albeit provisionally) as a generic and integrative umbrella term to encompass virtually all historical fiction related to the nineteenth century, irrespective of authors' or characters' nationalities, the plots' geographical settings, the language or composition or, indeed, the extent of narratives' self-consciousness, postmodernism, adaptivity, or otherwise' (2014, p. 27). While acknowledging the usefulness of this expanded conceptualisation, the neo-Victorian texts that I discuss throughout this book are united in their 'self-consciousness' about their status of adapting nineteenth-century historical figures and culture. However, as I seek to demonstrate, this does not mean that the ideological messages exposed in these 'rememberings' are always revisionary.
7. There are some notable exceptions to this omission. See, for example, Rosario Arias's excellent chapter '(In)visible Disability in Neo-Victorian Families' (2011, pp. 343–64), and Monika Pietrzak's thoughtful article '"Those Ill Things": One Hidden Spectacles and the Ethics of Display' (2011, pp. 24–48).
8. As both Robert Bogdan and Rosemarie Garland-Thomson identify in their studies of freakery, while some performers did have physical conditions (conjoinment, gigantism, dwarfism) which by modern medical standards

would be considered as 'disabilities', other performers – particularly in the vein of the ethnographic exhibitions discussed in Chapter 1 – were constructed as freaks due to perceived cultural and racial otherness. Similarly, some freak show performers exhibited physical differences – extensive tattoos, or women with facial hair – which bear no relation to 'disability' from a medical perspective. To complicate matters even further, Nadja Durbach explains how 'the disabled' is a category of social identity which only comes into being at the turn of the nineteenth century (Durbach, 2010, pp. 16–17). However, the neo-Victorian representations of freak show performers are writing with knowledge of twentieth- and twenty-first-century conceptualisations of physical difference as a marker of 'disability', and hence the term does seem appropriate in this context.

9. See, for example, Jeannette King (2005), Cora Kaplan (2007), and Ann Heilmann and Mark Llewellyn (2010).
10. As Chapter 5 will discuss in further detail, Lynch's film – following Frederick Treves's memoir – replaces Joseph Merrick's first name with 'John'.
11. For example, see Paul Semonin, 'Monsters in the Marketplace: The Exhibition of Human Oddities in Early Modern England' (1996, pp. 69–81).
12. For one of Butler's clearest explanations of her deployment of the concept of 'performativity' in her work, see 'For a Careful Reading' (1995, pp. 127–43).
13. See Garland-Thomson for a summary of theories of the gendered and racialised gaze (2009, pp. 41–42).
14. See Davies, 2012.
15. See Cora Kaplan (2007, pp. 37–84), Lena Steveker (2014, pp. 67–78), and Eckart Voigts (2014, pp. 79–92) for their respective discussions of the genre of neo-Victorian bio-fiction. Marie-Luise Kohlke's recent article, 'Neo-Victorian Biofiction and the Special/Spectral Case of Barbara Chase-Riboud's *Hottentot Venus*' is particularly useful for offering three 'descriptive modes' in which to classify neo-Victorian life-writing: 'celebrity biofiction'; 'biofiction of marginalised subjects'; and 'appropriated biofiction' (2013, p. 4).
16. See David Andress, 'Truth, Ethics and Imagination: Thoughts on the Purpose of History' (1998, pp. 237–48).
17. See Rebecca Stern, 'Our Bear Women, Ourselves: Affiliating with Julia Pastrana' for a discussion of Pastrana's life and cultural afterlife (2008, pp. 200–33).
18. A cast of Chang and Eng Bunker's body and their shared liver are on public exhibition at The Mütter Museum in Philadelphia, United States. For an exploration of the history and politics of this display, see Cynthia Wu (2012, pp. 58–78). The Royal London Hospital Museum houses the skeleton of Joseph Merrick, but his remains are not on public display. For a more general consideration from a disability studies on the ethics involved in exhibiting human remains in medical museums, see Alice Domurat Dreger (2004, pp. 113–41).
19. For a discussion of the 'medicalization' of disability and an exploration of the politics surrounding terminology, see Simi Linton, 'Reassigning Meaning' (2010, pp. 223–36).
20. However, Shakespeare also outlines an important critique of the problematic aspects of the social model of disability. See Shakespeare, 2010, pp. 269–73.

21. For example, see the sexually abusive doctor figure in Michel Faber's *Crimson Petal and the White*, the attempts at manipulation and exploitation made by Dr Simon Jordan in Margaret Atwood's *Alias Grace* (1996), the Frankenstein-esque aspirations of Archibald McCandless in Alasdair Gray's *Poor Things* (1992), amongst many others. Nevertheless, as Chapter 5's consideration of the Jack the Ripper story will indicate, suspicions as to the moral 'monstrosity' of medical professionals were also an issue in the nineteenth century.
22. The notable exception here is Chapter 5's discussion of Joseph Merrick, which largely explores his representation in neo-Victorian film, graphic novels, and television. It is telling that visual re-memberings of Merrick have dominated his cultural afterlife; considering the extensiveness of his physical disfigurement, perhaps it proves irresistible to attempt to replicate his appearance in this way.

1 Mixing (re)Memory and Desire: Constructing Sarah Baartman

1. Baartman's given name at birth is unknown. As Deborah Willis explains, the variations which tend to be used for her first name are as follows: 'Ssehura (thought to be closest to her given name); Sartjee, Saartje, Saat-je, Saartji, Saat-Jee, and Saartjie (all derived from the Afrikaans pronunciation, diminutive forms of Sara); as well as the Anglicized Sara or Sarah. The Afrikaans diminutive ending "-tjie" is now generally regarded as patronizing, thus Sarah is one of the most common spellings currently in use' (Willis, 2010, p. 4). Following Willis, I will use the name 'Sarah' throughout this chapter, but if using sources which have other names I will reproduce the different appellations. The origin of her surname is uncertain; Willis suggests that this might have been given to her at her baptism in Manchester, England, 1811 (Willis, 2010, p. 4). Confusingly, this also tends to be spelled in different ways: Baartman; Bartman; Baartmann. According to Clifton Crais and Pamela Scully, 'her surname literally means "bearded man" in Dutch. It also means uncivilized, barbarous, savage' (Crais and Scully, 2009, p. 9). Sarah's name thus speaks of a complex history of colonial power imbalances and exploitation.
2. The year of birth often reproduced for Sarah is 1789. However, Clifton Crais and Pamela Scully's meticulously researched biography of Baartman offers compelling evidence for an earlier birth date. See Crais and Scully, 2010, p. 184 for further information.
3. Hendrik Cesars and his wife were Free Blacks, descended from slaves. See Crais and Scully, 2009, pp. 39–44, for a discussion of the complex race relations on the Eastern Cape of South Africa at this point in history. The spelling of Cesars's last name is also subject to variation: Cesar; Caesar; Cezar (Willis, 2010, p. 4).
4. See Crais and Scully for the conflicting reports of the date of Sarah's death, and the cause (Crais and Scully, 2009, p. 138).
5. For a detailed account of the circumstances, debates, and politics surrounding the display of Sarah's remains, see Sadiah Qureshi, 2004, pp. 245–51.

6. The original title of the play is *La Vénus hottentote, ou haine aux Françaises*; my analysis uses the translation of the play provided as an appendix to T. Denean Sharpley-Whiting's study, *Black Venus: Sexualised Savages, Primal Fears, and Primitive Narratives in French* (1999).
7. On debates about the genitals of 'Hottentot' women and the cultural meanings attached to this, see Rachel Holmes, 2007, pp. 140–41.
8. According to Rachel Holmes, some twelve years after Bullock's refusal to exhibit Baartman he did concede to putting a 'living family of Laplanders' on display in Piccadilly (Holmes, 2007, pp. 59–60).
9. See, for example, Bernth Lindfors's edited collection, *Africans on Stage: Studies in Ethnological Show business* (1999) which explores numerous instances of displays of 'natives' in nineteenth-century freak shows.
10. See Crais and Scully's comments on Baartman's role as a 'colonial woman' in South Africa, as evidenced by her attire: 'She wore skirts and tops and dresses, humble yes, but European clothing nonetheless' (Crais and Scully, 2009, p. 57).
11. Crais and Scully suggest that, although some of these letters were purportedly from Cesars, it is unlikely that he was the author due to his lack of education (2009, p. 89).
12. For a more detailed account of this process, see Crais and Scully, pp. 95–97.
13. See Crais and Scully's comment that Dunlop, in fact, might have been present (2009, p. 98).
14. See Crais and Scully, 2009, pp. 133–36 for a full account of Sarah's visit to the museum.
15. For an overview of some of the key tropes of 'haunting and spectrality' in neo-Victorianism, see Rosario Arias and Patricia Pulham (2010, pp. xi–xxvi). Tatiana Kontou's book-length study of spiritualism and women's writing offers an extended exploration of the significance of mediumship in neo-Victorianism (Kontou, 2009). Kate Mitchell considers the significance of the uncanny 'return of the repressed' for the genre of neo-Victorianism (Mitchell, 2010, pp. 35–36). Although not specifically engaging with neo-Victorianism, Dominick LaCapra's work on (re)writing traumatic history repeatedly invokes the metaphor of haunting (LaCapra, 2001, pp. 68–71), a usage which informs Marie-Lusie Kohlke and Christian Gutleben's discussion of neo-Victorianism's 'bearing after witness' to nineteenth-century trauma (2010, pp. 1–34).
16. Ashraf H. A. Rushdy defines 'rememory' as the process of 'interpersonal' memory, memory as 'communal property' (Rushdy, 1990, p. 304; p. 321–22). In Caroline Rody's terms, 'rememory' can be understood as representing the 'interconnectedness of minds, past and present' in dealing with historical traumas (Rody, 1995, p. 101).
17. See Crais and Scully's discussion on the way in which Cuvier's writings on Baartman influenced nineteenth-century evolutionary theory, and racist science (Crais and Scully, 2009, pp. 144–45) See also Karen Ruth Kornweibel for similar comments on the ambiguity of Sarah's naming in Parks's play which, in her terms, demonstrates 'her slippage in history – the fact that she is not known except in the various names she was given' (Kornweibel, 2009, p. 67).

18. It is worth noting that Cuvier was not made a peer until 1819, and it was after this that he became known by the title of 'Baron'. Bearing this in mind, both Parks's and Chase-Riboud's use of the title 'Baron' to refer to Cuvier in his interactions with Sarah perhaps functions as a polemical gesture, emphasising his status and privilege in contrast to her multiple sites of powerlessness.
19. See Greg Miller's analysis of the play, which also notes the ways in which the erasure of 'the division between stage and spectators' in the play's 'parallels between the freak show and respectable theatre' (Miller, 2002, p. 135).
20. See '"The Hottentot Venus": A Ballad', (Toole, 1962, pp. 333–36).
21. See Zine Magubane's thoughtful commentary on the ways in which the story of 'The Hottentot Venus' has been appropriated by both feminist and postcolonial critics in a way which sometimes occludes the complexities of how Baartman's gendered and racial identity might have been understood by her contemporary audiences (2010, pp. 47–67).
22. There is no historical evidence to suggest that Jane Austen did, in reality, visit one of Sarah's performances, although as Crais and Scully have noted, Austen would have been in London in close proximity to 225 Piccadilly in 1811 (Crais and Scully, 2009, p. 93).
23. For a brief account of McDaniels' life, see Drimmer, 1985, pp. 320–21.

2 Separation Anxieties: Sex, Death, and Chang and Eng Bunker

1. In popular culture the coining of the name 'Siamese Twins' has been attributed to P. T. Barnum. However, Irving and Amy Wallace's biography of Chang and Eng, *The Two*, includes a letter written by the brothers in 1832 where they sign as 'The Siamese Twins': 'While Phineas T. Barnum has been given the credit for coining the term "The Siamese Twins" in 1853, it is evident here that Chang and Eng coined the name themselves twenty-one years earlier' (Wallace and Wallace, 1978, p. 74).
2. The brothers assumed the surname 'Bunker' in 1840; according to their friend Judge Jesse Graves, this was inspired by a family they had become close to whilst in New York in the 1830s (Wallace and Wallace, 1978, p. 165).
3. See David T. Mitchell and Sharon Snyder (2001) and Ato Quayson (2007) for studies of the oppressive and alienating effects of disability as metaphor in narrative.
4. See Susan Gillman, *Dark Twins: Imposture and Identity in Mark Twain's America* (1989) and Susan Gillman and Robert Patten, 'Dickens: Doubles: Twain: Twins'. *Nineteenth-Century Fiction*, 39:4 (March 1985), pp. 441–58.
5. See Allison Pingree's reading of Chang and Eng's billing as the 'United Brothers' in a publicity pamphlet published in 1831 (Pingree, 1996, pp. 92–114).
6. For a sustained consideration of the ways in which nineteenth-century discourse on the Civil War appropriated Chang and Eng, see Cynthia Wu, 'The Siamese Twins in Late Nineteenth-Century Narratives of Conflict and Resolution'. *American Literature*, 80:1 (March 2008), pp. 29–55.

7. Biographies of Twain offer no evidence to suggest that he actually met Chang and Eng.
8. Interestingly, the objection of the Yates family to their daughters marrying the brothers was apparently based on concerns about miscegenation rather than the 'propriety' of marriage to conjoined twins. See Wallace and Wallace, 1978, p. 173, and Cynthia Wu, 2012, pp. 24. Wu's analysis of Chang and Eng is particularly significant for its focus on the ways in which the brothers were represented as being at a vexed margin between 'oriental' and American (Wu, 2012, pp. 15–35).
9. According to popular accounts of the twins, Twain actually confuses Chang and Eng here in relation to propensity for drinking; Chang was apparently the heavier drinker (Wallace and Wallace, 1978, pp. 193–94).
10. See Robert A. Wiggins, 'The Original of Mark Twain's *Those Extraordinary Twins*'. *American Literature*, 23:3 (November 1951), pp. 255–357. Wiggins is the first critic to identify the Tocci brothers as a source for Twain's story.
11. See Wu, 2008, p. 35. In Twain's original version of the twins, he places much more emphasis on the incongruities between their personalities, particularly in relation to alcohol abuse. In the final version of *Those Extraordinary Twins* the brothers' arrangement whereby one twin controls their shared legs for a week echoes Chang and Eng's practice of 'alternate mastery' (Twain, 2009, p. 158). In addition, Luigi is accused of assaulting a man by kicking him and put on trial (Twain, 2009, p. 177), an echo of Chang and Eng's charge and conviction for an assault in 1833.
12. See Chapters 3 and 4 for a discussion of the concept of 'maternal impression' and the concept that pre-natal exposure to extraordinary bodies could lead to birth defects (Bogdan, 1988, p. 110). Chang and Eng were for some time prohibited from being exhibited in France due to concerns about the adverse effect that their appearance might have upon pregnant women (Wallace and Wallace, 1978, p. 97).
13. See Anne P. Wigger, 'The Composition of Mark Twain's *Pudd'nhead Wilson and Those Extraordinary Twins*: Chronology and Development'. *Modern Philology*, 55:2 (November 1957), pp. 93–102, for a full account of the composition of both texts.
14. See Cynthia Wu, 2012, pp. 41–43 for a discussion of the wives' reluctance to allow the autopsy.
15. Pancoast's autopsy report gives considerable detail about the brothers' physical strength and accomplishments (Pancoast, 1875, p. 157).
16. This expression features on the book jacket blurb for Bogdan's *Freak Show: Presenting Human Oddities for Amusement and Profit* (1988), and, according to David Gerber, was an expression suggested to Bogdan by his colleague Douglas Biklen (Gerber, 1990, p. 16). However, Michael M. Chemers offers the following caveat to this 'controversial phrase': 'In *Freak Show*, Bogdan quotes his colleague Douglas Biklen of Syracuse University, then the head of the Center for Human Policy, with this comment; in personal email correspondence with myself and Dr. Bogdan (May 16–30, 2000) Dr. Biklen denied using this term, and Bogdan was unable to reproduce the source of the original quote' (Chemers, 2008, p. 147). For me, however, this expression is particularly suggestive of the combination of moral outrage and sexual prurience which has been associated with the freak show.

17. See Holly E. Martin, '"The Original Siamese Twins": Living, Dying and Continuing under the Spectator's Gaze'. *The Journal of American Culture*, 34:4 (December 2011), p. 385.
18. See Bodgan, 1988.
19. See David Gerber, 1996, pp. 38–54.
20. Rather predictably, the Wallaces' biography takes the opportunity to speculate on the twins' excursions to prostitutes: 'it was clear that during their eight-year American tour they were often attracted by the women they met, fell in love frequently, and may even have had sexual intercourse with prostitutes' (Wallace and Wallace, 1978, pp. 120–21).
21. The term 'singleton' is used by Alice Domurat Dreger throughout her study of conjoinment to delineate non-conjoined people (Dreger, 2004).
22. See Wu, 2012, pp. 15–35.
23. The inaccurate report of Christopher's death is based on fact; his family received the details of his death in August 1864, but he was actually taken as a prisoner of war (Wallace and Wallace, 1978, p. 244).
24. See Wu's excellent ethnographic analysis of the Bunker family reunions which take place annually in North Carolina (Wu, 2012, pp. 145–69).

3 Excessively Feminine? Anna Swan, Gendering Giantesses, and the Genre of the 'True Life Story' Pamphlet

1. See Judith Butler, *Gender Trouble* (1990). Butlerian theory has been regularly applied to Angela Carter's work. For such a reading of *Nights at the Circus* see, for example, Sarah Sceats, 2007, pp. 84–94.
2. As several commentators have noted, slippage between gender roles is often a feature of the construction of freakery. For instance, see Rosemarie Garland-Thomson (1996, p. 6) and Elizabeth Grosz (1996, p. 57). Indeed, in Garland-Thomson's terms, 'hybridity, along with excess and absence, are the threatening organisational principles that constituted freakdom', which is relevant to race, gender, and sexuality (1996, p. 6).
3. See Anne Renaud, 2013, for an excellent biography of Anna Swan which is written for children. See Shirley Irene Vacan, 2008, for a biography of Swan and another Nova Scotian 'giant' of the nineteenth century, Angus McAskill.
4. As with many of the 'true life story' pamphlets, the publication details of this text are obscure. The account of Anna's life that I am using was written during her lifetime and published alongside a 'true life story' of Martin Bates, under the combined title *Sketches of the Two Tallest People in the World*. The text is available online via The John Crerar Library in Chicago at the following web link: http://storage.lib.uchicago.edu/pres/2014/pres2014-0612.pdf (accessed 28 December 2014). The year in the frontispiece of this book is 1894, and so I use this for in-text citations.
5. In her 'Preface' to the novel, Susan Swan states that she is not a relation of Anna's, but that 'I knew about her as a child because we have the same name and because my branch of the family is tall' (Swan, 1988, n.p.).
6. See Marlene Goldman, 1997, p. 77; p. 94, and Teresa Heffernan, 1992, pp. 36–37.

7. For critical readings of *The Biggest Modern Woman of the World* which emphasise the novel's postmodern narrative devices, see, for example, Heffernan, 1992, pp. 24–37; Gittings, 1994, pp. 81–91, and H. Wylie, 2002, pp. 238–45.
8. The newspaper article is reproduced at the following website: http://epe.lac-bac.gc.ca/100/205/301/ic/cdc/aswan/storyindex.htm (accessed 28 December 2014).
9. See Shildrick 1997.
10. See Linda Hutcheon, 1988, p. 93. This aspect of Linda Hutcheon's 'historiographic metafiction' has much in common with neo-Victorianism's interest in problematizing the 'official' discourse of history.
11. See Joan Riviere, 'Womanliness as Masquerade' (1929). Riviere conceptualises the performance of femininity as a defensive strategy for women against patriarchal reprisals.
12. As Riviere explains with regards to her theorisation of 'womanliness as masquerade': 'Womanliness therefore could be assumed and worn as a mask, both to hide the possession of masculinity and to avert the reprisals expected if she was found to possess it [...] The reader may now ask how I define genuine womanliness and the "masquerade". My suggestion is not, however, that there is any such difference; whether radical or superficial, they are the same thing' (1986, p. 38).
13. See, for example, Goldman, 1997, pp. 63–100; Heffernan, 1992, pp. 24–37; and Smaro Kamboureli, 1991: http://journals.hil.unb.ca/index.php/SCL/article/view/8138 (accessed 28 December 2014). Aside from considerations of the postmodernist and feminist aspects of Swan's novel, a further key theme in extant criticism on the text is how it reflects the postcolonial relationship between America and Canada. The ways in which this might be developed from a freakery studies perspective deserve a greater deal of analysis than I am able to allow for here. However, it is worth noting that Anna's nationality as Canadian was an important trope in her presentation as a performer, as evidenced by the title of her 'true life story' pamphlet: *The Nova Scotia Giantess*. Indeed, Edward S. Wood's *Giants and Dwarves* offers some pseudo-scientific remarks on how height might be influenced by geographical region: 'Men living by the sea-coast and in level countries are larger in stature than the inhabitants of mountainous regions' (Wood, 1868, p. 69). These theories find resonance in Susan Swan's fictionalised version of Martin, who expounds his ideas on creating a 'race' of giants with Anna. For a reading of the novel which explore the gendered connotations of Martin's colonising impulse towards his wife, see Kamboureli, 1991.
14. 'The Angel in the House' is the title of Coventry Patmore's poem (first published in 1854) which idealises his wife, Emily, and which had a significant hold over the construction of a certain type of middle-class Victorian femininity.
15. For a medical account of the birth of Anna's second child, see George Burden and Dorothy Grant, 2004, pp. 45–48.
16. See Elisabeth G. Gitter, 1984, pp. 936–54.
17. As discussed in the Introduction to this book, the conflation of bodies/texts – and the political and metatextual implications of this – has been identified by Ann Heilmann and Mark Llewellyn as a notable theme in some neo-Victorian novels (Heilmann and Llewellyn, 2010, p. 108).

18. According to H. Wylie, after attending a book reading of Swan's novel, several members of Anna Swan's family wrote letters to Susan Swan – including a missive to *McLean's* magazine – questioning her right to use a historical figure as a subject of fiction and 'to subject that name to any flights of fantasy in which she might care to indulge' (as cited in Wylie, 2002, p. 241). Marlene Goldman also discusses the Swan family's outrage towards the novel (Goldman, 1997, p. 64). Both critics pertinently note the way in which this controversy dramatizes the blurred boundary between history and fiction. However, it also crystalizes most poignantly the ethical concerns of subjecting historical figures to fictionalised treatment, and, as I have hoped to demonstrate in this chapter, Susan Swan's re-membering of Anna and Martin does have some features which undermine a reading of the novel which is wholly progressive, from either a feminist or disability studies perspective.

4 Innocence, Experience, and Childhood Dramas: Charles Stratton and Lavinia Warren

1. Thomas's remark about Caligula and the Roman Army resonates with Charles Stratton's experience as a precocious child star adored by his audiences, for Caligula ('Little Boots') was, as a child, something of a mascot for the Roman army, which in part accounts for the Emperor's influence over the troops as an adult. I am indebted to Andrew Burford for pointing out this connection to me. For a summary and analysis of Caligula's reign, see Scarre, 1995, pp. 36–41.
2. For a recent biography of Charles Stratton which also contains some key details about Lavinia's life, see Eric D. Lehman, *Becoming Tom Thumb: Charles Stratton, P.T. Barnum, and the Dawn of American Celebrity* (2013).
3. Although this volume was only published in 1979, A. H. Saxon, who introduces and edits the text, suggests that it came to be written by Lavinia 'around the turn of the century' (Saxon, 1979, p. 12).
4. See Peter Hunt on the tensions between the perception of children as 'inherently evil' and the Romantic ideal of child purity in the Victorian era (Hunt, 2009, p. 56). Joseph E. Illick makes a comparable argument about conflicting ideologies of childhood in the context of nineteenth-century North America (Illick, 2002).
5. For a useful summary of the changes in the law in Industrial Victorian Britain which affected child labour, see The National Archives resource at the following link: http://www.nationalarchives.gov.uk/education/victorianbritain/industrial/timeline2.htm (Accessed 28 December 2014).
6. W. T. Stead wrote a series of articles for the *Pall Mall Gazette* in July 1885 under the heading 'The Maiden Tribute of Modern Babylon' to expose the ease with which a child might be purchased for sex. The moral panic about the proliferation of child prostitution which ensued did contribute towards the raising of the age of consent, yet, ironically, Stead's participatory research in the form of purchasing a child (albeit that he did not engage in any sexual acts) led to a brief spell in jail. For further details of the articles and their cultural impact, see Judith Walkowitz, 1992, pp. 121–34.
7. See James R. Kincaid's study of the 'erotic child' in Victorian literature and culture (1994). Charles Dodgson, better known by his pen-name Lewis Carroll, has become a controversial figure due to his 'friendships' with young

girls, most famously Alice Liddell who was the inspiration for Carroll's *Alice in Wonderland* stories. For a discussion of the debates surrounding Carroll's interest in children, see Karoline Leach, 2000, n.p.

8. According to *Sketches of the Life, Personal Appearance, Character and Manners of Charles S. Stratton*, Stratton was 9 and a half pounds at birth, but was supposed to have stopped growing around the age of 18 months (*Sketches*, 1863, para. 2). Lavinia details her birth weight of six pounds in her autobiography, and claims that she was 'of the usual size' until she was a year old, when her growth slowed dramatically, finally halting completely at the age of ten (Magri, 1979, p. 36).
9. See, for example, the description of Stratton in Edward S. Wood's *Giants and Dwarves*: 'He had light hair and complexion, a fresh colour, dark eyes, well-developed forehead, good mouth, great vivacity of expression' (1869, p. 413).
10. For details of Barnum's 'What is it' exhibit, which invoked some aspects of ethnographic showmanship combined with racist pseudo-science about non-white, non-Western people as 'missing links', see James W. Cook Jr, 1996, pp. 139–57.
11. See Eric D. Lehman for a full account of Stratton's first visit to the palace (2013, pp. 1–9).
12. See Michael M. Chemers for a discussion of the construction of 'Tom Thumb's' 'Yankee' persona (Chemers, 2008, p. 34).
13. The chapter in Barnum's third autobiography entitled 'Political and Personal' offers a fulsome account of his abolitionist views and his own political activities towards this campaign (1889, pp. 229–40).
14. In fact, Stratton did appear in full blackface for his role in the stage adaptation of Harriet Beecher Stowe's novel, *Dred: The Tale of a Dismal Swamp* in 1856. Problematic as casting a white actor in a black character's role may be (Stratton appeared as the enslaved 'Tom Tit'), the play was staunchly abolitionist in sentiment, as Michael M. Chemers's thoughtful analysis indicates (Chemers, 2008, pp. 45–49).
15. For an overview of the history, politics, and various implications of blackface performances in the nineteenth century, see the collection of essays *Inside the Minstrel Mask: Readings in Nineteenth-Century Blackface Minstrelsy*, (eds.) Annemarie Bean, Brooks McNamara, and James V. Hatch (1996).
16. For an analysis of the enduring legacy of racist sexual stereotypes of black masculinity, see Patricia Hill Collins, 2004, pp. 149–80.
17. See Lori Merish's discussion of the description of Lavinia in this pamphlet, which similarly highlights the ways in which she is constructed as 'neither child nor adult but rather both at once' (Merish, 1996, p. 191).
18. For critical accounts of the wedding which place the event in the context of the nineteenth-century's burgeoning cult of the celebrity and which note the historical backdrop of the American Civil War, see Lehman, 2013, pp. 119–39; Merish, 1996, pp. 192–97; and Bogdan, 1988, pp. 148–49.
19. See Ronald Pearsall on virginity before marriage being the norm for 'aristocratic' and middle-class Victorian women (1969, p. 174).
20. In my study, *Gender and Ventriloquism in Victorian and Neo-Victorian Fiction: Passionate Puppets*, I explore the ways in which neo-Victorianism can be understood as a genre of transformation via repetition (Davies, 2012, pp. 9–12).

21. This quotation is taken from the original newspaper interview, published in *The Western Australia Sunday Times* (Perth), 4 October 1901, p. 10. Saxon's biography does not reproduce this detail. A copy of the original newspaper report can be found at the following link: http://trove.nla.gov.au/ndp/del/article/32720833 (accessed 28 December 2014).
22. For a discussion of the way in which the Carroll/Liddell relationship has been interpreted in neo-Victorian fiction, see Kym Brindle's analysis of Kate Roiphe's 2001 novel, *Still She Haunts Me* (Brindle, 2014, pp. 118–46).
23. See Michael M. Chemer's description of Stratton's performances: 'Stratton would [...] imitate figures of heroism and sex appeal (a gladiator, a highlander) and, in a tight-fitting body suit to simulate nudity, would strike poses imitating famous classical statuary' (Chemers, 2008, p. 36).
24. See Jack Zipes, *The Trials and Tribulations of Little Red Riding Hood: Versions of the Tale in Sociocultural Context* (1993) for an extended discussion of the sexual overtones of this fairy tale.
25. There is a point of contrast here with the historical Lavinia's autobiography for, in her commentary on Barnum's encouragement of the child Stratton in taking up drinking wine and smoking, she remarks 'I am glad to be able here to say Mr. Stratton had manliness and will power enough to give up these years before he died' (Magri, 1979, p. 116). Benjamin's decision to include the detail of the lingering smell of cigar smoke – suggesting that Charles still smokes – is thus surely a way of emphasising the pernicious consequences of Barnum's moulding of his child star.
26. It is interesting to note here that Bogdan is making his own subjective value judgements about what constitutes an 'attractive' body, which might be considered to undermine his generally sensitive and politically-engaged exploration of the construction of freakery.
27. See Simi Linton for a useful summary of the terminology used for defining 'disability', and the political and ideological implications of these various appellations (Linton, 2010, pp. 223–36).
28. The compounded silencing of this black woman in Benjamin's text can be profitably interpreted via Gayatri Chakravorty Spivak's 'Can the Subaltern Speak?', where she considers the problems in 'giving voice' to non-white, non-Western women who have historically been silenced (Spivak, 1988, pp. 271–313).

5 The Strange Case of Joseph and Jack: Joseph Merrick and Spectacles of Deviance

1. Michael Howell and Peter Ford's biography of Merrick, *The True History of the Elephant Man* (originally published in 1980, with a third edition published in 1992) is widely regarded as the most thoroughly researched and reliable account of Merrick's life, and is notable for challenging various inaccuracies of Fredrick Treves's memoir which have passed into popular culture as 'fact' (including Merrick's first name, his relationship with his mother, and the circumstances of his death). On the theories surrounding the circumstances of Merrick's death, see Howell and Ford, 2001, pp. 140–152.

2. As Judith Walkowitz details, the moniker 'Jack the Ripper' for the Whitechapel killer came from a letter offering information about the murders, sent around 30 September 1888, which was signed with this name (Walkowitz, 1992, p. 199).
3. See Walkowitz, 1992, pp. 201–13 for a discussion of the various suspects – and ideological connotations of these accusations.
4. See Howell and Ford, 2001 pp. 29–30 for a commentary on the closure of Merrick's exhibition.
5. See, for instance, http://www.jtrforums.com/showthread.php?t=7327 (accessed 21th December 2014).
6. The popularity of Ripper plots and the presence of prostitutes in neo-Victorianism has, indeed, become something of a cliché, wryly acknowledged by Miriam Elizabeth Burnstein's (writing as 'The Little Professor') 'Rules for Writing Neo-Victorian Novels'. See her point 5: 'Any outwardly respectable man will a) have frequent recourse to Prostitutes, b) have a Dark Secret, and/or c) be Jack the Ripper', and point 6: 'There must be at least one Prostitute, who will be an Alcoholic and/or have a Heart of Gold' (Burnstein, 2006, n.p.). For a discussion of the significance of Jack the Ripper in neo-Victorianism, see Max Duperray, 2012, pp. 167–95. For an exploration of the role of prostitution in Michel Faber's *The Crimson Petal and the White*, which also considers the metatextual implications of 'selling sex' in neo-Victorianism more broadly, see Nadine Muller, 2012, pp. 39–60.
7. For detailed commentaries on the complexities of the discourses surrounding prostitution in Victorian Britain, see Lynda Nead (1988), Judith Walkowitz (1980), and Trevor Fisher (1997). See also Amanda Anderson on representations of the 'fallen woman' in Victorian literature and art (1993).
8. See Walkowitz (1980) for an extended discussion of the Acts and the repeal campaigns.
9. Interestingly, Elaine Showalter's exploration of the iconography of syphilis in Victorian culture makes reference to a wax museum in Blackpool owned by Louis Tussard, which 'displayed graphic models of hideous syphilitic disfigurement' (Showalter, 1992, p. 193). Such a spectacle offers a notable point of connection, then, with the wax models of the Ripper victims discussed at the beginning of this chapter.
10. Merrick's condition was initially diagnosed as being neurofibromatosis, but an article published in the *British Medical Journal* in 1986 by J. A. R. Tibbles and M. M. Cohen suggested Proteus syndrome as being a more probable cause of Merrick's disfigurements. See Tibbles and Cohen, 1986, pp. 683–85.
11. The references to Mayhew's work in this chapter are taken from Lee Jackson's reproduction of this volume of *London Labour and the London Poor* which features on his website 'The Dictionary of Victorian London'. See the following link for the full text: http://www.victorianlondon.org/crime1/mayhewprostitution.htm (accessed 28 December 2014).
12. Of course, this trope forms a crucial parallel to Robert Louis Stevenson's novella, *The Strange Case of Dr Jekyll and Mr Hyde* (1886). Unsurprisingly, the similarities did not escape the attention of a late-Victorian London desperately seeking a villain on which to blame the Ripper murders and, as

Mike Holgate details, the actor Richard Mansfield who played Dr Jekyll/Mr Hyde in the contemporaneous stage adaptation of Stevenson's text came under scrutiny as a Ripper suspect (Holgate, 2008, pp. 19–22). Furthermore, Holgate notes that the duality of the respectable doctor and his monstrous other finds resonance in the Treves/Merrick relationship (Holgate, 2008, p. 17), a connection which in invoked in Sinclair's novel and which I allude to in my title of this chapter.

13. The reasons as to why Treves – who obviously spent a considerable amount of time with Merrick – would alter his first name to 'John' remain obscure, but this re-naming of Joseph as 'John' has certainly had a formative influence on neo-Victorian representations of Merrick: he is called 'John' in Pomerance's play, Lynch's film, Moore and Campbell's graphic novel, and the Hughes Brothers' film adaptation of *From Hell*. For a thoughtful discussion of why Treves might have changed Merrick's name, see Graham and Oehlschlaeger, 1992, pp. 53–54.
14. For analyses of Treves's memoir which comment on his gendering of Merrick, see Graham and Oehlschlaeger, 1992, pp. 32–61; Andrew Smith, 2000, pp. 292–304; Christine Ferguson, 2008, pp. 114–33; and Nadja Durbach, 2010, pp. 33–57.
15. For an exploration of the ways in which the 'dandy' comes to signify as 'homosexual' in late nineteenth-century culture, see Alan Sinfield (1994). Considering that Treves was writing this memoir in the early twentieth century, he would have knowledge of these queer connotations.
16. The term 'pinhead' was freak show terminology for a performer with microcephaly, a neuro-developmental condition which, according to Robert Bogdan, is accompanied by 'a very small pointed head and small overall stature', and some level of cognitive impairment (Bogdan, 1988, pp. 111–12).
17. Howell and Ford's biography of Merrick suggests that, while Kendal was interested in supporting Merrick's cause, the historical figure was unlikely to have actually met Merrick (2001, p. 111).
18. The details about and analysis given of the life of Mary Merrick in Howell and Ford's biography suggest that she did attempt to support and provide for Joseph until her death in 1873 (Howell and Ford, 2001, pp. 42–45).
19. As with so many of the 'true life stories' of freak show performers, the veracity of Joseph's 'autobiography' remains questionable. For Howell and Ford's part, they do accord veracity to Merrick's authorship for this short text (2001, p. 79).
20. Graham and Oehlschlaeger also comment on the 'odious sexual overtones' of this scene, and give details which suggest that the imagery of this incident in the film's screenplay was even more brutally sexual (1992, p. 147).
21. Holladay and Watt's reading of the film also highlights the 'sexual ambivalence' in Bytes's violent possessiveness over Merrick (1989, p. 872).
22. The association of vampires with queer sexuality is a long-established cultural tradition. For a discussion of queer vampires in a cinematic context, see Barbara Mennel, 2012.
23. Interestingly, the Prince of Wales, Queen Victoria's eldest son, has also been named as a Ripper suspect (Holgate, 2008, pp. 13–15) and, as we shall see, his son Prince Albert Victor, becomes a key player in the Ripper plot which

forms the basis of Moore and Campbell's *From Hell*. Thus even in a film such as Lynch's which is at pains to present Merrick as a victim of sexual violence, the spectre of Jack is never too far away.

24. The historical Merrick constructed a model of St. Phillips Church, which still resides in the Royal London Hospital Museum as part of their collection his memorabilia (Howell and Ford, 2001, p. 169). The model also plays a 'central metaphor' in Pomerance's play: 'the groping toward conditions where it can be built and the building of it are the action of the play' (Pomerance, 1980, p. v).
25. It is certainly not the case that all sex workers in the nineteenth century were working class but, as Walkowitz's study indicates, women of limited means from working-class backgrounds might be more susceptible to entering into the sex industry to make money (Walkowitz, 1980).
26. The hat and veil which the historical Merrick wore are also part of the Royal London Museum collection and, as we shall see, are a recurring prop in neo-Victorian depictions of Merrick
27. See Elaine Showalter's gloss on the dynamics of 'veiling/unveiling' of the strip-tease, read via Roland Barthes's essay on 'Striptease' which features in his *Mythologies* (1957). Furthermore, in the context of the non-revelation of Merrick's penis, which is promised yet denied to the film's viewer, Jacques Lacan's work on the 'veiled phallus' is an interesting point of resonance. Gen Doy's gloss on Lacan's theories suggests: 'For Lacan, the phallus is always veiled and cannot be represented. The phallus is missing, a lack, therefore how can this missing object of desire be represented other than veiled? Neither the man nor the woman can ever possess the phallus (it is a symbol), though, according to Lacan, they have different positions with regards to its absence. The man's relation is related to "having" and the woman's to "being" the phallus (for the man)' (Doy, 2001, p. 131). Mapping this onto the film's representation of Merrick, he becomes the 'phallus' (woman) in this formulation, covered by the veil, and the object of 'desire' for the patriarchal medical audience.
28. This character is a fictionalised version of the author himself.
29. A Golem is a creature from Jewish folklore, made from clay and brought to life through ritual incantation. For a discussion of the significance of the Golem in Sinclair's novel and other neo-Victorian literature, see Patricia Pulham, 2010, pp. 157–79).
30. Both the graphic novel and film version of *From Hell* indulge in some gratuitous exhibition of the mutilated bodies of the Rippers victims. As Christine Ferguson's analysis of the misogyny of both sources suggests, while Moore and Campbell's book does make some attempts to acknowledge the horrific deaths of the historical women, the gruesome attention to detail which is devoted to Mary Kelly's brutalisation (which takes up the whole of Chapter 10) somewhat undermines the graphic novel's nods to feminist consciousness (Ferguson, 2009, p. 56). The ways in which the original media reports of the killings emphasised the grotesque spectacle of the victim's bodies surely lives on in such representations.
31. At the time of writing, the third series of *Ripper Street* is currently being screened on Amazon Instant Video, having moved from the BBC after the end of the second series. In series three, Reid's daughter is recovered, having

been found, seemingly traumatised by the accident, and kept captive by a childless couple. However, in Episode 4 (entitled 'Your Father My Friend') Mathilda Reid's trauma is revealed to run much deeper, for when living with her father she was accidently exposed to his case notes on the Ripper murders. Fleeing from the father she perceives as a monster, she revisits the locations of the murders in Whitechapel. In a sense, then, Mathilda can be understood as a traumatised neo-Victorian subject, compelled to repeat the details of the Ripper crimes in a vain attempt to make sense of the horror.

32. 'Phossy (sometimes spelled 'fossy') jaw' – the colloquial term for phosphorus necrosis of the jaw – was caused by the use of white phosphorus in the production of matches during the nineteenth century which produced facial disfigurements and also brain damage.
33. The episode's depiction of Merrick's journey across the city somewhat undermines the previous construction of him as a geographically mobile agent; he is pestered by a crowd and in the scuffle his travelling garb is removed, exposing his disfigured face to the assembled throng. He is 'rescued' by one of H Division's Inspectors, which momentarily reiterates the nineteenth-century trope of the risk of women making a 'spectacle' of themselves by wandering the streets.

Afterword: The Neo-Victorian Enfreakment of P. T. Barnum

1. For an excellent biography of Barnum, see A. H. Saxon's *P. T. Barnum: The Legend and the Man*. Of course, Barnum himself has left no less than three autobiographies of his life story.
2. Michael Howell and Peter Ford's biography of Joseph Merrick contains some useful contextual information about his most famous manager, Tom Norman, as well. They explain that Norman regularly 'invoked' the name of Barnum as also having featured some of his performers in his shows. At one exhibition, Barnum himself was in the audience, and met Norman afterwards: 'Barnum stretched out a hand to touch the festoons of Mexican and American silver dollars that Tom Norman habitually wore suspended from his watchchain and said to his companions with wry amusement, "The Silver King, eh?" [...] It was enough: from a moment of acute embarrassment Tom Norman characteristically salvaged triumph. He retained the nickname to the end of his days and claimed Barnum among his friends' (Howell and Ford, 2001 pp. 70–71).
3. For a commentary on these various perspectives on Barnum, see Eric Fretz, 1996, pp. 97–107.

Bibliography

Primary sources

Atwood, Margaret. *Alias Grace*. 1996; London: Virago, 1997.

Benjamin, Melanie. *The Autobiography of Mrs Tom Thumb*. New York: Delacorte Press, 2011.

Bleeker, Sylvester. *General Tom Thumb's Three Year Tour Around the World*. New York: A. Booth, 1872.

Carlson, Stacy. *Among the Wonderful*. Hanover, New Haven: Steerforth Press, 2011.

Carter, Angela. *Nights at the Circus*. 1984; London: Picador, 1985.

Chase-Riboud, Barbara. *Hottentot Venus: A Novel*. New York: Anchor Books, 2003.

Faber, Michel. *The Crimson Petal and the White*. Edinburgh: Canongate Books Ltd., 2002.

Ferrus, Diana. 'I've Come to Take You Home'. 1998. In (ed.) Deborah Willis. *Black Venus 2010: They Called Her "Hottentot"*. Philadelphia: Temple University Press, 2010, pp. 213–14.

Gray, Alasdair. *Poor Things*. London: Bloomsbury, 1992.

'The Hottentot Venus: A Ballad'. 1810. In (ed.) R. Toole. *Circus and Allied Arts*. Derby: Harper and Sons, 1962, pp. 333–36.

'The Hottentot Venus: A New Song'. 1811. In Lars Eckstein. *Reading Song Lyrics*. Amsterdam and New York: Rodopi, 2010, pp. 180–81.

Hughes, Albert, and Hughes, Allan [Dir.] *From Hell*, Twentieth Century Fox, 2001.

Lynch, David [Dir.] *The Elephant Man*, Brooksfilms, 1980.

Magri, Countess M. Lavinia. *The Autobiography of Mrs. Tom Thumb*. Hamden, Connecticut: Archon Books, 1979.

Moore, Alan, and Campbell, Eddie. *From Hell*. 1999; Marietta, Georgia: Top Shelf Productions, 2001.

Morrison, Toni. *Beloved*. 1987; London: Vintage, 1997.

The Nova Scotia Giantess, Miss Anna H. Swan, A Brief Account of her Birth and History. Publisher unknown, 1894.

Parks, Suzan-Lori. *Venus*. New York: Theatre Communications Group, 1990.

Pomerance, Bernard. *The Elephant Man*. 1979; London and Boston: Faber and Faber, 1980.

Shankland, Tom [Dir.] 'Pure as the Driven', *Ripper Street* (Season 2, episode 1), BBC, 28 October 2013

Shankland, Tom [Dir.] 'Am I Not Monstrous?', *Ripper Street* (Season 2, episode 2), BBC, 4 November 2013.

Sherman, Kenneth. *Words for Elephant Man*. 1983; Erin, Ontario: The Porcupine's Quill, 2012.

Sinclair, Iain. *White Chappell, Scarlet Tracings*. 1987; London: Penguin, 2004.

Slouka, Mark. *God's Fool*. London: Picador, 2002.

Sketch Of The Life, Personal Appearance, Character And Manners Of Charles S. Stratton, The Man In Miniature, Known As General Tom Thumb, And His Wife,

Lavinia Warren Stratton. New York: Press of Wynkoop & Hallenbeck, 1863 <http://www.disabilitymuseum.org/dhm/lib/detail.html?id=693&page=all> (accessed 28 December 2014).

Smith, Albert. *Hop-O'-My-Thumb, or The Seven League Boots: A Romance of Nursery History in Two Acts*. London: T Brettell, 1846.

Starling, Belinda. *The Journal of Dora Damage*. London: Bloomsbury, 2008.

Strauss, Darin. *Chang and Eng: A Novel*. London: Allison & Busby Limited, 2000.

Sullivan, Jane. *Little People: A Novel*. Melbourne: Scribe Publications, 2011.

Swan, Susan. *The Biggest Modern Woman of the World*. 1983; London: Pandora, 1988.

Théaulon, Dartois, and Brasier. *The Hottentot Venus, or Hatred of French Women*. 1814. In T. Denean Sharpley-Whiting, *Black Venus: Sexualized Savages, Primal Fears, and Primitive Narratives in French*. Duke University Press, 1999, pp. 127–64.

Treves, Sir Frederick. *The Elephant Man and Other Reminiscences*. London, New York, Toronto and Melbourne: Cassell and Company Ltd., 1923.

Twain, Mark. *Those Extraordinary Twins*, in *Pudd'nhead Wilson and other tales*. Oxford: Oxford University Press, 2009.

Twain, Mark. 'Personal Habits of the Siamese Twins'. *Packard's Monthly*, August 1869. <http://twain.lib.virginia.edu/wilson/siamese.html> (accessed 28 December 2014).

Waters, Sarah. *Tipping the Velvet*. 1998; London: Virago, 1999.

Waters, Sarah. *Affinity*. 1999; London: Virago, 2000.

Waters, Sarah. *Fingersmith*. London: Virago, 2002.

Secondary sources

Acton, William. *Prostitution, considered by its Moral, Social, and Sanitary Aspects*. Second Edition. London: John Churchill and Sons, 1870.

Adams, Rachel. *Sideshow U.S.A: Freaks and the American Cultural Imagination*. Chicago and London: The University of Chicago Press, 2001.

Adelson, Betty M. *The Lives of Dwarfs: Their Journey from Public Curiosity toward Social Liberation*. New Jersey and London: Rutgers University Press, 2005.

Anderson, Amanda. *Tainted Souls and Painted Faces: The Rhetoric of Fallenness in Victorian Culture*. Ithaca and London: Cornell University Press, 1993.

Andress, David. 'Truth, Ethics and Imagination: Thoughts of the Purpose of History', in (eds.) John Arnold, Kate Davies, and Simon Ditchfield, *Consuming the Past in Contemporary Culture*. Dorset: Donhead, 1998, pp. 237–48.

Arias, Rosario, and Pulham, Patricia. 'Introduction', in (eds.) Rosario Arias and Patricia Pulham, *Haunting and Spectrality In Neo-Victorian Fiction: Possessing the Past*. Basingstoke: Palgrave Macmillan, 2010, pp. xi–xxvi.

Arias, Rosario. '(In)visible Disability in Neo-Victorian Families', in (eds.) Marie-Luise Kohlke and Christian Gutleben. *Neo-Victorian Families: Gender, Sexual and Cultural Politics*. Amsterdam and New York: Rodopi, 2011, pp. 343–64.

Baker, Brian. *Iain Sinclair*. Manchester: Manchester University Press, 2007.

Barker, Clare. *Postcolonial Fiction and Disability: Exceptional Children, Metaphor and Materiality*. Basingstoke: Palgrave Macmillan, 2011.

Barnum, P. T. *The Life of P. T. Barnum*. New York: Redfield, 1855.

Barnum, P. T. *Struggles and Triumphs; or, Sixty Years' Recollections of P. T. Barnum, Including His Golden Rules for Money Making, Illustrated and Brought Up to 1889, Written by Himself.* Buffalo, New York: Courier Co., 1889.

Bean, Annemarie, Hatch, James V., and McNamara, Brooks (eds). *Inside the Minstrel Mask: Readings in Nineteenth-Century Blackface Minstrelsy.* Hanover, New Hampshire: Wesleyan University Press, 1996.

Bogdan, Robert. *Freak Show: Presenting Human Oddities for Amusement and Profit.* Chicago and London: The University of Chicago Press, 1988.

Brindle, Kym. *Epistolary Encounters in Neo-Victorian Fiction: Diaries and Letters.* Basingstoke: Palgrave Macmillan, 2014.

Burden, George, and Grant, Dorothy. *Amazing Medical Stories.* Fredericton, New Brunswick: Goose Lane, 2004.

Burnstein, Miriam Elizabeth. 'The Little Professor: Things Victorian and Academic'. 'Rules for Writing Neo-Victorian Novels'. 15 March 2006 <little professor.typepad.com/the_little_professor/2006/03/rules_for_writi.html> (accessed 28 December 2014).

Butler, Judith. *Gender Trouble: Feminism and the Subversion of Identity* (1990). New York and London: Routledge, 1999.

Butler, Judith. 'For a Careful Reading'. In Seyla Benhabib, Judith Butler, Drucilla Cornell and Nancy Fraser. *Feminist Contentions: A Philosophical Exchange.* New York and London: Routledge, 1995, pp. 127–43.

Chemers, Michael M. *Staging Stigma: A Critical Examination of the American Freak Show.* Basingstoke: Palgrave Macmillan, 2008.

Clare, Eli. *Exile and Pride: Disability, Queerness, and Liberation.* Cambridge, Massachusetts: South End, 1999.

Collins, Patricia Hill. *Black Sexual Politics: African Americans and the New Racism.* London: Routledge, 2004.

Cook, James W., Jnr. 'Of Men, Missing Links, and Nondescripts: The Strange Career of P. T. Barnum's "What Is It?" Exhibition', in (ed.) Rosemarie Garland Thomson. *Freakery: Cultural Spectacles of the Extraordinary Body.* New York and London: New York University Press, 1996, pp. 139–57.

Crais, Clifton and Scully, Pamela. *Sara Baartman and the Hottentot Venus: A Ghost Story and a Biography.* Woodstock: Princeton University Press, 2009.

Davies, Helen. *Gender and Ventriloquism in Victorian and Neo-Victorian Fiction: Passionate Puppets.* Basingstoke: Palgrave Macmillan, 2012.

Davis, Lennard J. 'Constructing Normalcy', in (ed.) Lennard J. Davis. *The Disability Studies Reader.* Third Edition. New York: Routledge, 2010, pp. 3–19.

Doy, Gen. *Drapery: Classicism and Barbarism in Visual Culture.* London and New York: I. B. Tauris, 2002.

Dreger, Alice Domurat. *One of Us: Conjoined Twins and the Future of the Normal.* Cambridge, Massachusetts: Harvard University Press, 2004.

Dreger, Alice. 'The Sex Lives of Conjoined Twins'. *The Atlantic* 25th October 2012 <http://www.theatlantic.com/health/archive/2012/10/the-sex-lives-of-conjoined-twins/264095/> (accessed 28 March 2013).

Drimmer, Frederick. *Very Special People: The Struggles, Loves and Triumphs of Human Oddities.* New York: Bell Publishing Company, 1985.

Durbach, Nadja. *Spectacles of Deformity: Freak Shows and Modern British Culture.* Berkeley, Los Angeles, and London: University of California Press, 2010.

Duperray, Max. '"Jack the Ripper" as Neo-Victorian Gothic Fiction: Twentieth-Century and Contemporary Sallies into a Late Victorian Case and Myth', in (eds.) Marie-Luise Kohlke and Christian Gutleben, *Neo-Victorian Gothic: Horror, Violence and Degeneration in the Re-Imagined Nineteenth Century*. Amsterdam and New York: Rodopi, 2012, pp. 167–77.

Eckstein, Lars. *Reading Song Lyrics*. Amsterdam and New York: Rodopi, 2010.

Ferguson, Christine. 'Victoria-Arcana and the Misogynistic Poetics of Resistance in Iain Sinclair's *White Chappell Scarlet Tracings* and Alan Moore's *From Hell*'. In Rebecca Munford and Paul Young (eds.), *Engaging the Victorians*, special issue of *LIT: Literature Interpretation Theory*, 20:1–2 (2009), pp. 45–64.

Fielder, Leslie. *Freaks: Myths and Images of the Secret Self* (1978) Harmondsworth, Middlesex: London, 1981.

Fisher, Trevor. *Prostitution and the Victorians*. New York: St. Martin's Press, 1997.

Foucault, Michel. *The Birth of the Clinic* (1963). Trans. Alan Sheridan. London: Tavistock Publications, 1973.

Foucault, Michel. *The History of Sexuality Volume 1: The Will to Knowledge* (1976). Trans. Robert Hurley. London: Penguin, 1998.

Fredricks, Nancy. 'Twain's Indelible Twins'. *Nineteenth-Century Literature*, 43:4 (March 1989), pp. 484–99.

Fretz, Eric. 'P. T. Barnum's Theatrical Selfhood and the Nineteenth-Century Culture of Exhibition', in (ed.) Rosemarie Garland Thomson. *Freakery: Cultural Spectacles of the Extraordinary Body*. New York and London: New York University Press, 1996, pp. 97–107.

Garland-Thomson, Rosemarie. 'Introduction: From Wonder to Error – A Genealogy of Freak Discourse in Modernity', in (ed.) Rosemarie Garland Thomson. *Freakery: Cultural Spectacles of the Extraordinary Body*. New York and London: New York University Press, 1996, pp. 1–19.

Garland-Thomson, Rosemarie. 'Foreword: Freakery Unfurled', in (ed.) Marlene Tromp. *Victorian Freaks: The Social Context of Freakery in Britain*. Columbus: The Ohio State University Press, 2008, pp. ix–xi.

Garland-Thomson, Rosemarie. *Staring: How we Look*. Oxford: Oxford University Press, 2009.

Garland-Thomson, Rosemarie. 'Integrating Disability, Transforming Feminist Theory', in (ed.) Kim Q. Hall, *Feminist Disability Studies*. Bloomington, Indiana: Indiana University Press, 2011, pp. 13–47.

Gerber, David A. 'The 'Careers' of People Exhibited in Freak Shows: The Problem of Volition and Valorization', in (ed.) Rosemarie Garland Thomson. *Freakery: Cultural Spectacles of the Extraordinary Body*. New York and London: New York University Press, 1996, pp. 38–54.

Gerber, David A. 'Pornography or Entertainment? The Rise and Fall of the Freak Show'. *Reviews in American History*, 18:1 (March 1990), pp. 15–21.

Gillman, Susan and Patten, Robert. 'Dickens: Doubles: Twain: Twins'. *Nineteenth-Century Fiction*, 39:4 (March 1985), pp. 441–58.

Gillman, Susan. *Dark Twins: Imposture and Identity in Mark Twain's America*. Chicago: University of Chicago Press, 1989.

Gitter, Elisabeth G. 'The Power of Women's Hair in the Victorian Imagination'. *PMLA*, 99:5 (October 1984), pp. 936–54.

Gittings, Christopher. 'A Collison of Discourse: Postmodernisms and Post-Colonialisms in *The Biggest Modern Woman of the World*'. *Journal of Commonwealth Literature*, 29:1 (1994), pp. 81–91.

Goldman, Marlene. *Paths of Desire: Images of Exploration and Mapping in Canadian Women's Writing*. Toronto: University of Toronto Press, 1997.

Grosz, Elizabeth. 'Intolerable Ambiguity: Freaks as/at the Limit', in (ed.) Rosemarie Garland Thomson. *Freakery: Cultural Spectacles of the Extraordinary Body*. New York and London: New York University Press, 1996, pp. 55–66.

Gould, George M. and Pyle, Walter L. *Anomalies and Curiosities of Medicine* (1897). London: The Rebman Publishing Company, 1898.

Graham, Peter W., and Oehlschlaeger, Fritz H. *Articulating the Elephant Man: Joseph Merrick and his Interpreters*. Baltimore: The John Hopkins University Press, 1992.

Harrison, Fraser. *The Dark Angel: Aspects of Victorian Sexuality* (1977).Glasgow: Fontana, 1979.

Heffernan, Teresa. 'Tracing the Travesty: Constructing the Female Subject in Susan Swan's *The Biggest Modern Woman of the World*'. *Canadian Literature*, 133 (1992), pp. 24–37.

Heilmann, Ann and Llewellyn, Mark. *Neo-Victorianism: The Victorians in the Twenty-First Century, 1999–2009*. Basingstoke: Palgrave Macmillan, 2010.

Hewitt, Martin. 'Why the Notion of Victorian Britain *Does* Make Sense'. *Victorian Studies*, 48:3 (Spring 2006), pp. 395–438.

Holgate, Mike. *Jack the Ripper: The Celebrity Suspects*. Stroud: The History Press, 2008.

Holloday, William E., and Watt, Stephen. 'Viewing the Elephant Man'. *PMLA*, 104:5 (October 1989), pp. 868–81.

Holmes, Rachel. *The Hottentot Venus: The Life and Death of Saartjie Baartman, Born 1789–Buried 2002*. London: Bloomsbury, 2007.

Howell, Michael and Ford, Peter. *The True History of the Elephant Man: The Definitive Account of the Tragic and Extraordinary Life of Joseph Carey Merrick* (1980). London: Allison & Busby, 2001.

Hunt, Peter. 'Children's Literature and Childhood', in (ed.) Mary Jane Kehily, *An Introduction to Childhood Studies*. Second edition. Maidenhead: Open University Press, 2009, pp. 50–69.

Hutcheon, Linda. *A Poetics of Postmodernism: History, Theory, Fiction*. London: Routledge, 1988.

Illick, Joseph E. *American Childhoods*. Philadelphia: University of Pennsylvania Press, 2002.

The Industrial Nation Timeline, The National Archives <http://www.nationalarchives.gov.uk/education/victorianbritain/industrial/timeline2.htm> (accessed 28 December 2014)

Joyce, Simon. *The Victorians in the Rear View Mirror*. Athens, Ohio: Ohio University Press, 2007.

Kamboureli, Smaro. '*The Biggest Modern Woman of the World*: Canada as the Absent Spouse'. *Studies in Canadian Literature* (June 1991) <http://journals.hil.unb.ca/index.php/SCL/article/view/8138> (accessed 28 December 2014).

Kaplan, Cora. *Victoriana: Histories, Fictions, Criticism*. Edinburgh: Edinburgh University Press, 2007.

Kawin, Bruce. '*The Elephant Man* by David Lynch', *Film Quarterly*, 34: 4 (Summer 1981), pp. 21–25.

Kincaid, James R. *Child-Loving: The Erotic Child and Victorian Literature*. London: Routledge, 1994.

King, Jeannette. *The Victorian Woman Question in Contemporary Feminist Fiction*. Basingstoke: Palgrave Macmillan, 2005.

King, Wilma. *Stolen Childhood: Slave Youth in Nineteenth-Century America*. Second Edition. Bloomington, Indiana: Indiana University Press, 2011.

Kohlke, Marie-Luise. 'Introduction: Speculations in and on the Neo-Victorian encounter'. *Neo-Victorian Studies*, 1:1 (2008), pp. 1–18.

Kohlke, Marie-Luise. 'The Neo-Victorian Sexsation: Literary Excursions into the Nineteenth Century Erotic', in (eds.) Marie-Luise Kohlke and Luisa Orza, *Probing the Problematics: Sex and Sexuality*. Oxford: Inter-Disciplinary Press, 2008b, pp. 345–56.

Kohlke, Marie-Luise, and Gutleben, Christian. 'Introduction: Bearing After-Witness to the Nineteenth Century', in (eds.) Marie-Luise Kohlke and Christian Gutleben, *Neo-Victorian Tropes of Trauma: The Politics of Bearing After-Witness to Nineteenth-Century Suffering*. Amsterdam and New York: Rodopi, 2010, pp. 1–34.

Kohlke, Marie-Luise. 'Neo-Victorian Childhoods: Re-Imagining the Worst of Times', in (eds.) Marie-Luise Kohlke and Christian Gutleben. *Neo-Victorian Families: Gender, Sexual and Cultural Politics*. Amsterdam and New York: Rodopi, 2011, pp. 119–47.

Kohlke, Marie-Luise, and Gutleben, Christian. 'The (Mis)Shapes of Neo-Victorian Gothic: Continuations, Adaptations, Transformations', in (eds.) Marie-Luise Kohlke and Christian Gutleben, *Neo-Victorian Gothic: Horror, Violence and Degeneration in the Re-Imagined Nineteenth Century*. Amsterdam and New York: Rodopi, 2012, pp. 1–48.

Kohlke, Marie-Luise. 'Neo-Victorian Biofiction and the Special/Spectral Case of Barbara Chase-Riboud's *Hottentot Venus*'. *Australasian Journal of Victorian Studies*, 18.3 (2013), pp. 4–21.

Kohlke, Marie-Luise. 'Mining the Neo-Victorian Vein: Prospecting for Gold, Buried Treasure and Uncertain Metal', in (eds.) Nadine Boehm-Schnikter and Susanne Gruss, *Neo-Victorian Literature and Culture: Immersions and Revisitations*. London: Routledge, 2014, pp. 21–37.

Kontou, Tatiana. *Spiritualism and Women's Writing From the Fin de Siècle to the Neo-Victorian*. Basingstoke: Palgrave Macmillan, 2009.

Kornweibel, Karen Ruth. 'A Complex Resurrection: Race, Spectacle, and Complicity in Suzan-Lori Parks's *Venus*'. *South Atlantic Review*, 74:3 (Summer 2009), pp. 64–81.

Knights, Stephen. *Jack the Ripper: The Final Solution* (1976). London: Grafton Books, 1985.

Kucich, John and Sadoff, Dianne F. (eds.), *Victorian Afterlife: Postmodern Culture Rewrites the Nineteenth Century*. Minneapolis and London: University of Minnesota Press, 2000.

Lacan, Jacques. 'The Mirror Stage as formative function of the I as revealed in psychoanalytic experience', in (trans.) Alan Sheridan, Écrits, *A Selection*. New York: W. W. Norton & Co., 1977, pp. 502–09.

LaCapra, Dominick. *Writing History, Writing Trauma*. Baltimore and London: The John Hopkins University Press, 2001.

Leach, Karoline. '"Lewis Carroll": A Myth in the Making'. *The Victorian Web*, 2000 <http://www.victorianweb.org/authors/carroll/dreamchild/dreamchild1.html> (accessed 28 December 2014).

Lehman, Eric D. *Becoming Tom Thumb: Charles Stratton, P. T. Barnum, and the Dawn of American Celebrity*. Middletown, Connecticut: Wesleyan University Press, 2013.

Lindfors, Bernth. 'Ethnological Show Business: Footlighting the Dark Continent', in (ed.) Rosemarie Garland Thomson. *Freakery: Cultural Spectacles of the Extraordinary Body*. New York and London: New York University Press, 1996, pp. 207–18.

Lindfors, Bernth (ed.) *Africans on Stage: Studies in Ethnological Show Business*. Bloomington and Indiana: Indiana University Press, 1999.

Linton, Simi. 'Reassigning Meaning', in (ed.) Lennard J. Davis. *The Disability Studies Reader*. Third Edition. New York: Routledge, 2010, pp. 223–36.

Llewellyn, Mark. 'Neo-Victorianism: On the Ethics and Aesthetics of Appropriation'. In Rebecca Munford and Paul Young (eds.), *Engaging the Victorians*, special issue of *LIT: Literature Interpretation Theory*, 20:1–2 (2009), pp. 27–44.

Magubane, Zine. 'Which Bodies Matter? Feminism, Post-Structuralism, Race, and the Curious Theoretical Odyssey of the "Hottentot Venus"', in (ed.) Deborah Willis. *Black Venus 2010: They Called Her "Hottentot"*. Philadelphia: Temple University Press, 2010, pp. 47–61.

Martin, Holly E. '"The Original Siamese Twins": Living, Dying and Continuing under the Spectator's Gaze'. *The Journal of American Culture*, 34:4 (December 2011), pp. 372–90.

Mayhew, Henry. *London Labour and the London Poor*, 1862 <http://www.victorianlondon.org/crime1/mayhewprostitution.htm> (accessed 28 December 2014).

Mennel, Barbara. *Queer Cinema: Schoolgirls, Vampires, and Gay Cowboys*. London and New York: Wallflower Press, 2012.

Merish, Lori. 'Cuteness and Commodity Aesthetics: Tom Thumb and Shirley Temple', in (ed.) Rosemarie Garland Thomson. *Freakery: Cultural Spectacles of the Extraordinary Body*. New York and London: New York University Press, 1996, pp. 185–203.

Miller, Greg. 'The Bottom of Desire in Suzan-Lori Parks's *Venus*'. *Modern Drama*, 45:1 (Spring 2002), pp. 125–37.

Mitchell, David, and Snyder, Sharon. 'Exploitations of Embodiment: *Born Freak* and the Academic Bally Platform'. *Disability Studies Quarterly*, 25:3 (2005) <dsq-sds.org/article/view/575/7527> (accessed 28 December 2014).

Mitchell, David, and Snyder, Sharon. 'Narrative Prosthesis', in (ed.) Lennard J. Davis. *The Disability Studies Reader*. Third Edition. New York: Routledge, 2010, pp. 274–87.

Mitchell, Kate. *History and Cultural Memory in Neo-Victorian Fiction: Victorian Afterimages*. Basingstoke: Palgrave Macmillan, 2010.

Mitchell, Robin. 'Another Meaning of Understanding the Gaze: Sarah Bartmann in the Development of Nineteenth-Century French National Identity', in (ed.) Deborah Willis. *Black Venus 2010: They Called Her 'Hottentot'*. Philadelphia: Temple University Press, 2010, pp. 32–46.

'Moral and Political Tendency of Modern Novels', *Church of England Quarterly Review*, 11 (1842), pp. 287–88.

Morey, Anne, and Nelson, Claudia. 'The Secret Sharer: The Child in Neo-Victorian Fiction'. *Neo-Victorian Studies*, 5:1 (2012), pp. 1–3.

Muller, Nadine. 'The (Feminist) Politics of Sex Work in Michel Faber's *The Crimson Petal and the White*', in (eds.) Joel Gwynne and Angelia Poon, *Sexuality in Contemporary Literature*. Amherst, New York: Cambria Press, 2012, pp. 39–60.

Nead, Lynda. *Myths of Sexuality: Representations of Women in Victorian Britain*. Oxford: Basil Blackwell, 1988.

The New York Tribune, 14 July 1865 <http://epe.lac-bac.gc.ca/100/205/301/ic/cdc/aswan/storyindex.htm> (accessed 28 December 2014).

O'Connell, Catharine. 'Resecting *Those Extraordinary Twins: Pudd'nhead Wilson* and the Cost of "Killing Half"'. *Nineteenth-Century Literature*, 57:1 (June 2002), pp. 100–24.

O'Riley, Michael F. 'Postcolonial Haunting: Anxiety, Affect, and the Situated Encounter'. *Postcolonial Text*, 3:4 (2007) <http://postcolonial.org/index.php/pct/article/view/728/496> (accessed 28 December 2014).

The Oxford English Dictionary 2nd edition. Oxford: Oxford University Press, 1989, <http://www.oed.com> (accessed 13 July 2013).

Pancoast, William H. 'Report on the Surgical Considerations in Regard to the Propriety of an Operation for the Separation of Eng and Chang Bunker, Commonly Known as the Siamese Twins'. *Transactions of the College of Physicians* (Philadelphia), 1, 1875, pp. 149–69.

Pearsall, Ronald. *The Worm in the Bud: The World of Victorian Sexuality*. Harmondsworth: Penguin, 1969.

Pietrzak-Franger, Monika. '"Those Ill Things": On Hidden Spectacles and the Ethics of Display'. *Neo-Victorian Studies*, 4:2 (2011), pp. 24–48.

Pingree, Allison. 'America's "United Siamese Brothers": Chang and Eng and Nineteenth-Century Ideologies of Democracy and Domesticity', in (ed.) Jeffrey Jerome Cohen, *Monster Theory: Reading Culture*. Minneapolis: University of Minneapolis Press, 1996, pp. 92–114.

Powell, Kerry. *Women and the Victorian Theatre*. Cambridge: Cambridge University Press, 1997.

Pulham, Patricia. 'Mapping Histories: The Golem and the Serial Killer in *White Chappell, Scarlet Tracings* and *Dan Leno and the Limehouse Golem*', in (eds.) Rosario Arias and Patricia Pulham, *Haunting and Spectrality In Neo-Victorian Fiction: Possessing the Past*. Basingstoke: Palgrave Macmillan, 2010, pp. 157–79.

Quayson, Ato *Aesthetic Nervousness: Disability and the Crisis of Representation*. New York: Columbia University Press, 2007.

Qureshi, Sadiah. 'Displaying Sara Baartman, The 'Hottentot Venus'. *History of Science*, 42 (2004), pp. 233–57.

Renaud, Anne. *The Extraordinary Life of Anna Swan*. Sydney, Nova Scotia: Cape Breton University Press, 2013.

Rieger, Christy. 'The Legacy of Medical Sensationalism in *The Crimson Petal and the White* and *The Dress Lodger*', in (eds.) Nadine Boehm-Schnikter and Susanne Gruss, *Neo-Victorian Literature and Culture: Immersions and Revisitations*. London: Routledge, 2014, pp. 153–64.

Riviere, Joan. 'Womanliness as Masquerade' (1929), in (eds.) Victor Burgin, James Donald, and Cora Kaplan, *Formations of Fantasy*. London and New York: Methuen, 1986, pp. 35–44.

Rody, Caroline. 'Toni Morrison's *Beloved*: History, "Rememory", and a "Clamor for a kiss"'. *American Literary History*, 7:1 (Spring 1995), pp. 92–119.

Rushdy, Ashraf H. A. '"Rememory": Primal Scenes and Constructions in Toni Morrison's *Beloved*'. *Contemporary Literature*, 31:3 (August 1990), pp. 300–23.

Russo, Mary. *The Female Grotesque: Risk, Excess and Modernity*. New York and London: Routledge, 1995.

Sánchez-Eppler, Karen. *Dependent States: The Child's Part in Nineteenth-Century American Culture*. Chicago and London: University of Chicago Press, 2005.

Saxon, A. H. 'Introduction', in Countess M. Lavinia Magri, *The Autobiography of Mrs. Tom Thumb*. Hamden, Connecticut: Archon Books, 1979, pp. 9–21.

Saxon, A. H. *P. T. Barnum: The Legend and the Man*. New York: Columbia University Press, 1989.

Scarre, Chris. *Chronicle of the Roman Emperors: A Reign-by-Reign Record of the Rulers of Imperial Rome*. London: Thames & Hudson, 1995.

Sceats, Sarah. 'Performance, Identity and the Body', in Helen Stoddart, *Angela Carter's Nights at the Circus: A Routledge Study Guide*. Oxon: Routledge, 2007, pp. 84–94.

Semonin, Paul. 'Monsters in the Marketplace: The Exhibition of Human Oddities in Early Modern England', in (ed.) Rosemarie Garland Thomson. *Freakery: Cultural Spectacles of the Extraordinary Body*. New York and London: New York University Press, 1996, pp. 69–81.

Shakespeare, Tom. 'The Social Model of Disability', in (ed.) Lennard J. Davis. *The Disability Studies Reader*. Third Edition. New York: Routledge, 2010, pp. 266–73.

Sharpley-Whiting, T. Denean. *Black Venus: Sexualized Savages, Primal Fears, and Primitve Narratives in French*. Duke University Press, 1999.

Shildrick, Margrit. *Leaky Bodies and Boundaries: Feminism, Postmodernism and (Bio) ethics*. London: Routledge, 1997.

Shildrick, Margrit. *Embodying the Monster: Encounters with the Vulnerable Self*. London: SAGE publications, 2002.

Shiller, Dana. 'The Redemptive Past in the Neo-Victorian Novel'. *Studies in the Novel*, 29:4 (1997), pp. 538–60.

Showalter, Elaine. *Sexual Anarchy: Gender and Culture at the Fin de Siècle* (1990). London: Virago, 1992.

Shuttleworth, Sally. 'Natural History: The Retro-Victorian Novel'. In Elinor S. Shaffer (ed.), *The Third Culture: Literature and Science*. Berlin: de Gruyter, 1998, pp. 253–68.

Sinfield, Alan. *The Wilde Century: Effeminacy, Oscar Wilde, and the Queer Moment*. London: Cassell, 1994.

Smith, Andrew. 'Pathologising the Gothic: The Elephant Man, the Neurotic, and the Doctor'. *Gothic Studies*, 2:3 (2000), pp. 292–304.

Spivak, Gayatri. 'Can the Subaltern Speak?' In Cary Nelson and Lawrence Grossberg (eds.), *Marxism and the Interpretation of Culture*. Urbana, Illinois: University of Illinois Press, 1988, pp. 217–313.

Stern, Rebecca. 'Our Bear Women, Ourselves: Affiliating with Julia Pastrana', in (ed.) Marlene Tromp. *Victorian Freaks: The Social Context of Freakery in Britain*. Columbus: The Ohio State University Press, 2008, pp. 200–33.

Steveker, Lena. '"Eminent Victorians" and Neo-Victorian Fictional Biography', in (eds.) Nadine Boehm-Schnikter and Susanne Gruss, *Neo-Victorian Literature and Culture: Immersions and Revisitations*. London: Routledge, 2014, pp. 67–78.

Stewart, Susan. *On Longing: Narratives of the Miniature, the Gigantic, the Souvenir, the Collection*. Durham and London: Duke University Press, 1993.

Strother, Z. S. 'Display of the Body Hottentot', in (ed.) Bernth Lindfors, *Africans on Stage: Studies in Ethnological Show Business*. Bloomington and Indiana: Indiana University Press, 1999, pp. 1–61.

Sweet, Matthew. *Inventing the Victorians*, London: Faber and Faber, 2001.

Tibbles, J. A. R., and Cohen, M. M. 'The Proteus syndrome: The Elephant Man diagnosed'. *British Medical Journal*, 293, 13 September 1986, pp. 683–85.

'Tom Thumb's Widow Reveals Secrets of the Show'. *The Western Australia Sunday Times* (Perth), 4 October 1901, p. 10 <http://trove.nla.gov.au/ndp/del/article/32720833> (accessed 28 December 2014).

Tromp, Marlene, with Valerius, Karyn. 'Introduction: Toward situating the Victorian Freak', in (ed.) Marlene Tromp. *Victorian Freaks: The Social Context of Freakery in Britain*. Columbus: The Ohio State University Press, 2008, pp. 1–18.

Vacon, Shirley Irene. *Giants of Nova Scotia: The Lives of Anna Swan and Angus McAskill*. Lawrencetown Beach, Nova Scotia: Pottersfield Press, 2008.

Voights, Eckart. 'Bio-Fiction: Neo-Victorian Revisions of Evolution and Genetics', in (eds.) Nadine Boehm-Schnikter and Susanne Gruss, *Neo-Victorian Literature and Culture: Immersions and Revisitations*. London: Routledge, 2014, pp. 79–92.

Walkowitz, Judith R. *Prostitution and Victorian Society: Women, Class, and the State*. Cambridge: Cambridge University Press, 1980.

Walkowitz, Judith R. *City of Dreadful Delight: Narratives of Sexual Danger in Late-Victorian London*. Chicago: University of Chicago Press, 1992.

Wallace, Irving and Wallace, Amy. *The Two*. New York: Simon and Schuster, 1978.

Warner, Sara L. 'Suzan-Lori Parks's Drama of Disinterment: A Transnational Exploration of Venus'. *Theatre Journal*, 60:2 (May 2008), pp. 181–99.

Wigger, Anne P. 'The Composition of Mark Twain's *Pudd'nhead Wilson and Those Extraordinary Twins*: Chronology and Development'. *Modern Philology*, 55:2 (November 1957), pp. 93–102.

Wiggins, Robert A. 'The Original of Mark Twain's *Those Extraordinary Twins*'. *American Literature*, 23:3 (November 1951), pp. 255–357.

Willis, Deborah. 'Introduction: The Notion of Venus', in (ed.) Deborah Willis, *Black Venus 2010: They Called Her "Hottentot"*. Philadelphia: Temple University Press, 2010, pp. 3–11.

Wood, Edward J. *Giants and Dwarfs*. London: R. Bentley, 1868.

Wu, Cynthia. 'The Siamese Twins in Late Nineteenth-Century Narratives of Conflict and Resolution'. *American Literature*, 80:1 (March 2008), pp. 29–55.

Wu, Cynthia. *Chang and Eng Reconnected: The Original Siamese Twins in American Culture*. Philadelphia: Temple University Press, 2012.

Wylie, H. *Speculative Fictions: Contemporary Canadian Novelists and the Writing of History*. Montreal: McGill-Queen's University Press, 2002.

Young, Jean. 'The Re-Objectification and Re-Commodification of Saartjie Baartman in Suzan-Lori Parks's *Venus*'. *African American Review*, 31: 4 (Winter 1997), pp. 699–708.

Zipes, Jack. *The Trials and Tribulations of Little Red Riding Hood: Versions of the Tale in Sociocultural Context*. New York and London: Routledge, 1993.

Index

Note: 'n' after a page reference denotes a note number on that page.

CPSIA information can be obtained
at www.ICGtesting.com
Printed in the USA
LVOW04*2037090216
474369LV00018B/594/P

9 781137 402554